THE AFRICAN DREAM

By the same author

THE BIG PUSH: *The Battle of the Somme*

ON TO KILIMANJARO: *World War I in East Africa*

THE YEAR THAT CHANGED THE WORLD: *The Tragedy of 1945*

UP THE LINE TO DEATH: *The War Poets 1914–18*

ALLENBY OF ARABIA: *A Biography*

THE TERRIBLE RAIN: *The War Poets 1939–45*

MAFEKING: *A Victorian Legend*

THE QUEST FOR TIMBUCTOO

CHURCHILL IN POWER

THE LION'S CAGE: *Cecil Rhodes and the Siege of Kimberley*

The African Dream

Brian Gardner

G. P. Putnam's Sons

New York

To All Old Colonial Servants

FIRST AMERICAN EDITION 1970

Library of Congress Catalog Card Number: 78–105603

PRINTED IN THE UNITED STATES OF AMERICA

Contents

Illustrations follow page 90

19682

Author's Note

This book is about the British in Africa: a remarkable breed of people, who plodded across, spread the word in, drank in, went to war in, saved life in, went bankrupt in, built railways in, administered justice in, made fortunes in, shot animals in, and engaged in a thousand other activities in Africa; most of the survivors of whom returned home—to modest villas on the chilly Channel coast and bleak shires, to live a few years of retirement, dreaming perhaps of other days in the far-off land which had beckoned them when young. It is about the *people,* mostly the British, but not forgetting the Africans, rather than about the treaties. But the people are presented in the framework of the main events, from slavery to one man, one vote, by way of explorers, missionaries, soldiers, hunters, administrators, and revolutionaries. For permission to quote, and to reproduce photographs, I am grateful to the following: Lord Cranworth; William Collins Sons and Co. Ltd.; Associated Press; the Imperial War Museum; and the Radio Times Hulton Picture Library.

B. G.

PART ONE

PROLOGUE

❖ I ❖

The Dark Continent

At each side of the Mall, in London, where that historic route ends before the façade of Buckingham Palace, stands a tall sentinel stone pillar, stark against the gentle foliage of St. James's Park. The two are relics of a once-great empire. At the top of one is simply inscribed "South Africa," at the top of the other "West Africa."

The dream of a vast African empire, owing allegiance to the British crown, started at the end of the eighteenth century. It did not start with conquering expeditions, with redcoats marching on native cities, with Union Jacks being hoisted over newly won territories, or with African hordes being decimated by disciplined rifle fire. That came later. It started over breakfast at a terrace house in an unfashionable London square.

It was a dream which came true. At its peak, the British Empire embraced nearly a third of the African continent, and it ruled more than 63,400,000 people from the Cape to Cairo, from Gambia to Zanzibar. But in the catalogue of empires, it was brief indeed. The British Empire in Africa lasted only 100 years. Its start was not so long ago. There are people alive today who knew people who were born before Britain had any territory in Africa at all. Much more than half of it was under the reign of one sovereign—the great white queen who ruled the black peoples, the remote mother figure who never saw her immense African domains, as large as all Europe.

It was a short generation before Victoria's reign when those who breakfasted at 32 Soho Square at the end of the eighteenth century dreamed of Africa. Their hopes for Britain in Africa were of wealth, territory, and glory. Their confidence allowed no doubts about the future. Their influence in Africa, however, was slight, for at that time British territorial possessions were nil.* Fewer than a dozen forts on the west coast flew the Union Jack. The only country with areas of the continent under control was Portugal, which had been slowly and painfully colonizing since the sixteenth century. The Portuguese had already established a tradition of secrecy about their African territories that was to last until the present day. In the north, from Algiers to the Nile, the continent was nominally under Turkish influence. In the northwest, the Moroccan empire was in decline. In the far south, a few thousand Dutch farmers had been settled for 150 years and had gradually pushed their territory inland, oblivious of the rest of the world. But all this was less even than a foothold. No continent was so little known, so mysterious, to Europeans. All that was known in the late eighteenth century was a coastline. The interior was a place of secrecy, hidden beyond impenetrable forests, mountain ranges, and huge rivers. Rumors about the interior of Africa had swept across Europe for two centuries; they told of two main things: great and powerful kingdoms and fantastic wealth, in particular an extensive supply of gold. No one had been able to verify these legends, but neither had anyone been able to disprove them, and there was some evidence to support them.

Sir Joseph Banks, who lived in the house in Soho Square, was irritated, even outraged, at this ignorance about such a large sector of the earth's surface, and he was not a man who suffered ignorance gladly. Although he has not found a place in British national memory, he was one of the most influential and important men in Europe. His was an age when the quest for knowledge was supreme, and leading the quest in many fields was Sir Joseph Banks. He had always been rich, and as a youth he had been strikingly handsome. Now he was fat, with a heavy face crowned by white hair; large, alert eyes glowed beneath black eyebrows. A big man, he had an intimidating manner and no small talk at all. Throughout his life he was bursting with both energy and curiosity, and in later years he had added to these a

---

* The "colony" of Senegambia, 1758–79, was no more than a few slaving posts. Tangier had been British, 1662–84, as the result of a royal dowry.

sound common sense, an ability to manipulate people and to get things done, and a wide circle of loyal and influential friends. Sir Joseph Banks was a very formidable person.

Scion of a wealthy landowning family, he had achieved early fame after spending three years with Captain Cook on the latter's tour of the world and exploration of Australia and New Zealand. His chief contribution on that famous journey had been in botany, but he had also brought back a great deal of other scientific information. On his return to London he had become a close personal adviser to George III and was acknowledged by the leading scientists of the day. At the early age of thirty-five he had been elected president of the Royal Society, which made him, as a contemporary said, "The Great Panjandrum of British Science—the president, the organizer, the lord justice of appeal." He held the position for forty-two years, becoming one of the most famous men in London.

> Lord, that's Sir Joseph Banks, how grand his look,
> Who sailed all round the world with Captain Cook.

Banks' house in Soho Square* contained the best scientific library in London; it housed collections of insects, minerals, plants, and other specimens that the universities could not match. The greatest men of the day, from all over Europe, met there, usually for breakfast. Banks was a great believer in the "working breakfast." On these occasions—almost every morning—there was an air of suppressed excitement, for all present were aware that they lived in an exceptional time, with men engaged in great discoveries and changes. Banks presided, with the authority of an experienced premier over a diverse and agitated cabinet. His wife, "a comely and modest young lady," hovered in the background.

Joseph Banks' need to find out about the world and the life in it dominated almost every moment of his day. His breakfast meetings went on till midday; after lunch he chaired various meetings or went out about the many administrative and organizational matters in which he was involved, all connected with his projects. On the rare occasions when he found himself outside his world of learned discussion he was not only bored, but completely at a loss. The novelist and socialite Fanny

* The house has been destroyed; 32 Soho Square is now the London office of Twentieth Century-Fox.

Burney met him at a tea party and noted in her diary: "So exceedingly shy that we made no acquaintance at all. If instead of going around the world he had fallen from the moon, he could not appear less versed in the usual modes of a tea-drinking party."

But there was another side to Banks. Although he appeared to keep clear of politics, he was, in fact, one of the most successful and well-concealed lobbyists of the eighteenth century. The lobby he led encouraged the spread of British influence around the world. It was Sir Joseph Banks who was to be behind the founding of the first British settlement in Australia and the early development of that land.

Before the 1780's Banks' interest in Africa had been mainly botanical; but in 1787 he began to express a close interest in "the interior parts of Africa," and he was to receive fairly frequent reports from a correspondent in Morocco. At that time his breakfast discussions must have been turning more and more to Africa and the responsibilities and opportunities there. He looked around for a more formal gathering, which he could use to get his views on Africa transformed into actions. His friendship with the monarch gave him the ear of many powerful men, and he was at that time a member of the exclusive Saturday Club, which met for dinner at the St. Alban's Tavern, just off Pall Mall. The "club" was restricted to twelve members, all of them interested in the sciences. Eight were Members of Parliament, but it was not politics that brought them together. In view of later history, it was entirely apt that six of the twelve were Scotsmen. Of the many branches of knowledge which they discussed, exploration held an important place. And what sector of the world begged more for exploration than Africa? At a time when curiosity obsessed all civilized men, nothing was more provoking than the continent whose legends had haunted mankind for centuries and whose map had remained blank for so long. "While we continue ignorant of so large a portion of the globe, that ignorance must be considered as a degree of reproach upon the present age," they declared.

On the summer evening of June 9, 1788, the Saturday Club met as usual at the St. Alban's Tavern. Three were unable to attend. Before they went home that night, the remaining nine—we may assume under the direction of Banks—had composed and passed the following resolution:

That as no species of information is more ardently desired, or more generally useful, than that which improves the science of geography, and as the vast continent of Africa, notwithstanding the efforts of the ancients, and the wishes of the moderns, is still in a great measure unexplored, the members of this club do form themselves into an Association for Promoting the Discovery of the Inland Parts of that Quarter of the World.

It was perhaps a little pretentious; it was certainly presumptuous. Nine men of the world, well stimulated with wine, had taken on themselves the unveiling of a whole continent, a prospect at which governments and even the richest business houses had balked. But it was a historic occasion, for although there was no word of empire or of territorial acquisition, there was more in the minds of Sir Joseph Banks' friends than the pursuit of knowledge. Had not Britain lost the American colonies only five years before?

It was the beginning.

Since the time of Elizabeth I, interest in Africa—which meant mainly West Africa—had been confined to trade. This trade had been done with the west and north coasts, at first in ivory, gold, and pepper. The steady trickle of gold dust had been enough to sustain interest and rumors and little else. England had played no greater part than the Dutch, the Portuguese, the Danes, the Swedes, the French, and the Prussians in slight development of trade with the African coast. Trading posts, connected with one another only by sea, had changed hands with bewildering frequency. William Pitt the Elder had shown the only official interest in the area, and that had been confined to rivalry with the French. Except for a few Portuguese and French, hardly a trader had thought it advisable or worthwhile to venture even a mile inland from the coast or riverbanks and the safety of the ships at anchor. The Portuguese, always aloof and secretive, had made it a criminal offense to show their maps to foreigners.

For nearly 200 years before the founding of the African Association, trade had become more and more dominated by the transportation of slaves from Africa to North America and the West Indies. By Sir Joseph Banks' time the trade in slaves had cast its shadow over the Atlantic, and interest in Africa was restricted to discussion on slavery—those decrying it being more vocal and apparently more numerous, but seemingly impotent against a well-entrenched and profitable activity which had powerful financial interests. It was a trade in which Britain, although by no means alone, was playing a very ignoble part. During the seventeenth century about 2,750,000 slaves had been transported across the ocean, mainly in Portuguese, Spanish, and Dutch ships. In the eighteenth century 7,000,000 made the same journey, more than half in British ships. This was strange, for in no country was denouncement of the trade more persistent or more eloquent. From Elizabeth herself ("a detestable act"), there were few prominent figures in England that had not gone on record against the slave trade. As early as 1620 the English navigator Richard Jobson, observing the trade in West Africa, had declared that his countrymen were "a people who did not deal in any such commodities, neither did we buy or sell one another, or any that had our own shapes." Later generations of Africans were to experience the mockery of that statement.

There is no evidence that the British were any less brutal in this business than their Portuguese and Spanish predecessors, only more efficient. Slaves were carefully fitted into the ships, lying in rows, so that every square inch was fully utilized; "cargoes" were carefully insured. John Newton, a captain of a slave ship, recalled in 1788:

> With our ships, the great object is to be full. The cargo of a vessel of a hundred tons, or little more, is calculated to purchase from two hundred and twenty to two hundred and fifty slaves. Their lodging-rooms below the deck, which are three (for the men, the boys and the women), besides a place for the sick, are sometimes more than five feet high, and sometimes less; and this height is divided towards the middle, for the slaves lie in two rows, one above the other, on each side of the ship, close to each other, like books up on a shelf. I have known them so close that the shelf would not easily contain one more. And I have known a white man sent down, among the men, to lay them in these rows to the greatest advantage, so that as little space as possible might be lost. Let it be observed that the poor creatures, thus cramped for want of room, are likewise in irons, for the most part both hands and feet, and two together, which makes it difficult for them to turn or move, to attempt either to rise or to lie down. . . . The heat and smell of these rooms, when the weather will not admit of the slaves being brought upon deck, and of having their rooms cleaned every day, would be almost

insupportable to a person not accustomed to them. . . . They are kept down, by the weather, to breathe a hot and corrupted air, sometimes for a week; this, added to the galling of their irons and the despondency which seizes their spirits when thus confined, soon becomes fatal. And every morning perhaps more instances than one are found of the living and dead fastened together. I believe nearly one-half of the slaves on board have, sometimes, died; and that the loss of a third part, in these circumstances, is not unusual.

This account omits that the travelers were usually naked, always branded, often flogged, flung overboard if in any way a nuisance, fed meager and often foul food, and supplied with sanitary arrangements that were, at best, primitive. On some ships the young girls were raped by the crew without mercy and without respite. About the only crime on humanity the British did not commit was the establishment of slave-breeding farms, as the Portuguese did in Angola for their Brazilian plantations, in the belief that Africans born in captivity were easier to ship and control than those captured or purchased. It was with such a background that the British set out in the nineteenth century to gain the goodwill of the Africans in the vast territories which by then they on paper at least administered.

It is true that Europeans were not alone in slavery. It is true that slavery had existed in Africa before the start of the Atlantic traffic. But in its scale, in its horror, in its losses, in its misery, in its effect on individuals, on families and on whole peoples, Africa had experienced nothing like it. Inland from the coast there existed states which, if not civilized by European stand-ards, were certainly far in advance of anything in Australia or North America before the white man. The moral effect of the slave trade on these relatively advanced societies was cata-strophic, with each sect fighting for superiority to take the others to the Europeans. Negroes and white men became not only degraded, but immutably scarred in their relationship to each other—for the white man had treated the black man as if he were closer to an animal than a fellow human.

Around company tables in London, comfortable merchants solemnly discussed ideas to ameliorate the conditions of their human cargoes. They made themselves, if no one else, happier by sending off instructions to their agents: "You are always to have sufficient of Provisions for such Slaves that they may have daily their Bellies filled with that which is most likely to give them the best Nourishment." What would those merchants have thought or done had they actually seen the slave trade in operation?

By the time of Sir Joseph Banks, condemnation of the trade was well in the majority in England. But it was a trade which had been going on for many generations and which seemed to have become an established, if shameful, aspect of society. It was a period which had taken Britain from the Middle Ages to the eve of Victoria's reign. What brought the matter to a head was the growing number of African slaves being brought to Britain itself. There were more than 10,000 African slaves in England.* Their presence outraged all liberal-minded people, of whom at that time there were a great many. After a test case, the Lord Chief Justice pronounced in 1772 that "the state of slavery is so odious that nothing can be suffered to support it." For most of the rest of the century the antislavery members of Parliament, led by William Wilberforce, fought the powerful West India plantation lobby. At first they failed, but at last the hideous stain of slavery, in British ships and possessions, seemed likely to be halted, if never to be completely washed from England's past.

The antislavery movement was closely allied to religion. That movement, together with the formation of the African Association and the continuing stories of gold, thus completed the three forces which were to fire the British conquest of Africa: exploration, trade, and religion.

Banks, as could be expected, galvanized the African Association into observing its grandiose resolution of the St. Alban's Tavern. He made the acquaintance of all travelers who had more than cursory knowledge of the African coast and collected a library of every important work that had ever been published on Africa—the most comprehensive collection of its kind in the world. In the first eleven years of its existence there was only one occasion when Banks was not present at a meeting of the committee of the African Association.

Membership of the African Association was restricted to the wealthy and the aristocracy. Only the wealthy could afford the

---

* About 1 in every 800 of the total population of some 8,000,000.

annual subscription of five guineas, and only the aristocratic and academic would feel at ease in the exclusive circle of Banks' friends. An inner group of the association continued to meet at the St. Alban's Tavern, then at the Star and Garter in Pall Mall, and afterward at the Thatched House in St. James's Street. Members who joined included the Duke of Grafton (an ex-Prime Minister), three other dukes and two marquesses, Thomas Coutts (a powerful banker), James Rennell (the greatest geographer in Europe), Edward Gibbon, John Hunter (the leading surgeon in London), Josiah Wedgwood, Henry Cavendish (an important scientist), and several professors from Oxford and Cambridge.

The committee consulted the blank map of Africa, the coastline marked here and there with the dot of a trading station, but empty within. It seemed natural that they should turn their attention first to the great bulge of West Africa, known as Guinea, for there Britain had made its tentative contacts with the edges of the "Dark Continent." Within days of its inauguration, the association had received two offers from explorers to penetrate the interior of Guinea. The association leaped into activity. After generations of slumber, Britain seemed suddenly to awaken her interest in Africa. There was no shortage of potential explorers in England and Scotland.

Simon Lucas was the son of a London wine merchant. He had been sent to Spain to learn the trade, but had been captured by Moorish pirates and sold as a slave at the court of Morocco. On his release he had made full use of his knowledge of Arabic and became the official interpreter at the royal court in London. Banks was able to secure Lucas' release from his official duties, on full pay, so that he could explore North Africa.

Only a week later a penniless itinerant American, in ragged clothing, stood on Banks' doorstep in Soho Square and asked to see him. His name was John Ledyard, and he was a world traveler, who had explored northwestern America, traveled with Captain Cook, and crossed Siberia. The association was impressed with this tough and determined American. One member wrote of "the manliness of his person, the breadth of his chest, the openness of his countenance and the inquietude of his eye." American characteristics were well to the fore in him: "Little attentive to differences of rank, he seemed to consider all men his equals and as such he respected them. Though unpolished," he was "neither uncivil nor unpleasing." The association noted with satisfaction that he was "adventurous beyond the conception of ordinary men . . . he appeared to be formed by nature for achievements of hardihood and peril."

Banks sent Ledyard to the newly appointed secretary of the association. With the map of Africa spread before him, the secretary traced with his finger a line from Cairo westward across the continent toward the Atlantic. "I told him that was the route by which I was anxious that Africa might, if possible, be explored." Ledyard was asked when he could leave. "Tomorrow morning," he replied.

In these two remarkable adventurers the association put its trust. They were to open up Africa for Britain—with £430 between them. By October, 1788, Lucas was in Tripoli and Ledyard in Cairo.

Simon Lucas was middle-aged, suffered from gout, and had led a fairly luxurious life at court. He set out from Tripoli, in Turkish dress, on a mule given him by the local ruler, his plan to delve into the Sahara. He took with him a copious supply of strong brandy, explaining that the sheikh he had to visit had a famous thirst. Troubled by the intense heat, beset by tribal warring, he had not gone more than a few miles before he turned back to Tripoli.

Lucas returned to London, with Africa unconquered. During his absence the association had learned, from one who had known Lucas in Morocco, that "he never has, nor never will, nor can if he pleased, tell you one word of the truth."

Ledyard was meanwhile having an uncomfortable time in Cairo. He knew no Arabic and adopted no disguise. Foreigners were unpopular, to say the least, and he was taunted and jeered at wherever he went. On November 15 he wrote to Thomas Jefferson, whom he had met before leaving America: "From Cairo I am to travel S.W. about three hundred leagues to a black king. There my present conductors will leave me to my fate. Beyond, I suppose I shall go alone. I expect to cut the continent. . . ." But he became sick, possibly with dysentery, before leaving Cairo, and an overdose of medicine resulted in his death in agony.

The grand hopes of the African Association had produced some expense and no exploration whatever. The continent was proving as intractable as many had feared. This was not a situation to please Sir Joseph Banks, and as the reputation of the association declined, disaster in Africa was matched by farce in London. A Moor living in the city was contacted and was offered the task of guiding an expedition to Timbuktu, which was one of the few places of the interior known by name in Europe; it had long been considered—without any proof—a capital city of great importance and astonishing wealth. While preparations were made for the expedition, the Moor ran up considerable debts and then disappeared.

As more members with business interests joined the association, the commercial aspect of its activities grew larger. Timbuktu, in particular, seemed to beckon. One member wrote: "We have heard of a city called Timbuktu—gold is so plentiful as to adorn even the slaves—if we could get our manufactures into that country, we should soon have gold enough."

Undeterred by its two failures, the association decided to send another explorer. This time the goal was Timbuktu itself, as well as the Niger River and the land of the Hausa. On July 5, 1790, Major Daniel Houghton offered his services to the association. On the same day, the committee met at Soho Square and accepted him.

At first glance Houghton seemed to be the man who would at last start filling in the map of Africa for Britain. He had as much experience of Africa as most and had spent three years in command of a post on the west coast. He had learned one of the major languages of the area, Mandingo, and had been on an official mission to Morocco. Even more to the point, so far as Houghton's selection was concerned, were his winning personality and considerable charm. The committee was impressed by "the order of his mind and the strength of his constitution." An Anglo-Irishman, retired from the army, bankrupt, with a wife and children to support, he was desperate for money.

Houghton asked for, and got, £260. In an attempt to get the government interested in its activities, the African Association arranged for him an interview with the Prime Minister himself, William Pitt the Younger. Houghton departed from London with Lucas' old Oriental clothes in his bag (Lucas had meticulously returned them to the association), leaving his wife and three children in "circumstances of great distress." He gambled on returning with a fame which would lead to fortune or at least to financial restoration.

He sailed up the Gambia River, known to the British since Elizabeth I. Then, with two Africans, he delved into the interior. At first things went well. "Am greatly caressed here," he wrote to his wife from a native town, "on account of my coming to make a settlement in their country which will enrich them all by trade, and I hope myself, too." But then Houghton lost his firearms, his ammunition, and one of his Africans, after moving only about 300 miles inland. Undaunted, he plunged on into the continent.

A few months later a scribbled note in pencil from him arrived in London: "Major Houghton's compliments—is in good health on his way to Timbuktu, robbed of all his goods. . . ." It was the last that was ever heard of Major Daniel Houghton. He is forgotten today, like many another early explorer of Africa, but he had succeeded in penetrating farther into West Africa than any European before him with the exception of a few Portuguese many years before. His widow found herself in debtors' prison.

The general meeting of the African Association had been held just before the news of Houghton's death. The news from the major had been so encouraging that it had been decided that the committee should "make whatever applications to the government they may think advisable for rendering the late discoveries of Major Houghton serviceable to the commercial interests of the Empire." The secretary of the association wrote, in his report of the year's proceedings: "Of all the advantages to which a better acquaintance with the inland regions of Africa may lead, the first in importance is the extension of the commerce and the encouragement of the manufactures of Britain." Thus the noble sentiments of the founding resolution had soon been transformed into more worldly motives. It was an era which insisted that competitiveness based on nationalism had no part in the quest for knowledge; but nationalism had long since become a basic emotion among Europeans, and no one could say Sir Joseph Banks was not a patriot, nor some of his friends inept in commerce. The association was doing all it could to involve the British government in Africa.

The next step of the African Association committee, as always prompted by Sir Joseph Banks, was to meet the Foreign Secretary. It was suggested to the government that a consul should be sent deep into the interior of West Africa. The Foreign Secretary consulted Pitt, and the Prime Minister agreed. Behind their decision was the ever-present fear of the ambitions of the French, with whom Britain was now at war. Thus Banks and his friends had subtly brought the government into positive action.

It was also necessary to choose a successor to Houghton. It was Banks' influence which resulted in the selection of a young Scots doctor, who was fortunate, among other things, to rejoice in the unforgettable name of Mungo Park.

Park, like everyone else who had been connected with the association, had been partly inspired by the publication, in five volumes, of the travels in Egypt and Abyssinia of James Bruce, also a Scotsman. Bruce's ambitions had been different from those that now lay behind the association. He had been solely interested in adding to knowledge; in particular, he had decided to solve the mystery of the source of the Nile, which in all recorded history had disappeared beyond Cairo to no one knew where. Bruce was a remarkable man, the first of the great modern explorers of Africa, with a presence that people seldom forgot. To Fanny Burney he was "Man-mountain—the tallest man you ever saw in your life—he has a very good figure and is rather handsome." Another observer wrote that "his walk was stately, his air stately and commanding." He was redheaded and spoke with a loud, commanding voice. In Egypt he had adapted Arab disguise, and it was noted that "he was attentive to his dress and was particularly successful in wearing that of the nations through which he passed in an easy and graceful manner." He had prepared himself thoroughly, at his own expense, and spoke Arabic fluently.

Bruce had penetrated Abyssinia from the Red Sea. He had reached the capital and had so impressed the Abyssinians with his air of natural superiority that he had become commander of the royal cavalry and had taken part in local wars. He had returned to Europe, by way of the Sudan and Egypt, after an absence of ten years. Bruce had worked on his account of his travels for years; with its publication he claimed to have filled "a great chasm in the history of the Universe." In fact, he grossly overrated his contribution, but he had succeeded in traveling farther in Africa than any European before him.

Such was the man who inspired Mungo Park. Bruce had set a high standard. Could anyone even equal his achievement and emulate his gift for survival?

Park had qualified as a doctor at Edinburgh University but had no interest at all in medicine and was too ambitious to settle down to the life of a general practitioner. He was twenty-three years old, with a finely chiseled nose, tall and thin, extremely religious, and with a cold, reserved personality. To satisfy an interest in natural history, he had served as a ship's surgeon in the East Indies.

On Banks' recommendation, Mungo Park was interviewed by the committee, which found him "a young man of no mean talents." He was accepted as the man to follow Houghton's trail and then to press on for himself. It was agreed that he should receive 15 shillings for every day he spent in Africa, with £200 expenses. He was to travel with the new British consul to West Africa. But the consul was reluctant to depart, and when it was discovered that he was already proving more expensive than even the highest estimates before as much as setting foot in Africa, his appointment and the whole project of a consul were canceled. Park set out alone, well aware of the terrible task ahead of him, but fortified by his ambition to become famous, by his faith, and by his strangely unemotional character. "I wish you may be able to look upon the day of your departure," he wrote to a friend, "with the same resignation that I do on mine."

On December 3, 1795, Mungo Park, with an interpreter and servant, left the Gambia River for the interior. Like Houghton, his object was to reach the Niger, visit Timbuktu, and report on what nature of civilization existed in Africa, if any. His chances of survival were thin. It was typical of Park that he made things as difficult for himself as he could by insisting on wearing European clothes and by not preparing himself in Arab or Moslem customs, although it was well known that there was Moslem influence in the interior. He took with him food for two days, beads and tobacco for buying provisions, some fire-arms, clean shirts, a compass, a thermometer, a sextant, and an umbrella.

News of the progress of the white man spread in the thick forest and bush. On arrival at each village, Park was begged to remain, but he was a man of exceptional, almost suicidal, resolution. At one village he came across the practice of Mumbo Jumbo, in which an unsatisfactory wife was beaten with a rod, after a wild communal dance. He made good progress and just before Christmas passed the place where the wretched Major Houghton had died. Native kings dispossessed him of his few belongings, and what was left was seized by robbers.

Later Park was taken prisoner by a Moor chief and was brutally ill-treated—kept in a hut with a wild hog, the object of great curiosity. His journal reveals: "The surrounding attendants, and especially the ladies, were most inquisitive; they asked a thousand questions, inspected every part of my clothes, searched my pockets, and obliged me to unbutton my waistcoat and display the whiteness of my skin—they even counted my toes and fingers, as if they doubted whether in truth I was a human being." The ladies were intrigued to know whether circumcision was practiced among white men. "I observed to them that it was not customary to give ocular demonstrations in such cases before so many beautiful women; but that if all of them would retire except the young lady to whom I pointed (selecting the youngest and handsomest), I would satisfy her curiosity."

Park managed to escape, with his horse, after more than a month's captivity. Without food and water, he eventually was unable to continue. He thought: "Here, after a short but ineffectual struggle, I must end all my hopes of being useful in my day and generation; here must the short span of my life come to an end." On the point of death, a storm came, and Park survived by sucking the water from his clothing. For three weeks he struggled on. Then, nearly eight months after starting his journey: "I saw with infinite pleasure the great object of my mission—the long-sought-for majestic Niger glittering to the morning sun, as broad as the Thames at Westminster. I hastened to the brink and, having drunk of the water, lifted up my fervent thanks in prayer to the Great Ruler of all things."

Park waited outside the walls of Segu, at that time one of the great cities of West Africa, but was not allowed admittance. His position was extremely dangerous. No one for hundreds of miles had ever seen a white man before. His clothes, though ragged, were strange and unfamiliar. He could speak only a few words of any language that could be understood. Above all, he seemed to have no acceptable reason for his journey, and it was widely rumored through many districts that he was a sinister spy.

Park decided to end the expedition. "Worn down by sickness, exhausted by hunger and fatigue, half-naked, and without any article of value by which I might get provisions, clothes or lodging, I felt I should sacrifice my life to no purpose, for my discoveries would perish with me."

He began the long and dangerous journey to the coast, in an almost perpetual daze through fever. Here and there he found help and compassion and eventually met a caravan of slaves, led by a merchant who had experienced contact with Europeans. He reached a British trading station on the coast after an absence of two years and nine months, having traveled nearly 2,000 miles. He had suffered terribly in mind and body, often through his own stubbornness. Had he at anytime used his medical training on an African with a minor ailment which he could have been confident of curing, his progress might have been transformed to one full of welcome and interest rather than of suspicion. But not once on the entire journey, so far as is known, did he make use of his background in medicine.

In London, Mungo Park was feted with some joy. It was ten years since the foundation of the African Association, and in that time it had fathered nothing but chaos, farce, and tragedy. Now, at last, there was something practical to show for all the expense and all the earnest talk. Banks proudly showed off his protégé at dinner parties and at his breakfast discussions. Park submitted to the adulation with a sullen resignation. One fashionable hostess wrote in her diary: "He has neither fancy nor genius, and if he does fib, it is dully." Like many explorers after him, he must have found the transition from the rigors and adventures of the wilderness to the trivialities of society an irritating one. But Park did not, in fact, fib. The publication of his account, partly ghostwritten, was an immediate success, owing in the main to its transparent honesty and also to its brevity, compared with Bruce's work. It became a classic.

Before returning home to Scotland, Park attended the general meeting of the association at the Star and Garter. There he was presented with great satisfaction as a kind of prize exhibit. It was May 25 ,1799—a significant date for the British Empire in the coming century. If anyone had still believed that the object of the association was entirely limited to the quest for knowledge, Banks' speech would have quickly disillusioned them:

We have already, by Mr. Park's means, opened a gate into the interior of Africa, into which it is easy for every nation to enter and to extend its commerce. . . . A detachment of 500 chosen troops would soon make that road easy and would build embarkations [*i.e.,* boats] upon the Niger—if 200 of these were to embark with field pieces they would be able to overcome the whole forces which Africa could bring against them. The trade which the Moors carry on to the interior is always directed to the towns situated on or near the river—it is said to produce an annual return of about a million sterling—much of it in gold. . . . It is easy to foretell that if this country delays much longer to possess themselves of the treasures laid open to them by the exertions of this Association, some rival nation will take possession of the banks of the Niger and assert by arms her right of prior possession.

It was agreed that the government should be approached immediately about sending an armed expeditionary force to the Niger. Some of the most respected and influential men in the land were crowded into that room at the tavern just off Pall Mall. The resolution was carried unanimously.

At the same time that the African Association was congratulating itself in London, a colony was actually being established on the west coast. It was a weird affair, very different from the colonial aspirations of Sir Joseph Banks. The judgment which had made slavery illegal in England had automatically freed more than 10,000 Africans in London and the provinces. Most of these were thus suddenly destitute, and apparently few householders were interested in them as wage earners. A London doctor suggested that they should be established on the coast at Sierra Leone—"a permanent and comfortable establishment in a most pleasant, fertile climate." The doctor explained that the place was a virtual paradise: "A man possessed of a change of clothing, a woodaxe, a hoe and a pocket-knife may soon place himself in an easy and comfortable situation."

It seemed an excellent and humanitarian solution to the color problem of the day. Guilt would be assuaged, responsibility fulfilled, and a social nuisance disposed of. The scheme gained much support, and the government promised free transport. About 350 Africans left Portsmouth in the first shipload. With them were 70 white women "of dubious reputation." Because of the war with France, the government even provided a naval escort. On arrival at the west coast of Africa, the naval commander negotiated a chunk of land for the settlers from the local chief, King Tom. The ships then departed.

The freed slaves had for the most part worked in England as flamboyantly dressed and heavily powdered flunkies at stately homes and town mansions. To have had such a slave had been a considerable status symbol. Compared to the slaves of the Americans, their lot had been positively agreeable. Their experiences on their home continent were disastrous. Many of them died during the torrential downpours of the first rainy season. Others died when they were attacked by a neighboring tribe. When another shipload arrived, there were few of the original party left. More reinforcements—1,200 strong—arrived from Nova Scotia, where they had been languishing after making the mistake of supporting the English side in the American War of Independence. A company was set up, financed by middle-class investors from all over Britain. Company officials were sent out, and gradually the chaotic, rough little settlement began to look more durable. It even managed to survive a comprehensive sacking by a squadron of French ships.

The African Association kept somewhat aloof from this venture. It dispatched another explorer, Frederick Hornemann, a German, into Africa. Hornemann followed the direction that Ledyard had intended to take. From Cairo he traveled across the continent almost to the Niger, but like Houghton and Ledyard, he never returned. He was followed by W. G. Browne, who explored the Sudan on his own initiative.

By the end of the century the British had undertaken more activity in the interior of Africa since the start of the African Association twelve years before than they had in all their previous history. Now it was time for military conquest. The French had already occupied Egypt, and this act had prompted the British government to send an expeditionary force there. Egypt was one way to the greatest prize of all—India. There had been hard fighting before the French had sailed for home; but the government had no real wish to remain in Egypt. After two years of mild, ineffective, and inconclusive occupation, the British force sailed out of Alexandria in March, 1803.

After the African Association resolution about the conquest of the Niger lands, Banks had written to Lord Liverpool, a minister, asking that the Cabinet be informed of the association's view. He wrote in the most energetic terms of the likely benefits:

> As the trade with the negroes for manufactured goods is already firmly established and as gold is found in abundance [the government ought] to secure to the British throne, either by conquest or by treaty, the whole of the coast of Africa from Arguin to Sierra Leone. [The British could be expected to] govern the negroes far more mildly and make them far more happy than they are now under the tyranny of their arbitrary princes, [and] would become popular at home by converting them to the Christian religion by inculcating in their rough minds the mild morality which is engrafted on the tenets of our faith and by effecting the greatest practicable diminution of the slavery of mankind upon the principles of natural justice and commercial benefit.

What Lord Liverpool read—and the Cabinet considered—was the first expression of the code of British rule in Africa. Nothing was omitted: Commercial gain for Britain would bring gain for the natives; British rule would be enlightened and would benefit the natives morally and practically; such rule would spread Christianity and end slavery. This was a glimpse of the future, a prediction of the attitude of the white man's burden, in which lofty sentiments expressed self-justification and half hid commercial interest.

Mungo Park idled in Scotland, supported by the proceeds of his book. He married and had three children, toyed with the idea of becoming a farmer, and considered, with some distaste, taking up the life of a country doctor. He also kept in touch with Sir Joseph Banks.

The Establishment in London was increasingly agitated by the continuing stories of the vast riches in Africa, almost always connected with the name of Timbuktu.

Meanwhile, Banks had gained an important ally. The government, reluctant to take the initial step in building a new empire in Africa, had to be ceaselessly goaded and lobbied. The undersecretary of state at the Colonial Office had become a supporter of Banks' view, since Sir Joseph had shown him a copy of a recently published French book which advocated "a plan of operations" in West Africa, including "one sole administration, firm, wise and enlightened" backed by "a well-organized land force." Writing to the Colonial Office, Banks pointed out that the book was "written with the clear intention to induce the French to colonize" in Africa. He added, ominously: "I am clear that His Majesty's Ministers should be aware of the contents, and hold in mind what will happen, which is that whoever colonizes in that part of Africa with spirit will clearly be able to sell colonial products of all kinds in the European market at a cheaper price."

Mungo Park, on his return from Africa, had promised he would go back to the Niger if the government should "think fit to establish a colony on its banks." He was summoned to London but was not now so enthusiastic to revisit Africa. He was deeply in love with his wife, adored his children, and he was famous. But he had become a country doctor, and he seemed to believe that the nation owed him more than that. He was also getting short of money. He agreed to go on the conditions that a pension of £100 a year would be provided to his wife if he did not return and that any bad news would be kept from the newspapers so that she would not read it. In his own words: "My sweet wife, you are everything that I could desire, and wherever we go you may be sure of one thing, that I shall always love you." He also extracted from the government "the most solemn promise that in case of my success I shall be put into a comfortable situation at my return."

An ambitious plan, involving a considerable expeditionary force, was worked out, but after a change of government this was whittled down. Park, accompanied by a small force, was to act as "an envoy of the British Government," make treaties by which Britain could establish trading depots along the Niger, and establish the location of the mouth of the Niger to determine if it was navigable from the sea. Throughout its planning and execution, the least enthusiastic backers of this scheme were the political leaders of Britain. Seldom, if ever, has a government set out on the course of imperialism so reluctantly.

On January 31, 1805, Mungo Park and his little party embarked at Portsmouth to claim one of the richest and most populous areas of the African continent for Britain.

Forty-four Europeans, mostly soldiers, and a large party of African bearers and guides set off for the interior under Park's leadership. None of them could have realized what lay ahead or they might not have gone. Park had been given the rank of captain in the army and led the expedition as he imagined a military affair should be conducted. He knew nothing of military life and expected his men to follow him blindly, without showing much interest in them or displaying the exceptional qualities of leadership which were demanded. He was impatient. Knowing full well the dangers of the rainy season, he could not wait for it to pass over. "If all goes well," he wrote, "this day six weeks I expect to drink all your healths in the water of the Niger."

The column progressed slowly but successfully until, after a few weeks, distant lightning heralded the start of the rains. "The rain had not commenced three minutes," wrote Park, "before many of the soldiers were affected with vomiting; others fell asleep and seemed as if half-intoxicated." Unknown to the abstemious Park, they were probably wholly intoxicated. Every mile became a sodden misery. Park hurried on ahead, and when he camped at the end of each day, the weary soldiers, in their disintegrating red coats, stumbled in one by one, hours behind him. Every few days a redcoat was left behind in a native village, wasting with disease, never to be seen or heard from again. Park would stop for no one, while the expedition, feverish and exhausted, tramped and slithered through the forest, stretching for miles behind him. It had become an ill-disciplined rabble. The second-in-command had discovered native liquor and was seldom sober: "Whitbread's beer is nothing to what we get at this place, as I feel by my head this morning, having been drinking all night."

With death and disaster all around him, Park kept up a series of cheery dispatches home, presumably to reassure his wife. In reality he must have been disheartened and probably conscious of his fate. After nearly four months and 500 miles, the remnants of the expedition reached the northern bank of the Niger. It was ten years since Park had last seen the great river. The proud party which had left the coast to claim the Niger for Britain had been reduced to a pathetic rabble that could hardly have impressed the most unsophisticated native. Only one of the carpenters, who had been attached to the party for building the boats, had survived, and he was dying. Still, Mungo Park was as indomitable as ever, although he admitted now that his prospects were "somewhat gloomy . . . I had proudly flattered myself that we should reach the Niger with a very moderate loss."

With the only one of the remaining redcoats who could still stand, Park joined together two half-rotten canoes and made a 40-foot craft. It took nearly three weeks to complete. Park then sent what was to be his last note: "I am far from desponding." The Union Jack was hoisted, and the party embarked. Of the original forty-four Europeans, five remained (one of them mad). They and four Africans sailed downriver into the unknown.

What happened will never be exactly known, but what is certain is that Park spilled much African blood as he progressed, firing away at the banks when approached by natives. It was unexpected, for, as Park had written, throughout the overland journey "I had always been able to preserve the most friendly terms with the natives." The tales of the destruction of the tall white man, in his strange craft, were recounted over a large part of Africa for generations. The English were indelibly marked, not as friends, but as enemies. Perhaps Park did it out of determination to reach the sea and safety, perhaps out of self-preservation, perhaps, with the flag flying above him, in some half-crazed dream of colonial conquest. Whatever the reason, the result did incalculable harm to the dreams of Sir Joseph Banks and the African Association. Another explorer, twenty years later, coming across the results of Park's work, exclaimed: "How imprudent, how unthinking! I may even say how selfish it was in Park to attempt to make discoveries in this country at the expense of the blood of the inhabitants, and to the exclusion of all after communication." Thus the first official British expedition into Africa was a disaster: Not one man returned, no territory was claimed, no commercial benefit resulted, the mouth of the Niger remained a mystery, and the Africans of the Niger region had been alienated.

Park's widow, who lived till 1840, refused to accept her husband's death. Twenty-one years later she sent one of her sons to trace him, convinced that he was a captive of the natives. He, too, perished in the interior.

A year after Park's death, the British were back in Africa with military force. In 1807 an expedition of nearly 5,000 men disembarked at Alexandria without opposition. The intention was not conquest but the stabilization of the regime after the vacuum left by the end of the French occupation. Marching south, a column was ambushed, and it regained Alexandria only after very severe losses. The heads of the slain British soldiers were fixed on spikes lining each side of a road in Cairo. The advance guard of the main column, nearly 750 strong, was surrounded and destroyed; the remainder regained Alexandria, having suffered 900 casualties. Six months after its arrival, the expeditionary force left Alexandria, leaving many hundreds of British heads on display in Cairo. The reputation of British military expertise it left behind on the Nile was not high.

In the same year the abolition of slavery in British territories and by British subjects was passed in the House of Commons by a vote of 283 to 16. It was the result of several long debates in Parliament stretching over a number of years—the most noble debates ever to have been held at Westminster. The government paid £20,000,000 compensation to the owners of West Indies plantations. It did not mean the end of the slave trade in Africa; it did not even herald it, but it did mean that the British had prepared themselves morally for a humanitarian aspect of any future colonialism in Africa.

For the British had just taken over an African territory, not through negotiation and not through treaties, but through armed intervention. It was not in that part of Africa which had most interested the statesmen, Egypt; it was not in that part which had intrigued the African Association, the west coast; it was in the farthest part of the continent, the remote and distant Cape of Good Hope.

The Dutch colony in South Africa had existed for a century and a half. It was the only well-defined European colony in Africa. By 1810 it extended nearly 200 miles inland. But Holland had never shown much interest in the place except as a calling station on the way to the East. The settlers had suffered for many generations from harsh and unsympathetic government by the home country. A great many of them, moreover, were not of Dutch stock at all but were German and French. In order to escape taxes and administration, they had developed the system of pushing ever farther away from Cape Town, trekking, which had led to the expansion of the colony. The European population was different in a very important respect from that in most other colonies of the world since American independence: It had not come to Africa to exploit the people, to set up plantations, or to open up trade. It had come to escape from Europe, for a variety of reasons, but mainly because of religious persecution. Whatever the Dutch government and merchants thought about it, the intention of the settlers was not to colonize, but to start a new country. They considered themselves as African as the natives—Afrikaners. Most of the territory had been purchased from the African chiefs, and when the British arrived, as a result of the war with France (in which Holland had become involved), there was already a move for independence from the home country. The British military occupation had been astounded "at the almost incredible ignorance of the world without." The British governor had written to London: "Of the importance of this colony I need say nothing to you, but it grows in it every hour. It is and will become the centre of commerce with India, America and Europe." When peace had been made, the British had left. But on the resumption of war with Napoleon they returned in 1806. A battle was won outside Cape Town, where a 2,000-strong Cape army, facing 4,500 British troops, fled when the British artillery opened fire. Ten days later the colony capitulated.

This time the British showed no sign of leaving the Cape of Good Hope. They were there primarily because of its strategic importance, halfway to India and the East. With the renewed interest in the East, since the loss of the American colonies, they surely would not again leave a place of such vital importance to a scattered and reviving empire.

Britain was in Africa.

The loss of Mungo Park and the setback to the ambitions of the African Association in West Africa had an inevitable effect on the association. Although interest in its activities began to wane, it sent out two more explorers, Henry Nicholls and J. L. Burkhardt. They fitted a few more tiny pieces of the jigsaw of Africa in place, but no commercial advantages ensued. The association started to decline. Many of the original founder members died, and regular meetings were no longer held at the Star and Garter; nor were there any new subscribers. But the association had done its work. It had given the momentous push that aroused the British government to the possibilities of Africa and to the danger of rival powers colonizing there. When the next important explorer, Henry Salt, visited Ethiopia, he did so as a personal emissary of the Foreign Secretary and at public expense.

The early African explorers—Bruce, Houghton and, above all, Mungo Park—had played their part in this reversal of policy. This extraordinary breed of men—madly adventurous, inexhaustibly ambitious for self and country, and with iron determination—had set a standard of bravery, if not of scientific method, of which all future explorers of the continent would be conscious. It was they who gave African exploration of the nineteenth century its flavor. But most important had been the man who had directed the whole operation from his home in Soho Square, Sir Joseph Banks, who knew that the government was sufficiently involved to ensure that he would get his way, although not quite for the reasons that he would have wished. If Britain had made clear to the world its interest in Egypt and the Cape of Good Hope, it was only because these were the two gateways to India.

But there was no escaping the fact that the British army had marched beside the Nile, was stationed at the Cape, and was now in West Africa, where the government had taken over responsibility for the small ailing settlement of Sierra Leone. The Cabinet had committed itself, at some expense and considerable loss of life, to obtaining the lands of the Niger for British influence. It had all happened in less than thirty years. For most of that time the authorities in Britain had been distracted, and the energies of the country sapped, by the war with France. With a long peace in Europe, it would be different.

Africa, almost inviolate for centuries, ruled by Africans or Arabs over nearly all its vast surface, awaited the onslaught of the men from the faraway island, a mere fraction of its own size, off the coast of Europe.

PART TWO

WHITE MAN'S GRAVE

✤ II ✤

The Way to Timbuktu

BRITAIN emerged from Napoleon's wars with confidence restored after the shattering loss of the American colonies. Her people felt, and were, powerful once more. They had good claim to being the most powerful country in Europe. The British navy had asserted itself as the most important single factor of power in the world, a situation which was to last throughout the new century. The Industrial Revolution had given the nation a useful start in new skills and capital. There were many opportunities, particularly in India, which seemed to hypnotize the minds of both the ruling class and a rapidly expanding middle class—to the fury of those trying to turn the government's attention to Africa. But the African Association had given the push, and the government had committed itself and its successors, in West and South Africa.

The navy was remarkably successful in enforcing the act abolishing the slave trade in British ships. And Britain, proud of her newly won self-respect and conscious of her self-imposed economic sacrifice, pestered other countries to follow her example and abolish slavery. The result was an economic decline of British trading posts on the west coast of Africa. Serious and determined efforts to replace the trade in slaves with legitimate trade met at first with little success, although some merchants had been conducting such trade for years. Only in Sierra Leone, to which the government had dispatched troops, and at the free-enterprise area at what was (unknown at the time) the Niger Delta, was there much legitimate trading. Despite the British abolition, the slave trade lingered on. So long as a profitable market existed in America, European and American ships could be found to transport Africans across the ocean.*

Sir Joseph Banks had done his best, but now he was immersed in many other projects: a reform of the coinage, the troubles of the colony in New South Wales, progressive agriculture, the chairmanship of many committees, and his usual involvement in science. He had lost the use of his legs and had to be carried about by his servants or pushed in a wheelchair. Only one other founder member of the association was still alive. The Saturday Club had faded away.

A new group had been set up in 1807: the African Institution. This consisted mostly of those who had fought for abolition and who wanted to continue their interest in Africa now that their battle had been won. They were in the main different from Banks' friends, especially in their motives: "Deeply impressed with a sense of the enormous wrongs which the natives of Africa have suffered in their intercourse with Europe; and from a desire to repair those wrongs, as well as from a general feeling of benevolence, [the institution] is anxious to adapt such measures as are best calculated to promote their civilization and happiness." This is yet another early statement of the burden which some English men, probably sparked by guilt, felt they were obliged to bear.

Banks died on June 19, 1820, and was buried unostentatiously, at his own request, not in St. Paul's or in Westminster Abbey, but in the parish churchyard at Heston, Middlesex. Eulogies of him soon appeared throughout Europe. Banks would have been unimpressed. He once wrote: "My disposition is not of a nature inclined to wish for the control of any man's sentiments. . . . We shall certainly be esteemed by the world in proportion to the truth or justice of what we speak or print." There is no doubt that he always spoke what he believed to be true.

A year after Banks' death the British government took another tentative step toward Africa. The old posts of the Gold

* Until the Second World War there was still a colony of old first-generation slaves, near Mobile, Alabama, who had come to America, as children, seventy-five years before.

Coast, struggling to survive, were taken over from private enterprise. But the most important upheaval taking place in West Africa did not result from the British at all. It was the spread of the empire of the Fulani, in what is now Nigeria, and the rise of a proud people, called the Ashanti, in what is now Ghana.

One reason for the deterioration of the African Association was that the government had taken over responsibility for expeditions into the interior—a fact which most members would have rightly considered a success for the association. Beginning in 1816, various expeditions were sent out from the west and north coasts. In 1822 a party of three, two Scotsmen and an Englishman, was sent to make contact with the native kingdom of Bornu. They were better chosen than some of the adventurers whom the African Association had picked. Hugh Clapperton, a brawny, adventurous naval officer, was the tenth child of a Dumfriesshire doctor. Walter Oudney was a serious Royal Navy doctor from Edinburgh. Dixon Denham was an army major who had fought at Waterloo. Oudney was studious, Clapperton was fond of the bottle, and Denham was fond of the ladies.

Denham wrote: "We were the first English travellers who had determined to travel [from the north] in our real characters as Britons and Christians and to wear our English dress: the buttons on our waistcoats and our watches caused the greatest astonishment." Within days they all were down with fever. A few generations later they would have been considered invalids who would not have been allowed out of the hospital to cross the road, let alone the Sahara Desert. Three months later they sighted Lake Chad across the billowy sand dunes—the first Europeans known to have done so. Leaving Denham at Chad to explore that area, the other two continued. Oudney died of fever, but Clapperton continued on his lonely way, reaching the important trading city of Kano—one of the largest cities in Africa. Surveyed with bewilderment and suspicion by the population, Clapperton entered the walls. "Arrayed in what was left of my naval uniform, I made myself as smart as circumstances would permit." Clapperton was given a hut beside a stagnant swamp that acted as an open sewer. In one of his few phrases of

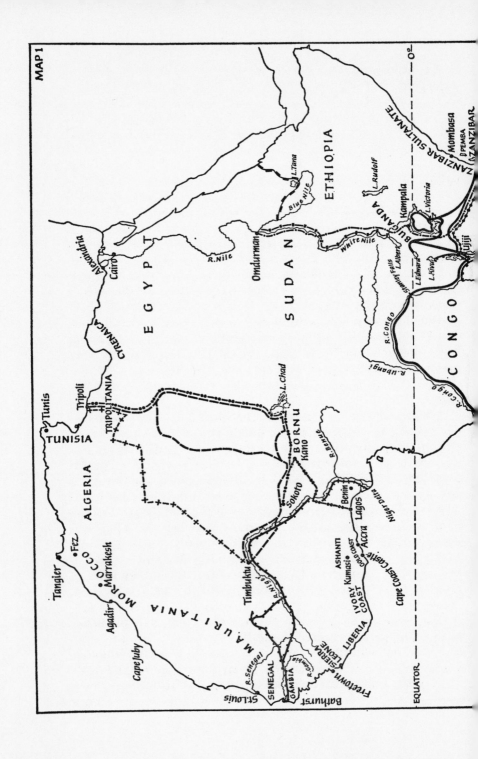

MAP 1

Bruce 1768-73
Mungo Park 1795-7, 1806
Clapperton 1823-5, 1825-7
Landers 1830
Barth 1850-5
Livingstone 1851-73
Speke & Grant 1862
Burton & Speke 1857-9
Baker 1862
Stanley 1871-2, 1874-7
Laing 1825

AFRICA—The Explorers

discontent, he complained of "an abominable stench." His condition was improved by the safe arrival of three bottles of port from Denham.

The two men met again after a nine-month absence. Having done rather more than his fair share of the expedition, Clapperton was half-dead with exhaustion. Relations between the two deteriorated, and Denham reported to London that Clapperton was having a homosexual affair with one of the Arab attendants. They returned to Tripoli nearly three years after they had left it.

Clapperton and Denham were able to fill in a section of the map and to report on untapped trading potential at Bornu. Of Timbuktu, they could report little, but Clapperton confirmed that it was a source of gold.

The government now decided that it was in the national interest to solve the Timbuktu mystery. For the task they picked yet another Scotsman, Gordon Laing, the son of an Edinburgh headmaster. Laing was probably the most remarkable of all the explorers of Africa. At Edinburgh University he had been a star pupil, and eventually he became a schoolmaster. But Laing was plagued with restlessness and taunted by ambition. In 1811 he joined the army and was stationed in Sierra Leone. Unpopular in his regiment and feeling restricted by military life, he began to bombard the authorities, including the Colonial Secretary, with letters suggesting he should try to reach Timbuktu. After five years he had made such a nuisance of himself that he got his way.

For years he had suffered from ill health, he spoke no Arabic, and he knew nothing of the desert. When he arrived at Tripoli, in 1825, heading the grandly named Timbuktu Mission the British consul there, Hanmer Warrington, was alarmed at his wan and sickly appearance. Warrington reported to London: "He is both gentlemanly and clever, and certainly appears most zealous in the cause he has undertaken, although I much fear the delicate state of his health will not carry him through his arduous task." Laing rejected the idea of taking a doctor with him. He was determined to be the first European to visit Timbuktu and to share the fame with no one.

Laing fell desperately in love with the consul's lovely daughter, a granddaughter, out of wedlock, of George IV. The atmosphere of Laing's departure from Tripoli for the unknown could not have been more extraordinary. The intense and hotheaded Scotsman demanded Emma Warrington's hand in marriage. Warrington, outraged, wrote to the Colonial Secretary: "I must allow a more wild, enthusiastic and romantic attachment never before existed. I found my wishes, exertions, entreaties and displeasure quite futile and of no avail." British consuls had the right to conduct the marriage service, and the couple persuaded him to marry them. Warrington, however, refused to allow the marriage to be consummated. From the moment of the service he arranged that his daughter should never leave his sight or that of his wife.

Two days after the ceremony Laing made off into the desert. With virtually no preparation at all by modern standards, he was attempting the most terrible journey that the world had to offer. He carried with him a letter of introduction from the government of the United Kingdom to "The Sultan of the Kingdom and Territory of Timbuktu." Against all odds, the obscure, sickly junior officer from the hopelessly unfashionable regiment had succeeded in his life's ambition: "I shall do more than ever has been done before, and shall show myself to be what I have ever considered myself, a man of enterprise and genius."

A race to be the first to reach Timbuktu had been developing for some months. An Italian had died trying to reach it from the west coast. A Frenchman was now preparing himself for the effort. The Geographical Society of Paris had announced a 10,000-franc prize to the first man to return from Timbuktu. And before leaving Tripoli, Laing had learned that Clapperton intended to return to Africa in order to visit Timbuktu. Laing wrote, coldly: "Should he succeed in reaching Timbuktu, which I doubt much, I shall have much pleasure in meeting him."

Laing progressed slowly, continually delayed by money wrangles, sickness, and the deceit of his guides. He plodded on across the wastes of the Sahara, an unwanted stranger, from oasis to oasis. Every few months, letters from him, often infuriatingly full of irrelevant material, such as his obsession about being promoted, amazingly got back to Tripoli:

> Pray say nothing to Emma about the detention I have met with, as it will only cause her to fret and to suppose that I may be much longer on the journey than I expected. . . .

For heaven sake, my dear Consul, do endeavour to let me hear occasionally from Tripoli. If I can only know that my Emma is well, I will answer for my successful completion of this journey, but if I am left to conjecture and despondency the state of my mind may prove much more prejudicial to the state of my health than the climate of Africa. The road has for the most part been a complete desert, and for the last three days we ran very short of water, and entirely so of provisions. . . . The heat has been almost intolerable; since I left you the thermometer at noon standing not infrequently at 120 degrees Fahrenheit. . . .

I admit that common sense is more necessary for conducting the petty affairs of life than genius or enterprise, but the man who roams into the regions of speculation should never be hampered by it. Had I been gifted with that quality which the bulk of mankind consider so inestimable, I might now have been a jolly subaltern on half-pay, or perhaps an orthodox preacher in some country kirk. . . . I must say I am very desirous to reach this wonderful capital. . . .

When I write from Timbuktu I shall detail precisely how I was betrayed and nearly murdered in my sleep; in the meantime I shall acquaint you with the nature and number of my wounds, in all amounting to twenty-four, eighteen of which are exceedingly severe. To begin from the top: I have five sabre cuts on the crown of my head. . . . All will yet be well. . . . I am recovering rapidly, but am subject to dreadful pains in my head. Love to my dearest Emma, whom may heaven bless.

A year and one month after leaving Tripoli, Gordon Laing entered Timbuktu, having crossed the Sahara from north to south—the first European to have done so—and having covered a distance of 2,650 miles, almost all of them across loose sand. It was an incredible achievement, accomplished by almost inhuman determination and nothing else. It should have secured him the lasting fame he so desperately sought. His object had always been "to rescue my name from oblivion."

Laing's arrival at Timbuktu must have seemed to him the final twist of some cruel fate that was determined to sacrifice him. For what he saw was not a great metropolis steeped with learning and roofed with gold, but a squalid and unimportant slave market, made up of low mud buildings.

On the third night after leaving Timbuktu on the return journey, Laing was attacked by robbers while he slept and he was decapitated. His journal and papers were never discovered and became a recurrent source of dissension between Britain and France for half a century, because the British suspected that the journal had found its way to the French consul at Tripoli. There was an official and inconclusive French inquiry in 1910.*

It is the nature of exploration that its end cannot be foreseen, and Laing's discoveries were minor indeed. And thus, although he suffered and endured more than any other explorer in the history of African exploration, his efforts did not succeed in dragging his name from the oblivion which he feared. He has remained virtually unknown.

Clapperton had been probing for Timbuktu from the other side of the continent. The government had sent with him several companions, including a short, stocky Cornishman named Richard Lander—a man of "great muscular strength and iron constitution." Within a few months only Clapperton and Lander were left; the others had died of disease. Progress, however, was good: Clapperton distributed a goodly number of umbrellas as they went, and his easygoing manner made friends all the way. One chief was so enthralled with him that they had great difficulty in getting away. They were entertained liberally. "This morning," Clapperton wrote, "when I was with the sultan his breakfast was brought in, which I was asked to partake of. It consisted of a large grilled water-rat with the skin on, some very fine boiled rice with dried fish stewed in palm oil, and fried or stewed alligators' eggs." Clapperton gradually weakened; he seemed to lose the will to move on or to go back. He must have regretted his rashness in returning to Africa after only two months in London, his fame already established. One morning he called Lander to him: "Richard, I shall shortly be no more. I feel myself dying." He begged Lander to leave all their belongings but somehow to get his journal back to London. When Clapperton died Lander buried him with ceremony. "Amidst showers of tears, I read the impressive funeral service of the Church of England over the remains of my valued master—the English flag waving slowly and mournfuly over them at the same moment. Not a single soul listened to this peculiarly distressing ceremony, for the slaves were quarrelling with each other the whole of the time it lasted."

* Emma died of consumption three years later. Articles which had belonged to Laing were still appearing in the western Sudan well into the twentieth century.

Lander, a humble manservant, was alone deep in the hinterland of an unexplored continent. Somehow he managed to survive and seven months later reached the coast.

The government was suitably impressed by Lander's fortitude. Less than two years later he was back in Africa with his brother John, their mission to reach Mungo Park's place of death and carry on from there till they reached the mouth of the Niger. After three and a half months they reached the point on the Niger where Park was believed to have perished. The only relics of Park they found among the Africans were his logarithm tables, the hymnbook of his brother-in-law, a tailor's bill, and an invitation to a party in the Strand. The brothers loaded two native canoes with provisions, including two large bags of corn and one of beans, and two sheep. Surviving rapids and hostile natives on the banks, they heard within two months "the welcome sound of the surf on the beach."

The Niger exited into the Gulf of Guinea. The mystery of its termination had been solved, after a lapse of 2,500 years since the river had first been recorded by Herodotus, and it was two simple sons of a Cornish publican who had solved it.

The effect of the Landers' discovery was immediate. A company of merchants was formed in Liverpool to exploit the Niger. The instigator was Macgregor Laird, a kindly, rich shipbuilder. Two steamers were prepared for the purpose of entering the river, and Richard Lander agreed to accompany the expedition of forty-eight Europeans. The only interest the government showed was the attachment of a naval officer, a strange reaction after spending so much money and so many lives in discovering the course of the Niger. But this was in keeping with its policy of encouraging, but not otherwise interfering with, legitimate private enterprise. It was the age of laissez-faire.

One of the craft, a paddle steamer of 55 tons, was the first iron vessel to make an ocean voyage. The steamers puffed about in the intricate channels of the delta, the crews, struck with fever, crawling along on the decks. They found the area "uninviting, repulsive, dangerous, horrible and loathsome." One steamer spluttered and wheezed to a standstill in the great heat. The men ran out of oil for the engine and had to use pork fat; "extremely annoying," said Macgregor Laird. After many disappointments the expedition reached the town of Rabba, but

Macgregor Laird did not find the trade he had expected. Although the coast at the delta had traded with Europeans for generations, the interior was deeply set in its own pattern of trade, which allowed no room for the acquisitive men from Liverpool. The ships went up the river three times in attempts to make trading deals, but the local merchants, intimidated by the Fulani, were not interested. Lander was attacked and died of his wounds, and the expedition limped back to Liverpool with only eight of the Europeans surviving.

The attempt to open up the Niger had been a disastrous failure. But Laird was remarkably single-minded, and he did not give up easily. Still convinced that there was immense trading potential in the area around the Niger, he spent the rest of his life promoting his belief, although he never returned to Africa. In later years he persuaded the government to sign contracts for ships specially built for navigation of the Niger and began a shipping service to the west coast. And undismayed, other Englishmen were soon thinking of the possibilities of the Niger Basin.

The Niger was now established as an area of British interest, although no territory had been claimed. The grandly named West African Settlements consisted of no more than Sierra Leone, which was only one shantytown, the tiny settlement at Gambia, and the Gold Coast. It was the Gold Coast which was proving most tiresome.

Although the gold of the Gold Coast had been known for centuries and the sources were less than 100 miles inland, no European was known to have seen them. The Africans guarded their secret with tenacity, well aware of its value. The British had made the fatal, if inevitable, mistake of being involved in tribal competition. They had supported the claims of the inland Ashanti over the coastal Fanti. This was the humiliating result of an attack on a British fort by the Ashanti, which resulted in the loss of two-thirds of its garrison. The suspicious Ashanti were not satisfied with the British interpretation of this agreement.

As a result of their earlier moral victory, the Ashanti were full of confidence. They had an army of 10,000 fierce warriors, while the British could muster only 500 men from along the coast. Their Fanti allies were unreliable, and the British were overwhelmed. The governor himself, Sir Charles M'Carthy, was slain, and his skull was taken home by the Ashanti and used as a drinking cup.

Fighting continued for two years. Finally a Fanti-British force defeated the Ashanti, after great slaughter, near Accra. The Ashanti agreed to the frontier enforced on them.

The First Ashanti War did not command much attention at the time, but it was not without its significance. Despite all their protestations of goodwill, the British authorities had set a precedent of maintaining their interest by force. They had beaten a courageous and resourceful enemy by vastly superior firepower. The bitterness that was left in the Gold Coast would never be fully erased while the British remained—the useful traders had turned into conquerors. The British government, for its part, decided that the taxpayer could no longer be expected to pay for wars in Africa in the interests of trade.

On the coast, there was an uneasy, grim peace.

The government nominated a Committee of London Merchants to run the old Gold Coast forts. As local governor it appointed Captain George Maclean. It was firmly impressed on Maclean that his jurisdiction was confined to the forts and trading stations—the government, stung once, wanted to have nothing further to do with the interior of the Gold Coast.

George Maclean was the first of a line of dedicated and energetic public servants who, while serving the British, tried to serve the Africans too. As administrator, judge, and friendly ally, this tough Scotsman set a standard for all future British rulers in Africa—a standard not all were able to reach. For fifteen years he presided over the whole area—not just the forts—with paternal firmness and avuncular wisdom. He was the first senior administrator to profess to the white man's burden, and like most of the successful public servants in British Africa, he had to fight his own government all the way.

After peace was restored between Fanti and Ashanti, trade was increased. The slave trade was virtually stamped out. British law came to be understood and respected. Maclean was judge, as well as administrator, and chiefs sent petitioners from hundreds of miles to be judged by him—he became a kind of supreme court. Throughout the length of the West African coast there was a passionate love of litigation, a love which is not altogether absent today.

Maclean believed that the ancient customs of Africans should not be rudely destroyed in attempts at Europeanization; for this reason he did nothing about domestic slavery. News of this brought him many enemies in London, particularly from the still-powerful abolitionists, most of whom had never seen Africa. Since the abolition of the trade, no people were more condemnatory of slavery, more prone to see it everywhere, than the British—competition to be regarded as an abolitionist was intense.

Maclean's wife was a wildly popular, romantic poet. She had married Maclean after a giddy affair, having been enthralled by the notion of this already almost legendary figure, ruling the west coast as "the great white king." Her fans much resented her marriage to a man who they believed encouraged slavery and her departure for the "Dark Continent." When she died soon after her arrival, rumors that she had been murdered by Mclean spread through London.

Prejudice had its day, as it usually does. Maclean was recalled to London and was the subject of inquiry of a select committee of the House of Commons. The result was vindication and recognition of Maclean's work, especially his "useful, though irregular, jurisdiction." The government took over the Gold Coast from its committee of merchants, and Maclean was left to perfect his system of British equity and tribal law—a system which lasted for more than a century.

Around the coast, at the Niger, another expedition was taking place. Macgregor Laird had typified the tenacious new interest of British commerce in Africa. The latest sortie typified the other aspect of British interest—humanitarianism.

Three steamers and a sailing boat entered the Niger, with a total of 145 Britons aboard. Their object was twofold: one, to make trade treaties with African chiefs who would promise to give up domestic slavery; second, to establish a model farm on the Niger bank. The farm was intended to expand into a major settlement—"a city built under the protecting wings of Great Britain, to become ere long the capital of Africa." The goodwill behind the project was massive, and the phrases uttered in its support could not have been more noble. Victoria's prince consort was connected with it, and the government, contrary to its attitude to Laird, felt it safe and proper to support it in every way, including financially.

Few of the white men in the expedition—kindly, well-meaning but portly gentlemen—were physically ideal for the venture facing them. Within three weeks of entering the Niger, most of them were seriously ill, many of them dying. Nevertheless, the place picked for the farm, over a map on a table in London, was reached, and the materials—carts, plows, farmhouse furniture, and quantities of agricultural implements, most of them totally unsuitable for African conditions—were landed. Thirty-three freed slaves, who had been brought along for the purpose, were disembarked. Not only were they appalled by the reptiles crawling everywhere, but they had no idea how to use the farming equipment with which they were supplied. After two days they were back on board.

All the paraphernalia was reembarked, and a new place, a mile away, was chosen. After a week ashore seven men were dead and eighteen dying. Treaty-making, meanwhile, progressed briskly. A local chief, named by the expedition "King of Iddah," was considered to be a particularly good catch. He was received in a tent, accepted the gifts which were showered on him, and promised everything that was asked of him. To lend dignity to the occasion, one of the party dressed in the uniform of a trooper in the Life Guards (a regiment to which he had formerly belonged), which he had thoughtfully brought with him from home, and proudly clasped the Union Jack. The chief indicated that he was ready to cede territory and to marry the Queen of England, if a supply of guns and ammunition could be forwarded to him, since he had some recalcitrant neighbors he wanted to be rid of: What he wanted more than anything else, however, but did not get was the Life Guards helmet. A document was carefully signed, on the back of one of the party (there being no table), by the light of some oil blazing in a frying pan. A few days later one of the king's sons came alongside the British ships and tried to sell three slaves. The newly signed treaty, abolishing slavery, was gravely read to him in English, not a word of which he understood.

The expedition, decimated, was forced to return home. The model farm was abandoned, the "only produce of the steaming soil that the vessels brought off being a boatload of wan, half-dead people, including superintendent, farmer, schoolmaster, surgeon and gardener." Forty of the whites on the expedition had died of malaria. There was much indignation at home, and the government was not pleased. It ratified the treaty with Iddah, a modest collection of grass huts, the influence of which spread no more than a few miles, but noted coldly that "Her Majesty declines the sovereignty of any territory in Central Africa" and rejected any land offered to her by the "King of Iddah."

There was yet another, and natural, withdrawal of interest in Africa after this costly fiasco. But the Africa lobby was indefatigable and not to be denied. Above all, the great mystery of Timbuktu remained as elusive as ever, for Laing had managed to get no conclusive news back, and a Frenchman who had been to the city was regarded as an impostor. The Foreign Secretary was now Lord Palmerston; he was not interested in British expansion in Africa. He was, however, an exceedingly dedicated antislaver. He gave his assent to a mission to the interior to discover details of the internal slave trade, at public expense.

The expedition consisted of James Richardson and Heinrich Barth. They were the first of a new generation of African explorers: prepared, cautious, and scientific. Richardson wrote: "We should take especial care not to attempt too much at once; we should proceed very slowly, feeling our way. . . . African travel can only be successfully prosecuted piecemeal, bit by bit, here a little and there a little, now an island, now a line of coast. . . ." Mungo Park and Laing would have been astonished at such a modest approach. Barth was a giant of a man, of great physical strength, nearly six feet and a half, fluent in Arabic, a fitness fanatic, and a considerable scholar.

Richardson died close to Lake Chad. Barth continued, interviewing chiefs, discussing treaties, compiling detailed reports, with a meticulous loyalty for his employers. He was given up for dead, but after five and a half years he reappeared at Tripoli. Within four weeks of leaving the dreaded Sahara, Barth was discoursing with Palmerston in Downing Street. He wrote a massive account of his travels, supplied a great deal of information about African life, filled in details of the map, threw light on political matters and slave routes, and finally laid to rest the Timbuktu myth.

In London, Barth received the attention that returning astronauts were to receive a century later. The queen awarded him the Order of the Bath, and Oxford conferred an honorary degree on him, but Barth was not happy. "I have been accustomed to the desert," he wrote. "To infinite spaces, where I have not had to worry about the trivialities that stifle men." He never returned to Africa and died a few years later in Berlin, aged forty-four.

It was ironic that for its most successful traveler in Africa, Britain had been obliged to hire a German. It was fortunate, too, for Barth set the new style; the buccaneering days, when reports were thin and life was cheap, were over.

By mid-century the British possessions in Africa still consisted of no more than the old Dutch colony in South Africa and the settlements on the west coast. Despite the presence of the army in Sierra Leone and the Gold Coast, frequent visits from the antislavery patrols of the Royal Navy, and the gradually increasing legitimate trade, the British west coast of Africa was a ramshackle affair. The government had long considered it more a nuisance than anything else.

In Gambia, at Bathurst, there were more French than British, and business was mainly in French hands. In Sierra Leone, the senior colony, the sole desire of most white men was to survive and eventually to return home; between 1822 and 1830 about 1,400 Europeans had died of a floating population of fewer than 2,000. Governors came and went at the rate of about two a year. One of them was Dixon Denham, who died a few days after taking up his post, aged forty-two. Freetown, in Sierra Leone, had become for a period a sort of capital for British interests on the coast. Drunkenness was the main cause for concern in Freetown, where the majority of the population was sober only when sleeping. The place was "roaring with drink," as one governor put it. The delta of the Niger was still the home of slaves and various "palm-oil" rogues out to gamble for a quick fortune against an early death from malaria. As late as 1851 a naval expedition was sent to Lagos to abolish human sacrifice. Tribal warfare continued unchecked around the British settlements. The ill-paid employees of the companies were often there for no better reason than debts at home. Some went "half-native," became corrupt, and most died of disease or drink.

The first half century of official British settlement on the west coast of the African continent had been largely sordid, farcical, or sad. It signally lacked that imperial majesty and grandeur that would have pleased the queen. Gallant white men selflessly fighting and educating black hordes, as certain adventure novels and romances were now beginning to portray, were all that most people knew of Africa. It was satisfying to know that Britain was engaged in such good work. The sooner the poor savages were civilized, the sooner they would become grateful customers for the industries of Birmingham, Manchester, and Leeds. And perhaps this could be more easily done if territory were actually taken over, after all.

✧ III ✧

The Great Trek

Six thousand miles from Whitehall, a new British colony was basking under a hot but pleasant sun. Farms and settlements spread for hundreds of miles northeast from Cape Town. Bullock carts pounded down the long tracks which snaked through the gentle hills. Compared with West Africa, the climate was kind to Europeans. Rains came in from the glistening Indian Ocean, producing a potentially hospitable land. Far inland, over the mountains, the vast, dry veld stretched away—an apparently endless expanse of land, tempting and waiting.

Cape Colony was an area which had been settled and developed by the Dutch. The British were conscious of this, but they had little idea what to do about it. Problems were inevitable, and policy was remote and out of touch. The white population numbered more than 25,000, nearly all Afrikaner. Cape Town was the largest white town on the African continent; about 20,000 people lived there, of whom more than 6,000 were Europeans.

The British occupation was formalized in 1815, at a meeting between the prince regent and the King of the Netherlands. The Cape was transferred to British sovereignty in part payment for the expense of defending Holland against Napoleon, but the British had been there for nearly ten years, anyway, and had no intention of departing. As his final act before leaving, the last Dutch governor had written a private and confidential letter to the British general in command:

Allow me, sir, to recommend to your protection the inhabitants of this colony, whose happiness and welfare ever since I have been here were the chief objects of my care, and who conducted themselves during that period to my highest satisfaction. . . . They have their faults, but these are more than compensated by good qualities. Through lenity, through marks of affection, and benevolence, they may be conducted to any good.

It had a nice ring. But relations between governors and governed in South Africa had never been marked by "affection." The British, however, did not expect trouble. In Africa they never did. Soon British officials took the place of Dutch in the administrative posts, and the Union Jack fluttered proudly over every outpost. But British people showed no desire to emigrate to the new colony. A curious, mixed administration ensued. The local dialect of Dutch remained the official language, for hardly anyone spoke English. The Dutch legal system remained much as it had been. On the other hand, British rule brought a new freedom in trade, unlike the strict monopoly that had been demanded by the Dutch East India Company. It also brought an administration quite as authoritarian as that of the Dutch had been and more determined to get its way. Censorship of the Cape Town press was instituted.

Most Afrikaners were of French and German blood and were not immediately hostile to the British, having had so much trouble with Holland. They were an independently minded people, who did not feel a strong patriotic pull to the home country. How would the British, who had not shown themselves very imaginative rulers in various part of the world, react to the hardy Afrikaners?

The main interest of the Boer farmers, who were descendants of the original Dutch and Huguenot settlers of the seventeenth century, in the new regime was to see how it would treat the native problem. As the Afrikaners had advanced their territory, to escape authority and increase their grazing lands, conflict with the African tribes had increased. The natives in the immediate hinterland of Cape Town had been relatively passive and docile, but they were now coming into contact with proud and fierce peoples, with well-defined societies, that were as avaricious of land as the Afrikaners themselves. These were the Bantu—of whom the Zulu had recently become a powerful and bellicose clan. The Dutch had made treaties, but the Africans were more concerned with an increasing land hunger than with pieces of paper. This had already led to one Kaffir War.

In London the situation seemed far clearer than it did to the authorities in Cape Town. The doctrine of laissez-faire still ruled government thinking, and thus the less official interference there was with territorial matters, the better. Allied to this there was the powerful feeling that the Africans must be "protected," rather than exploited and ruled—in the same way as the government had always shown more encouragement to humanitarian rather than commercial ventures in West Africa. There was also a prejudice in favor of the African in any dispute with the European, a result of the still-prevalent post-abolition mood.

The Boers, particularly those on the periphery of the colony, were not impressed with the handling of native affairs. There was little communication between the new rulers and the Afrikaner subjects and little attempt at understanding. A small group of up-country farmers rebelled. They were arrested, after a short fight, and brought to trial; five were condemned.

The place of execution was to be Slachter's Nek. A large crowd of the rebels' countrymen were ordered to the scene in order to witness the penalty for rebellion against the British crown. Great efforts were made to get the sentence commuted. The Boers who had assisted the British in the capture of the men were horrified; they had expected no such penalty as this. If there was a case for mercy, the governor, Lord Charles Somerset, did not perceive it. The future history of South Africa stretched ahead—and Lord Charles remained unmoved.

At the last moment friends and relatives of the condemned pleaded and begged for mercy. Amid tears and wailing, they made their last farewells. As the men were about to be hanged, the specially constructed gallows collapsed under their weight. The rebels, half-choked, lay writhing on the ground. The gallows were reerected, amid further pleas for mercy.

At the second hanging the men died, to the groans of the appalled crowd. Release of the bodies was refused to their respective families; and they were instead burned under the scaffold.

The British had gone into South Africa in the interests of the defense of the route to India, and they had done so with nothing but goodwill toward the inhabitants. This had been their first major act: a firm decision, given in the interest of respect for law and British rule. The hatred it engendered passed with generations of Boers from father to son. Britain's rule in Africa might be long or it might be short, but it would always be of a suspicious and unfriendly people. With unerring precision similar decisions were made across the continent for a hundred years.

The immediate result of Slachter's Nek was a strengthening of the cause of the rebels who had died. An idea to trek far away from British rule into the hinterland became a plan. The African tribes waited. After more fighting, great parties of them were pushed into an area known as the Transkeian Territories.

For a while the part of the colony behind Cape Town progressed peacefully. Villages sprang up. Cape Town developed, and the economy struggled and slowly improved. There the Afrikaners were more content; they cultivated their farms, while the "trek Boers," far out in the distant plains, grew more restless every year.

The British government's reaction to these difficulties was uncomplicated. The colony would have to be populated with people of British stock. Already there had been a trickle from Scotland, and 800 soldiers and sailors had been discharged in the colony after the war with France. More Britons would have to be sent out. In that way the troublesome Boers could be leavened with more tractable colonists. Parliament voted £50,000 for this purpose. Unemployment had followed the Napoleonic Wars, and there were 90,000 applicants anxious to start a new life on the African continent; of these, 4,000 were selected. These British emigrants to Africa were landed at Port Elizabeth, 400 miles up the coast from Cape Town. They were taken inland and dumped on the plain. Half a century later one of them recalled: "It was a forlorn-looking plight in which we found ourselves, when the Dutch waggoners had emptied us and our luggage on to the greensward and left us sitting on our boxes and bundles under the open firmament of heaven. Our roughly-kind carriers seemed, as they wished us goodbye, to wonder what would become of us. There we were in the wilderness; and when they were gone we had no means of following, had we wished to do so. Towns, villages, inns, hostelries, there were none. We must take root and grow, or die where we stood." While still in their best clothes, the women in long, high-waisted dresses and straw bonnets, the men in tail-coats, they began to work. Within a few weeks farms and settlements had been founded. "After a while," the same source recorded, "a great variety of fragile and grotesque-looking huts and cottages began to arise." As well as these officially sponsored immigrants, there was a trickle of more prosperous settlers from England: "Elderly gentlemen of upper-class connections, and retired officers from various departments of the king's service."

It all seemed an exciting beginning, like the settlement of North America. The London *Times* declared that the "natural advantages" were greater than in North America: "Our noble station at the Cape of Good Hope has the finest soil and climate in the world."

But this influx of British blood did not ease the problems of Cape Colony. The newcomers were mostly settled in an area reserved for them, so they did nothing to leaven the long-established Boer society; there were few instances of mingling or of intermarriage. Most of them were ex-soldiers, who knew little of farming. Their arrival and presence only made the Afrikaners more dubious than ever about the prospects offered them in a British colony. Most important of all, the newcomers, far from supporting the authority of Cape Town, were imbued with the current European liberalism and found Cape Town rule too authoritarian for their liking. They had the ear of Whitehall, which the Afrikaners did not have, and they were able to have censorship and the ban on public meetings raised. However, many of them also had a liberal approach to native affairs and were inclined to support British missionaries, who had been the bane of the Afrikaners for some years.

The Afrikaners watched the newcomers with increasing unease. An executive council which tended to be dominated by the British was formed to restrict the governor. Afrikaners were discouraged from speaking their own tongue, and the Dutch language began to be replaced in official proceedings. English schools were opened in all the small towns for Afrikaner children. (Most of the teachers were from Scotland, and for generations many Afrikaners spoke English with Scottish accents.) Anglican churches began to appear. The Cape was no longer just a stopping place on the way to India; it was an extensive British colony, a not insignificant part of a growing empire, a place to be administered, to be taxed, and to receive the protection of British military power.

The struggle for land continued. In 1834 the African tribes struck at the colony and penetrated for many miles. Bands of them rampaged the countryside, burning, looting, and killing. Up to 20,000 of them poured across the ill-defined frontier, destroying 456 farms and attacking many others. Boer farmers saw two decades of toil devastated and gathered for safety at Grahamstown, where a British column from Cape Town at last came on the scene. The African horde retreated into the wilds, taking with it 112,000 head of horned cattle.

Then there was the abolition of slavery. The Afrikaners were astounded. What would the British do, or not do, next?

Slaves in Cape Colony were treated with strict paternalism and served as agricultural workers or domestic servants. There were 37,745 of them, valued by their owners at £3,000,000, or £85 a head. The government offered £1,200,000, in compensation payable in London. After agents' and legal fees the owners got little, and sometimes nothing at all. Freed slaves left the farms and roamed the countryside as vagabonds or squatted outside the towns. Unable to support themselves, they naturally turned to crime. The farmers had lost their labor force, pushing the economy to the brink of chaos.

At the same time, the home government was making it clear that it tended to support African claims. It was suggested that the tribes had been justified in making war and that the colony should deflate its territory, rather than expand. The Boers thought the English were arrogant and fools. The English thought the Boers were cruel and bigots.

The Afrikaners had already noted that every time there was a Kaffir War the governor was recalled. Clearly official British policy and innate Afrikaner views and fears could not be reconciled. Cape Colony was no longer a place for trek Boers. A measure of oppression had made the Afrikaners—deserted by the Dutch—more self-conscious and proud than ever before; it had sown the seeds of nationalism. More than a century of isolation had molded their defiance of the opinions of others. Over the mountains lay the vast plateau of southern Africa, stretching away into the unknown. In 1835 the exodus began.

The idea of the Great Trek had often been discussed, but few could have visualized what it would entail. The Boers were an obstinate people, but the waiting tribes were dangerously insecure and some had become ferocious.

It began with pious sentiments and boundless hopes. Pieter Riethof, one of the leaders of the trek, stated:

> We solemnly declare that we leave this country with a desire to enjoy a quieter life than we have hitherto had. We will not molest any people, nor deprive them of the smallest property, but if attacked we shall consider ourselves justified in defending our persons and effects to the utmost of our ability against the enemy.

In great convoys, stretching for miles, the bullock carts trundled toward the mountains in vast clouds of dust. Over the Orange River, through the mountain passes that scouts had mapped, onto the veld. They found a dry, cruel plain of brown grass, continuing for hundreds of miles; they found a land to claim, but they did not find "a quieter life." The Zulu attacked the white intruders with terrifying savagery.

The Zulu had been organized into a formidable native force, that was feared from the Indian Ocean to the Limpopo. They had defeated rival Bantu tribes; even the Matabele, from the north, had been vanquished. Zulu tactics were to lead the enemy onto treacherous terrain, to face him in a crescent or surround him, and then to annihilate him. With headdresses, shields, and spears, the Zulu charged the Afrikaner convoys, leaving masses of dead around the wagons. The Afrikaners huddled together in their circular laagers, the wagons lashed together with chains, and blazed away with their elephant guns. Sometimes the laagers were overrun; massacre followed. More often the Zulu left the field, leaving a carpet of dead and a laager pincushioned with thousands of spears. At one battle 3,000 Zulu dead were left behind, whereas the trekkers had suffered 3 wounded. Andries Pretorius, with 600 men, defeated a force of 12,000 Zulu. But the trekkers also took the offensive. One Afrikaner party of 107 men surprised a Matabele camp and killed 400 Africans. After a battle between 135 Afrikaners and

12,000 Matabele, the natives were pushed across the Limpopo, leaving the veld to the trek Boers.

The British authorities viewed all this with languid interest. Their main concern was what appeared to be the settling of the Afrikaners near the Natal coast. This had to be discouraged because that coast overlooked the precious route to India. For several years American traders with the East had been showing an interest in the Natal coast. American shipping was prominent in the Indian Ocean. In London, the India Board had set up a secret committee to study the situation. When an American ship had called at the tiny station of Port Natal and made contact with the Zulu, there had been considerable alarm in Cape Town. The governor had written to the Colonial Office: "With reference to the possibility of the United States forming a settlement in Natal, it is hardly necessary to remark how embarrassing such neighbours might actually prove to this colony." Then 190 Cape businessmen had petitioned the government, declaring that "it is generally believed that the American Government has some intention of forming a small establishment" in Natal. This had been only two years before the Great Trek. The prospect of an American-Boer axis on the Cape Colony's border was not attractive. An army detachment was sent up the coast from Cape Town. Most of the Boers traveled on, and Natal was annexed to the Cape. In less than four years 4,500 immigrants arrived from England and Scotland, to establish villages, schools, courts, and churches. The colony was distinctly British in character. However, the few Afrikaners that remained were not discontented. Although they were less than half the European population of 8,000, Dutch law was respected. In 1856 Natal became a separate colony, and the northern hinterland was left to the brooding Zulu.

The trekkers who had settled across the Orange River had been followed by British troops, under the orders of an irate governor who believed that British subjects could not opt out of their citizenship (and who also believed he was conducting a holy war). Under Pretorius, the Afrikaners fought back. London, alarmed at the cost of protecting the extra territory against the Bantu, overruled Cape Town once more, and the Orange Free State was established in 1854. The more adventurous Afrikaners, who had fought their way as far as—and even beyond—the Limpopo River and who had defeated the Matabele, formed themselves into the South African Republic; it came to be known as the Transvaal.

The Great Trek was over. The republicans began to settle, farm, and organize their new lands. The trek had a lasting effect on the Afrikaners: It made them more than ever conscious of an independent heritage, and it filled them, coming from the comparative safety of the Cape, with deep feelings of insecurity about the Bantu peoples, who so vastly outnumbered them.

For Cape Colony, Natal, Orange Free State, and the Transvaal, the basic problem was always the same: African native insurgence and war. War was a constant threat—a match held over a sea of fuel. The Europeans were widely spread out, and they were outnumbered 12 to 1.

The old colony was having an even worse time than the new republics. A native stole an ax. On his way to trial, while he was handcuffed to another prisoner, a band of his tribesmen appeared, hacked off the arm of the fellow prisoner, and rescued their friend. The chief of the tribe refused to surrender him to the authorities. It did not seem an incident of great importance, but British and natives were intransigent. Thus, in 1846, began the War of the Ax. A British column, three miles long with its supply train, approached the offending tribe. It was a vulnerable target, and when the Africans struck, most of the supplies were lost in the hasty retreat. Seeing the white man humiliated aroused neighboring tribes. The frontier could not be held against the overwhelming warlike masses pressing on it, and the government was forced to seek aid. Troops arrived from India, England, Ireland, and Gibraltar. It took an army of 14,000 men, British and Cape Boer, to defend the colony.

Four years later the frontier flared up again. The inhabitants of the villages near the border were slaughtered. Peace was restored at the cost of 400 Europeans. Two years after that, in 1852, a column of 2,500 redcoats was sent to quell the Basuto who had been raiding and harassing the border for years and who not unnaturally resented the continuing diminution of their lands. The expedition found the Basuto well placed in a mountain stronghold. Their chief, who was not a fool, for years had been playing a skillful game of exploiting the conflict between British and Afrikaner to his own advantage. He caused some surprise by arriving at the British camp in European dress; there he rejected a demand for 10,000 cattle and 1,000 horses as compensation for destruction in territory claimed by Britain. In the fighting that followed, the half-armed Basuto by no means came off the worse. The wily chief wrote a letter (missionaries had been percolating a smattering of education through the tribes) that enabled the column to retreat without loss of pride and even as victors: "This day you have fought against my people and taken much cattle. As the object for which you have come is to have compensation . . . let it be enough, I pray you, and let me no longer be considered an enemy of the Queen." The general, worried about his supply line, was not ungrateful for the opportunity of returning at once to Cape Town. A few years later, Basutoland came under British "protection."

Contemplating the turmoil of empire building, in which colonialism, republicanism, and tribalism struggled, a Victorian historian, Sir John Robert Seeley, was to declare that Britain had gained its territory "in a fit of absence of mind." He was wrong. Several motives, some of them conflicting, had gone into the expansion of the Cape: the route to India; protection of the Boers from the Africans; protection of the Africans from the Boers; expansion of lands for immigrants; treaties and conquests to maintain a frontier. It was the conduct of the British that revealed an absence of mind.

In face of the size, potential, and population of South Africa, all the motives seemed inadequate. Immigration from Britain continued. People came from Yorkshire, from Scotland, from South Wales, from London, from Ireland, intending to build a great British land in southern Africa. Soon there were more than 50,000 British in the Cape and Natal, and the Colonial Office established an Africa department. The dream of those who had lobbied so long for a British Africa seemed to be coming true. But the thought of British territory stretching north from Table Bay to the Mediterranean, the length of the continent, was beyond everyone's dreams.

✤ IV ✤

Beyond the Zambezi

THE coming British domination of Africa was born of a curious mixture: the Bible, the gun, the treaty, and the factories of Manchester and Birmingham. The mid-nineteenth century was the time of the Bible. The missionaries were a formidable body of men and women: determined, tough, self-righteous, and, above all, earnest. They did a great amount of good. But to some of them the practices of the Africans were abominable and ignorant. They were mostly unappreciative of African culture, of any innate and perhaps essential part that native customs played in African society, and by attempting to demolish Africanism in Africa, they helped sow the seeds of much future distress. The peoples of Africa, however, were extraordinarily resilient and would not totally succumb to Europeans, as, for instance, did the native inhabitants of the Western Hemisphere.

The missionaries had begun by following the flag. They had gone first to Sierra Leone, then to the Gold Coast, then to the Niger. Wesleyans, the Church Missionary Society, Baptists, and Presbyterians. But in South Africa they were now going ahead of the flag, and there, particularly, their influence was adding much on the credit side. They were tackling disease, fighting slavery, and spreading Christianity.

In South Africa the basic difficulty of the British missionaries was with the Afrikaners. The Afrikaners did not accept the equality of black and white and viewed the spread of such an idea as a threat to their society. The missionaries, therefore, had so far restricted their activities to the borders of Cape Colony.

and to the tribal areas beyond its frontiers. The only practical way north was along the strip of land between the Kalahari Desert and the Transvaal border. This became known as the Missionaries' Road; it was much the same as the route taken by the present road and railway to Rhodesia.

The London Missionary Society had its most important post deep in the lands belonging to the Bechuana people—at a place called Kuruman, 100 miles from the British border. To this mission, in 1840, had come a dour, wiry Scotsman from the banks of the Clyde, with a drooping mustache, wavy auburn hair, and twinkling eyes. His name was David Livingstone, and he was to be the central figure of the great burst of exploration that was now to take place in southern, eastern, and central Africa.

Livingstone was the son of an impoverished mill worker. At the age of ten he had begun work in the same cotton mill as his father. He must have been a remarkable boy. With his first pay he had bought a Latin grammar and begun to educate himself— no mean task, for he worked for fourteen hours a day, giving him little leisure time for reading. He devised a system to read while at work "by placing the book on a portion of the spinning-jenny so that I could catch sentence after sentence as I passed at my work. I thus kept up a pretty constant study, undisturbed by the roar of machinery." With long hours at work and concentration on his studies, he had little opportunity for spending his meager wages. He was thus able to support himself at the Glasgow medical school. His education had cost no one a penny except himself.

His family was deeply religious, and young Livingstone was not a renegade, but he longed to escape from the humdrum life of the Clyde, preferably as a missionary. In London he continued his medical studies, along with divinity, and within a few months he was accepted by the London Missionary Society. He was an ideal choice: adventurous, pious, qualified, and possessed of an almost frenzied curiosity—a curiosity which had spurred him to educate himself.

Livingstone was delighted with Africa. He worked hard at Dr. Robert Moffat's Kuruman mission and then at a branch. Moffat, a gardener from near Edinburgh, was a remarkable man who for fifty years taught the Bechuana tribes many crafts and

English, as well as religion. Livingstone enjoyed traveling: "So much freedom in our African manners," he wrote. "We pitch our tents and make our fires wherever we choose; walk, ride or shoot at all kinds of game, as our inclination leads us." It was an exhilarating change from the slums of the Clyde. In due course he married one of Moffat's daughters and built the house they lived in. Livingstone provides a good picture of a missionary's life in Africa in the mid-nineteenth century:

> We rose early because . . . the morning was deliciously refreshing. After family worship and breakfast between six and seven, we went to keep school for all who would attend, men, women and children being all invited. School over at eleven o'clock; while the missionary's wife was occupied in domestic matters, the missionary himself had some manual labour as a smith, carpenter or gardener, according to whatever was wanted for ourselves or for the people. . . . After dinner and an hour's rest, the wife attended her infant school—generally a hundred strong; or she varied that with a sewing class, having classes of girls to learn that art. . . . After sunset the husband went into the town to converse with anyone willing to do so; sometimes on general subjects, at other times on religion. On three nights a week, as soon as the milking of the cows was over and it had become dark, we had a public religious service, and one of instruction on secular subjects aided by pictures and specimens. These services were diversified by attending upon the sick and prescribing for them, giving food, and otherwise assisting the poor and wretched.

The influence of such people as David and Mary Livingstone was great. They spread European civilization with tremendous energy and patience. In spreading their religion, they were less successful. Livingstone was told: "We like you as well as if you had been born among us. But we wish you to give up that everlasting preaching and praying; we cannot become familiar with that at all." Livingstone believed a missionary's life should be more than sending home dubious statistics of dubious conversions. He thought they had a responsibility as pioneers. There were other frustrations, for although he admired the Afrikaners in some respects, he could not get on with them. He found them "sober, industrious and most hospitable," but "the great objection many of the Boers had, and still have, to English law is that it makes no distinction between black men and white." It was this sort of frustration, together with his insatiable curiosity, that decided him to push northward into the unknown.

The map of the interior of Africa, from Kuruman in the south to Timbuktu in the north, was still blank.

After nine years of missionary work, Livingstone set out across the Kalahari Desert. He crossed the desert three times, twice with his wife and three children, all of whom suffered atrociously. On the third occasion the family did not return to the mission. They continued deep into Africa; "It was the end of June, 1851," Livingstone wrote, "that we were rewarded by the discovery of the Zambezi in the centre of the continent." They were the first white people ever to have been seen by the tribesmen, who were friendly.

Livingstone wanted to discover more about the great river, but by now it was obvious that exploring with a wife and family was hardly practical. They reached Cape Town, and Livingstone packed the family off in a ship to England. He then began his formidable career of exploration, plodding through Central Africa, in constant danger, plagued with dysentery, alone among strangers, covering immense distances with uncomplaining fortitude.

David Livingstone was not a hurried explorer. He lingered with tribes for months, communicating with them and studying every detail of their lives; Mungo Park, Hugh Clapperton, and Gordon Laing would have found him irritating and leisurely. In fact, he was immensely industrious. His advice to children was, "Fear God and work hard."

He progressed up the Zambezi, eyed by astonished Africans, with three books, a rug, a small tent, and a tin box containing a spare shirt, trousers, shoes, a few scientific instruments, and twenty pounds of coffee. "Excessively hot," he wrote. "The atmosphere is oppressive both in cloud and sunshine." He suffered abominably from fever but was tenderly treated by his attendants. After six months' traveling, he reached the Portuguese town of Loanda. Livingstone was a living skeleton. As they neared the Portuguese town of Loanda, his attendants—who came from the other side of the continent—were understandably nervous. Livingstone reassured them: "We have stood by each other hitherto and will do so to the last." They staggered into the town on the Atlantic shore.

One Englishman, engaged in the antislavery movement, was in Loanda. He gave up his bed to the emaciated explorer, who noted: "Never shall I forget the luxury I enjoyed in feeling myself again on a good English bed after six months sleeping on the ground." An English warship was lying off the coast. Livingstone's loyal African companions were entertained on board. The explorer himself was begged to return home, with his discoveries. But he wanted to discover more, and he felt he had to return his Africans to their home.

After a rest of three and a half months, Livingstone began the return journey. It took him a year. When the party arrived at the village which they had left eighteen months before, they were greeted with great excitement. Livingstone was a local hero.

He decided to descend the Zambezi to the sea. After only a few days, Livingstone reached the great falls, which he named the Victoria Falls after the queen. "Five columns of water," he wrote, "appropriately named smoke, bending in the direction of the wind, appeared to mingle with the clouds. The whole scene was extremely beautiful. It had never been seen before by European eyes."*

Almost everywhere he went the people were friendly and hospitable. "Great numbers came from all the surrounding villages and expressed great joy at the appearance of a white man and harbinger of peace." Livingston was supplied with quantities of food; in return he doctored the children, who were suffering from whooping cough. He loved all Africans, whom he described as "an imperishable race." But nearer the coast there was unrest, caused by slave trading and Portuguese Kaffir Wars. He left his faithful followers at a Portuguese post, promising to return one day and take them home. They believed him.

At last he saw the Indian Ocean. He had crossed Africa, the first man ever to do so. David Livingston boarded an English gunboat for home. One of the Africans refused to be left behind; the poor man was terrified of the sea but survived as far as Mauritius, where he became insane and hurled himself overboard.

David Livingstone returned to England, a few days before

---

* This was a confident claim, but it is unlikely that the Portuguese had not ascended the Zambezi that far, and an English hunter, Thomas Baines, may have seen the falls.

Christmas, in 1856, after an absence of sixteen years. He had left as an obscure missionary; he returned as a famous explorer. Honors were showered on him, receptions and banquets were held for him, and the queen entertained him at Windsor Castle. No one could have been less likely to be spoiled by such attention and flattery than the tanned, dapper, single-minded, reserved man from the Clyde. He lectured at Cambridge University; his subject "I Beg to Direct Your Attention to Africa."

A thousand miles north of where Livingstone had crossed Africa, another expedition was attempting to discover the great lakes of Central Africa. These lakes had been heard of from Arab and Portuguese traders. A German missionary had brought reports of an enormous inland sea. A Frenchman had recently died in the quest for it. The Foreign Office, prompted by the Royal Geographical Society, chose two of the most famous travelers of the day to solve the mystery—two Indian army officers: Richard Burton and John Speke.

Burton had become a national hero the previous year on the publication of his book detailing his feats in reaching the forbidden city of Mecca, although he had not been the first European to do so. A self-taught linguist in Oriental languages (he had been expelled from Oxford), he was a restless, emotionally immature, eccentric wanderer, proficient in disguise and with a masochistic taste for squalor. To the mid-Victorians he was a dashing, swashbuckling Englishman of a kind they loved to read about in popular romances.

John Speke was a well-built man, with an aquiline face and neat beard, who had crossed the Himalayas and visited Tibet. With Burton, he had recently returned from Somaliland where both of them had been wounded. Speke had something of the need for fame and the desire for posterity's attention that had so obsessed Gordon Laing in his search for Timbuktu.

The two men left the offshore island of Zanzibar in 1857. There they had found among the European traders the disregard of the interior that was typical of those along the entire coastline of Africa. Said Burton: "We could obtain no useful information from the European merchants, who are mostly ignorant of everything beyond the island."

They had not progressed far before both were stricken with malaria. Swaying on the backs of donkeys, they continued for months. At last, from a mountain range, Burton saw Lake Tanganyika before him. Speke, in the depths of malaria and probably sunstroke, was almost blind and could see nothing but a mist. Burton was convinced they had found the source of the Nile, a feat greater even than his visit to Mecca, for the source of the Nile had fastened on to the public imagination since Bruce, and was second only to Timbuktu itself as a matter for conjecture. The two men recuperated at the lakeside village of Ujiji.

Speke crossed the lake in a huge canoe paddled by twenty Africans. He went to a hut for some rest but was attacked by a horde of beetles. One penetrated his ear, causing considerable agony. Suffering intensely, he returned across the lake, where he found Burton completely succumbed to fever and unable to move.

Speke, still suffering, went off on his own to find another lake, which the natives spoke of. He found it quickly, and without much difficulty, less than 200 miles from Lake Tanganyika. He first saw the lake from the summit of a hill:

> The vast expanse of the pale-blue waters of the Nyanza [lake] burst suddenly upon my eyes! It was early morning. The distant sea-line of the north horizon was defined in the calm atmosphere. . . . A sheet of water extended far away to the eastward. The view was one which even in a well-known country would have arrested the traveller by its peaceful beauty. But the pleasure of the mere view vanished in the presence of those more intense emotions called up by the geographical importance of the scene before me. . . . This magnificent sheet of water I have ventured to name Victoria.

Beyond the lake, Speke was told, lay a great and mysterious kingdom. It was called Buganda.

Speke returned to Burton after six weeks' travel, having tramped some 450 miles. Burton was glad to see him, since he had thought he might never see him again and be left alone. "I laughed over the matter," wrote Speke, "but expressed my regret that he did not accompany me, as I felt quite certain in my mind I had discovered the source of the Nile." Burton was not amused. He insisted that the lake which he had been the first white man to see—Tanganyika—was the source of the Nile. A coldness developed between the two. They reached the coast, but Burton was too ill to travel farther than Aden. Speke parted from him with some satisfaction. He reached London, where he made his claim, turning the argument into a bitter dispute. Both men wrote books, making contradictory claims. Burton said Speke had "an immense and abnormal fund of self-esteem." This was probably true, but it might just as well have been said of himself.

Before Speke or Burton arrived in London, David Livingstone had gone back to Africa. He had stayed at home little more than a year, and his missionary zeal was now rivaled by the competitiveness of exploration. The government, slowly shifting its gaze in Africa, was taking an interest in him: Once it had been the west coast, then the Cape, now it was East Africa. It had taken half a century, but by about 1860 the whole continent was coming under Whitehall's scrutiny.

Livingstone resigned from the London Missionary Society in 1857. In 1858 he accepted the government's invitation to be "Her Majesty's consul for the eastern coast and the independent districts in the interior, and commander of an expedition for exploring eastern and central Africa." His mission was "to extend the knowledge already attained of the geography of eastern and central Africa and to encourage trade." With a small party, including his brother, he was taken to near the mouth of the Zambezi in H.M.S. *Pearl*. This area had been claimed by Portugal for many decades, but its administration was weak and mostly confined to the coast. Slavery was still rampant.

The faithful African companions of Livingstone's previous expedition were waiting patiently for him. He repatriated as many as wished to go home. For months he carefully explored the Zambezi and its tributaries. A great lake in the interior was known to the Portuguese, and Livingstone decided to find it. He followed a network of tracks: "They are veritable footpaths, never over a foot in breadth, beaten as hard as adamant by centuries of native traffic. Like the roads of the old Romans, they run straight on over everything, ridge and mountain and valley." On September 16, 1859, he saw a sheet of water which was the beginning of Lake Nyasa. Now all three of the great lakes of Africa had been seen by British explorers. "How far is it to the end of the lake?" he asked. "The other end of the lake?

Whoever heard of such a thing? Why, if one started when a mere boy to walk to the other end of the lake, he would be an old grey-headed man when he got there." Lake Nyasa was, in fact, more than 360 miles long. Livingstone realized its potential as a route for trade with the farther interior. He hoped to open up a trade for ivory in return for manufactured goods from home, and even considered the possibility of coal mining. "Something must be done to prevent the country being overrun by the Boers," he wrote to his brother-in-law, John Moffat, who was in what is now Rhodesia with his wife (their child, born in 1860, was the first white Rhodesian). Livingstone, by relentlessly directing attention to that quarter, was the father of modern Malawi (formerly Nyasaland), where his name is still respected.

Livingstone's reports of slavery prompted other missionaries to go to the area. His wife joined him, only to die of malaria three months later. To lose the loved companion with whom he had shared so much in Africa was a difficult blow. His attempts to open up the lake with a little steamer which had been brought from England were not a success. After two years he returned to the coast. He went back to England, only his second return in twenty-four years. There he learned that his son, who had fought on the Union side in the American Civil War, had been killed in the Battle of Gettysburg.

While Livingstone had been rediscovering Lake Nyasa, Speke had not been idle. With Burton away in California, he had become the current favorite of the authorities and of the armchair experts on Africa in London. The government decided to send him back again, with considerable financial support. His mission was ostensibly to settle the argument about the source of the Nile, but he was not to neglect a report on the mysterious and perhaps rich kingdom of Buganda, which had still not been visited. Interest in the source of the Nile was not purely academic, for whoever controlled its source controlled Egypt. An old Indian army friend, Captain James Grant, was to go with Speke. Grant, yet another Scot in Africa, was a tough, heavy man with a vast bushy beard.

After the two left London, it took them nearly ten months to reach the place which Burton and Speke had used as a base near Lake Tanganyika. First Grant was ill, then Speke. Speke suffered from continual coughing, and his limbs were so emaciated that they were "reduced to the appearance of pipesticks." Grant was able to go no farther. After a Christmas dinner of roast beef, Speke struggled on alone to reach Buganda, going right around Lake Victoria.

Buganda was a considerable surprise. The British public was determined to believe that the interior of Africa was peopled by uncivilized savages. Some of it was. But when Speke entered Buganda messengers from the Kabaka (the king) reached him. He was told that from then on he was to buy no more food; when he stopped each day, local officers would supply him. Clearly here was an organized state, one which existed without ever having been touched by European civilization. The roads were "as broad as our coach roads, cut through the long grass straight over the hills and down through the woods. The temperature was perfect. The whole land was a picture of quiescent beauty."

Speke was not impressed with the hut provided for him at the Kabaka's capital. But when he went to visit the Kabaka, preceded by a bearer carrying the Union Jack, he found a sophisticated court. Everyone was clothed in flowing robes, apart from the lesser royal wives—who were naked. The king, with a pet dog on a lead, was cosseted by tradition and a rigid system of etiquette. No one—except for the wives—was allowed to show an inch of skin when they crawled before the royal presence. A glance at the wives, naked or colorfully draped, resulted in certain death. A well-organized navy of canoes on the lake were at the Kabaka's disposal.

Grant, carried in a litter, joined Speke in Buganda. After further searching at last they discovered the Nile—issuing from Lake Victoria. "I stood on the brink of the Nile," wrote Speke. "Most beautiful was the scene, nothing could surpass it—a magnificent stream from six hundred to seven hundred yards wide, dotted with islets and rocks, the former occupied by fishermen's huts, the latter by crocodiles basking in the sun. I told my men they ought to bathe in the holy river, the cradle of Moses."

The explorers wanted to continue north, to the Mediterranean, so that "an uninterrupted line of commerce might exist between England and Buganda by means of the Nile." But the Kabaka was suspicious. A European had never visited his country before and he was not certain what these white men foreshadowed. But eventually he gave permission. Grant wrote: "The moment of triumph has come at last and suddenly the road is granted." The two men bade a formal farewell to the Kabaka. "We rose with an English bow, placing the hand on the heart, whilst saying *adieu;* and whatever we did the king, in an instant, mimicked."

Sometimes overland and sometimes on the river, the pair traveled slowly northward, across a poor country, through swamps and high grass, threatened by buffalo and lions, and then into the Sudanese desert—claimed by the Turkish Empire. On February 15, 1863, they staggered into a river port. When they were still 1,500 miles from the sea, they were greeted with a fantastic and unexpected sight: "We saw hurrying on towards us an Englishman."

The man who dashed toward them, arms outstretched, was Samuel White Baker, a forty-year-old engineer who had come up the river in the hope of meeting his friends Speke and Grant or of discovering their fate. He had founded an agricultural colony in Ceylon and had built the first railway in Turkey, but he had no experience of African exploration. Baker was a boisterous, jovial, pleasant man. He wrote a vivid account of the meeting:

> Report that two white men had come—could they be Speke and Grant? Off I ran and soon met them; hurrah for old England. They had come from the Victoria Nyanza from which the Nile springs. The mystery of ages solved! With a heart beating with joy I took off my cap and gave a welcome hurrah as I ran towards them! For the moment they did not recognize me . . . my sudden appearance in the centre of Africa appeared to them incredible. Speke appeared to me the more worn of the two. He was excessively lean; he had walked the whole way from Zanzibar, never having ridden once during that wearying march. Grant was in rags, his bare knees projecting through the remnants of trousers.

Speke was overjoyed: "What joy this was I can hardly tell. We could not talk fast enough, so overwhelmed were we both to meet again. We soon learned everything that could be told. I now first heard of the death of H.R.H. the Prince Consort. . . . Nobody had dreamt for a moment it was possible we could come through."

There never was a greater journey in African exploration

than that of Speke and Grant, but they have not received the measure of immortality accorded to Park, Livingstone, Burton, and Stanley.

When he reached Alexandria, Speke cabled home: THE NILE IS SETTLED. And so it should have been—except for lesser aspects —but controversy raged as before. The proud and fiery Burton never accepted it. On Speke's return home, the two men were due to meet at Bath to wrangle in public over the source of the Nile. Speke shot himself—it was said accidentally—the day before. Grant lived to an old age and nearly saw the twentieth century, almost unique among African explorers. As a faithful friend of Speke, he always declined to meet Burton.

Samuel Baker was not deterred by the success of Speke and Grant. He decided there was more to do. When they left for Cairo and Alexandria, he continued on his journey. "From my youth I had been inured to hardship," he wrote, "and endurance in tropical climates, and when I gazed upon the map of Africa I had a wild hope that I might by perseverance reach the heart of Africa." Baker was anxious to see his name among the already famous band of African explorers, and he was also an inveterate optimist. The most extraordinary aspect of his journey was that his pretty young Hungarian wife insisted on going with him. "It was in vain that I implored her to remain, and that I painted the difficulties and perils still blacker than I supposed they really would be; she was resolved to share all dangers and to follow me through each rough footstep of the wild life before me."

On March 26, 1863, they mounted two camels to cross the Sudan. They departed in splendor, with a bevy of servants. "We commenced our desperate journey in darkness about an hour after sunset. I led the way, Mrs. Baker riding by my side and the British flag following close behind us." Baker had not painted the perils any blacker to his wife than they were to be. They took neither guide nor interpreter and suffered appallingly from heat, famine and fever. Mrs. Baker collapsed with sunstroke and was carried unconscious for seven days through rainy swamps.

At one point Baker lay on the ground, "weak as a reed," unable to go on. But just when it seemed they were both to die, they discovered a hitherto unknown lake. They tottered to the water's edge. It was yet another source of the Nile.

The glory of our prize burst suddenly upon me! It is impossible to describe the triumph of that moment. . . . I determined to honour it with a great name. As an imperishable memorial of one loved and mourned by our gracious Queen, I called this great lake "the Albert Nyanza" . . . I rushed into the lake and, thirsty with heat and fatigue, I drank deeply from the sources of the Nile. My wife, who had followed me so devotedly, stood by my side pale and exhausted—a wreck upon the shores of the great Albert Lake that we had long striven to reach. No European foot had ever trod upon its sand, nor had the eyes of a white man ever scanned its vast expanse of water.

Using a large tartan cloth as sail, they explored the new lake. During another terrible journey, they again crossed the swamps and the Sudan. At least once even the amiable Baker had given up all hope of surviving. But thanks to a local chief, they regained Egyptian territory after an absence of two years: two living skeletons, their clothes in shreds. No woman achieved more in African travel than Mrs. Samuel Baker.

Livingstone had also been caught up in the prevailing obsession about the source of the Nile. Despite the frightful hardships he had already endured in Africa, he was cheerful about returning there. He was now the most famous living explorer—a situation which slightly exaggerated his work, although not his dedication. His books, well known in America, as well as in Britain, had brought him some prosperity. He was thus largely able to finance his next expedition himself. But he was supported by the government-backed Royal Geographical Society (which had taken over the work of the old African Association of Sir Joseph Banks), and the government itself contributed £500. He was officially declared "Her Majesty's Consul, Inner Africa."

As usual, Livingstone landed on the coast claimed by Portugal—one of the unhealthiest areas of Africa. He seems to have had little thought of ever returning to Europe. It was not a lavish expedition; he once wrote: "I have always found that the art of successful travel consisted in taking as few impedimenta as possible, and not forgetting to carry my wits about me." With thirteen Indian soldiers, some Africans (including one named Susi), some animals, a poodle, and the Union Jack fluttering to the fore, he delved into the interior once more. "I feel quite exhilarated. The mere animal pleasure of travelling in a wild, unexplored country is very great. Brisk exercise imparts elasticity to the muscles, fresh and healthy blood circulates through the brain, the mind works well, the eye is clear, the step firm, and a day's exertion makes the evening's repose thoroughly enjoyable." It was a sturdy attitude typical of the new generation of explorers, but it had little relevance to reality. One after the other, men and beasts went down with sickness. Porters dropped their loads and returned to the coast. The poodle was drowned in a marsh. The medicine chest was stolen.

Livingstone reached Lake Nyasa again. He then turned north into what became Northern Rhodesia and beyond into the future Belgian Congo. "Northwards," he wrote, "through almost trackless forest and oozing bogs—I am frightened at my own emaciation." A few months later: "Every step I take jars my chest and I am very weak; I can scarcely keep up the march." He joined a party of slave-trading Arabs and discovered new lakes. He found a great, broad river. Was it the Nile?

"Very ill all over—cannot walk. Pneumonia of right lung, and I cough all day and all night. I am carried several hours a day on a frame. The sun is vertical, blistering any part of the skin exposed, and I try to shelter my face and head as well as I can with a bunch of leaves." He stayed with cannibals; one man had ten jawbones hanging on a string over his shoulder—mementos of past meals. At last Livingstone reached Lake Tanganyika and the village of Ujiji, which Speke and Burton had visited.

Livingstone had been away for five years and nothing had been heard of him for two years. It was widely rumored that he was dead, lost, or held captive. The Royal Geographical Society was more optimistic, and on its urgings the government allocated £1,000 to enable Livingstone to return home.

It was the idea of James Gordon Bennett, manager of the New York *Herald,* to send a reporter to find Livingstone or to learn of his fate—a journalistic idea on the grandest scale. For the task he chose Henry Morton Stanley, an illegitimate son of obscure parents, born in Wales twenty-eight years before. Stanley had been adopted by a wealthy American broker and had become a well-known and well-traveled reporter. He was in Madrid when he got a cable from Bennett: COME TO PARIS ON

IMPORTANT BUSINESS. Five hours later, he was on his way: "The roving correspondent meets the command that may send him to his doom. To the battle or the banquet, it is ever the same—get ready and go." At the Grand Hôtel, Paris, Stanley found Bennett in bed.

"Who are you?"

"My name is Stanley."

"Ah, yes! Sit down. I have important business on hand for you. Where do you think Livingstone is?"

"I really do not know, sir."

"Do you think he is alive?"

"He may be, and he may not be."

"Well, I think he is alive, and that he can be found, and I am going to send you to find him."

Stanley was given other assignments to accomplish on the way, but he eventually arrived at Zanzibar, where he prepared a lavishly equipped expedition. After 900 miles of trekking toward Lake Tanganyika, losing many of his men and becoming involved in tribal wars, he heard of a white man in Ujiji. "God grant me patience," he wrote, "but I do wish there was a railroad, or at least horses, in this country." He bribed his men to undergo a nonstop march.

Through a lane of excited African crowds, the Stars and Stripes carried aloft by a bearer beside him, Stanley entered Ujiji. The native Africans appreciated the drama of the moment as much as the two white men. "I did not know how he would receive me," Stanley wrote, "so I did what cowardice and false pride suggested was the best thing—walked deliberately to him, took off my hat and said, 'Dr. Livingstone, I presume?' " Livingstone, who had heard of Stanley's approach but had expected a Frenchman, raised his cap in return and replied, "Yes." Seeing the style in which Stanley was traveling, not without numerous kitchen utensils and a tin bath, Livingstone dryly noted: "This must be a luxurious traveller and not one at his wit's end, like me."

The two men became extremely friendly. Livingstone, avid for news, learned for the first time that the Suez Canal had been completed. Together they explored the lake, pondering always on the Nile's source. Had Burton been right and Speke wrong? Was Lake Tanganyika the Nile's source after all? They traveled in two craft, each bearing the appropriate flag. Stanley was meticulous in ensuring his boat was always slightly to the rear of Livingstone's: "Was it not England's place to be in first place? She won the right to it by discovering the Tanganyika."

Stanley tried to persuade Livingstone to return to Europe, but Livingstone seems to have been determined to end his life in Africa. Stanley reached Zanzibar safely. Brilliant journalist that he was, he turned his story into the greatest scoop of the century. One of the most remarkable aspects of his feat was that he had been away for only fourteen months. An official expedition to find Livingstone had not left the coast by the time of Stanley's return. Within weeks, Stanley's story was in the New York *Herald;* within six months his book on the journey was in the shops.

From Zanzibar, Stanley sent plentiful supplies back to Livingstone, at his newspaper's expense. Livingstone left Ujiji, refreshed and stimulated by the meeting with Stanley, but soon he began to ail again. When his donkey died, he stumbled forward on foot, still trying to settle the mystery of the Nile. After a year and two days of painful and comparatively unproductive wandering, he wrote in his diary: "Knocked up quite." It was his last entry. He died sprawled out in a native hut. For thirty-three years David Livingstone had been traveling about in "Darkest Africa"; in all that time he had received no wound from a native, and he died peacefully in his sleep.

The faithful Susi organized the return of Livingstone's body to the coast. For hundreds of miles for five months, the body, carefully preserved and tenderly handled, was borne to the sea. There it was handed over to white men, who identified it by the scar of a lion wound of more than a quarter of a century before. It was then transported over the sea and buried, with ceremony, in Westminster Abbey. H. M. Stanley was the chief pallbearer at the funeral.

For thirty years from Livingstone's first journey the continent was crossed and crossed again by fervent Englishmen and by the Anglo-American Stanley. The map of the interior was fitting nicely into place. There is something immensely impressive about those bearded Victorians trudging through thousands of miles of African jungle, plains, and down raging rivers, under their Union Jacks, with inadequate knowledge of medicine and mainly ignorant of tropical disease, sometimes faced by hostile tribes, but always trusting in their own fortitude, in God, and in human hospitality in a strange world (which more often than not was, in fact, forthcoming). All were fired with a deep and simple patriotism. The white man in the African interior, if not familiar, was coming to be known—known confusingly as a man who brought beads, who brought cures, who brought death, and who brought talk of a strange God. Far more than those of any other European nation, the tentacles of Britain had probed the continent. Individuals were pushing Britain into Africa, as they had since the days of the African Association more than half a century before, in face of periodic opposition from Parliament (a select committee, in 1865, had recommended withdrawal "except, probably, Sierra Leone") and with spasmodic encouragement and occasional financial support from the government. While the missionaries, explorers, and journalists had been penetrating from the east, the traders and businessmen had been slowly establishing themselves in the west. The Niger region had been further explored, under Dr. W. B. Blaikie, and, owing to the use of quinine, not one life had been lost. Macgregor Laird had been persevering in trade from his Liverpool office. These men believed in the African dream.

The meeting of Stanley and Livingstone, the death of Livingstone, the moving loyalty of his servants in bringing his body to the coast, his noble funeral in Westminster Abbey had brought Africa before the public's imagination more than ever before. Livingstone had brought home to his countrymen the primitive state of much of Africa, where genocide, famine, and ignorance were coupled with high human qualities; he had projected a sense of the dignity of man, whether black or white. But the real nature of African society was little understood, for it was always seen in European terms.

Britain was reaching unprecedented heights of power. A great empire was emerging. Her people were streaming out all over the world. Her industrialization was forging ahead. The City of London was the center of the world's finance. The British navy ruled the waves of every ocean. The army, under General Sir Robert Napier, with supreme arrogance had marched nearly 300 miles into unexplored parts of Ethiopia to release a few captives at Magdala; they then razed the place to the ground and returned to the coast.*

The two political leaders were William Gladstone and Benjamin Disraeli. Gladstone believed that territorial acquisitions were "false phantoms of glory." Disraeli, who was more in tune with the public mood, believed in the benefits of imperialism for all, and in a special mission for Britain. He had bought a large shareholding in the Suez Canal, on a £4,000,000 loan from the Rothschilds (at about 13 percent per annum) —in a desire to forestall France. After the deal, he had rushed off a note to the admiring queen: "It is just settled; you have it, Madam." Although ships continued to go to India via the Cape, the journey via Suez was some thousands of miles shorter and weeks less. In future Cape Colony and Natal would have to stand as colonies in their own right; they could not be excused as necessary stopping places on the way to India. Victoria wrote: "Egypt is VITAL to us."

The new imperialism was now to begin. In Africa, not everyone was to oblige. The great kingdom of the Matabele still barred the way north. The slave caravans still wound their ways through central and north Africa. In northern Nigeria and Buganda, powerful empires ruled hundreds of thousands of people. In the Gold Coast the angry Ashanti were bellicose again. In the far south the Zulu were bristling with signs of war. It was a new era; the age of the Bible was giving way to the age of the gun.

* The gallant Sir Robert, a great Victorian hero, was the father of nine sons and six daughters.

✤ V ✤

The Drums of War

FROM 1872 to 1902 Britain was continually involved in war, skirmishes, and frontier "incidents" throughout her growing domains in Africa. British troopships plowed down the Atlantic and across the Indian Ocean, carrying famous regiments to fight in Africa from Natal to the Nile. As Rudyard Kipling was to write:

> We're foot-slog-slog-slog-sloggin' over Africa—
> Foot-foot-foot-foot-sloggin' over Africa.

The old trading posts on the Gold Coast had now been drawn together, with a belt of the immediate interior about 50 miles deep, into the Gold Coast protectorate. In 1850 the Danes had sold their Gold Coast posts, which they had held for two centuries, to Britain. In 1871 the remaining Dutch posts were bartered to the British in exchange for rights in the East Indies. The Gold Coast protectorate had been invaded by the Ashanti. The fetishes and cruelties of this great tribe were a byword in Victorian Britain. The horrors and bloodlust of the Ashanti, bad enough, were wildly exaggerated and breathlessly related in clubs and drawing rooms.

To deal with these fearsome people, the government sent its brightest young star: Major General Sir Garnet Wolseley—forty years old, the half-educated son of an impoverished major, onetime Dublin surveyor's clerk, and relentlessly ambitious. Wolseley had served in four campaigns in India and Canada, in each of which he had received wounds and distinction. He was

not popular, for unlike most of his contemporaries, he believed
that soldiering was a serious affair, that there was more to military life than sport, travel, and social activities. He had pleased
the government by suggesting he could settle the Gold Coast,
once and for all, for less than £150,000.

Wolseley left Liverpool on September 12, 1873. His expedition consisted of thirty-six junior officers, one sergeant, one
lance sergeant, one private soldier, and sundry items of equipment, including thirty foghorns, a hundred railway-guard
whistles, and a library of books. The mayor of Liverpool delivered a short address.

Wolseley was a little man, with a weak-looking chin and
drooping mustache, who always appeared kindly and fey. He
did not look like an impressive commander. A colleague recalled; "He had the talent of giving commands in such a way
that they gave pleasure to those who received them." His
manner to young officers was "inexpressibly gracious." But
appearances were deceptive. Sir Garnet Wolseley wished to get
on in the world, and he knew that failure would not increase his
prospects. Unlike not a few of the 400 generals on the Army
List, Sir Garnet was not a fool. The foghorns and whistles were
for communicating in jungle war and the books were relevant
to the coming campaign. The officers were a carefully picked
selection from the best in the army; among them were the stolid
Captain Redvers Buller and the witty Irishman Captain William Butler, whose careers, like Wolseley's, were to be inex-
tricably caught up in British history in Africa.

Wolseley's orders were to try to raise a force from the tribes
on the coast, led by his party of officers, defeat the Ashanti,
march into their country, force a favorable treaty on them, and
obtain a large indemnity of gold as punishment for their having
entered the British "protectorate." This was widely applauded
in Britain, but a few people abhorred the expedition on ethical
grounds, and some others were not satisfied about the legality of
the British position in the Gold Coast protectorate, anyway.
Wolseley believed the only way to fulfill his orders was "by
the seizure and destruction of Kumasi," the Ashanti capital,
which lay 150 miles inland, through thick and steamy bush and
forest. The route was virtually unmapped, the country largely
unknown. Paths were narrow, and the forests provided excellent cover for ambush and ample opportunity for a column to

become lost or surrounded or both. Through years of trading, the Ashanti were known to have accumulated a considerable arsenal of muskets, rifles, and ammunition.

The local tribes showed little interest in the scheme when Wolseley called a gathering of the chiefs. He told them that the great white queen was concerned for their safety and had sent him to help them push the Ashanti back. But only 1,200 Fanti from a possible 60,000 warriors were forthcoming. The British garrison in the various coastal forts numbered 130, of whom 22 were fit for duty. Wolseley had always wanted British troops for the operation; he now sent home for them.

Meanwhile, with notebooks, camp beds, supplies, port, and sun helmets, the press arrived. The march to Kumasi was to be the first fully reported war in the history of Africa. It was an indication not only of a growing mass readership, but of the importance of Africa in the British consciousness; hitherto the gaze of most of the empire builders of suburban villa and downland farm had been directed at India. Wolseley was horrified by the swarm of heavy-drinking, brash, questioning correspondents that descended by ship on his base camp. He considered them "those newly invented curses to armies who eat the rations of fighting men and do no work at all." He contemptuously divided them into "One Who Knows," "The Man on the Spot," and "The Man Who Has Been There." The *Times,* the *Standard,* the *Daily Telegraph,* and the *Illustrated London News* all sent reporters, and at least four other newspapers hired local correspondents. In their own way, such men were quite as important as Wolseley in establishing a British fixation on Africa.

The most formidable of them all arrived a few weeks after Wolseley. Stanley's vividly written book *How I Found Livingstone* had sold more, on both sides of the Atlantic, than any previous work on Africa. It had made him the most sought-after expert on African affairs. Once again he was in Spain when the New York *Herald* sent him off to the Gold Coast. The *Herald,* well aware that its staff man was now a celebrity, provided a steam yacht for his personal use.

On arrival at the capital—Cape Coast—Stanley received an immediate invitation to Government House, a modest, whitewashed building around which stood pretentious statues of antelopes. There Wolseley was living in considerable style. Dinner, with the officers in full-dress uniform, with "wax lights twinkling through well-filled decanters," was a formal and sumptuous affair. Stanley, who had been skeptical of the whole expedition, was impressed. The general seems to have applied his well-known charm. "He is the very reverse of my conception," wrote the famous reporter. "I should judge him to have made a first-class special correspondent."

To the rest of the company in the Gold Coast, however, H. M. Stanley was not so cordial. The young officers were "overgrown boys from Sandhurst." The army doctors had "a high idea of their mission." His fellow correspondents received his "sympathy," "while they cannot at once stride into the enchanted land" and had to be content with "its outskirts." As the most famous man on the continent, Stanley wandered around with some condescension. "I have been through all this," he said. Such an attitude did not make him the most popular man in the camp.

Ship after ship arrived from England. Excited soldiers splashed ashore under the blazing sun. Many of them had never before been out of Britain. They were fit, well trained in all the conventional formations, underpaid and excellent at parade-ground drill. They belonged to famous regiments. The Royal Welch Fusiliers, with their famous goat mascot, arrived; so did the Forty-second Highlanders, the Rifle Brigade, the renowned Black Watch, and two battalions of the West India Regiment, which had often supplied the garrisons in West Africa. There were detachments of Royal Marines, Royal Engineers, and Royal Artillery with some light guns. The engineers arrived with axes and tools in neat leather cases; one of their officers was immediately returned owing to "heat apoplexy." An officer of the infantry came ashore with his face covered by a veil—to keep out malaria. The fusiliers' goat breathed its last after leading a ceremonial march through the town.

To the astonishment of old soldiers, Wolseley fussed over his troops with parental attention. He had already caused a stir by insisting that the campaign should be fought in special clothing: the men in loose gray uniforms, the officers in Norfolk jackets, breeches, and gaiters. As a young officer, Wolseley had fought a campaign in the steaming Burmese jungle dressed in a scarlet jacket buttoned up to the chin, heavy trousers, and immaculate white buckskin gloves; he had not forgotten the experience.

Wolseley had 100 pamphlets printed, for distribution among the troops. Its contents were positively revolutionary, among men accustomed to floggings for breaches of eccentric regimental traditions. It read: "Never allow the body to suffer from a chill. . . . The officers must see that tea or chocolate, with a little biscuit, is provided for the men. . . . During the heat of the day, or when marching late in the morning, commanding officers may, at their discretion, allow jackets to be taken off and carried. . . . If any irregularity of the bowels is experienced, go at once to the doctor for a dose. . . . Never expose the head uncovered to the sun."

The first act of the war came as something of a surprise to Wolseley's clever and formidable young staff. The Ashanti took the initiative. They all went home. Despite a serious outbreak of smallpox and dysentery, the invading Ashanti army had conducted an orderly retreat. One of Wolseley's officers grudgingly remarked: "The army of a civilized nation need not have been ashamed of a retreat conducted with such skill and such success."

Without delay, Wolseley's force marched off into the interior. For men straight from the red-brick streets of British garrison towns, it was a strange wilderness they entered, but soldiers of the queen had to be prepared to fight in the most unlikely places across the globe. The first trouble encountered was one of supply. More than 5,000 native bearers were needed to follow the column. Metal-lined boxes, clearly marked "Fortnum & Mason," were carefully carried on African heads, but as soon as the bearers were taken on, they vanished—and they did not leave their bundles behind. Stanley suggested an answer to this problem. The government, he said, should acquire and send out 500 sets of slave chains; the porters should be bound into gangs of 50, "each controlled by a non-commissioned officer with a long whip." After the campaign, the government could compensate in some way "for the annoyance of being collared with iron bands." Wolseley rejected the suggestion.

When the first Ashanti village was reached, it was something of a surprise. It was unexpectedly spacious and orderly. There the column waited for signs of capitulation at Kumasi. As interpreter, the Ashanti king used a native former missionary named Joseph Dawson. A scribbled note from Dawson arrived: "Please see 2 Corinthians, chap. ii, ver. 11." Consulting a Bible, Wolseley discovered the text: "Lest Satan should get an advantage of us: for we are not ignorant of his devices." Wolseley took this to mean that the Ashanti were prepared for battle and were waiting ahead.

The advance guard found the Ashanti army nearly 20 miles outside Kumasi. Wolseley realized that he could not now avoid a fight. It was not an enticing prospect. More than a 100 miles inland from his base on the coast, he was convinced he would be attacked from the flanks and rear, while an attempt was made to stop his advance—the favorite Ashanti tactic. This the enemy could easily do owing to its immense superiority in numbers and to Wolseley's isolation. He decided to advance, therefore, in the form of a large square, with headquarters, hospital, and artillery in the center. "My little army breakfasted early," he wrote, "and moved off at daybreak." The pipers of the Black Watch sent their chilling battle call swirling through the thick undergrowth. The British Expeditionary Force to the Gold Coast marched briskly off to do battle with the queen's enemies.

Owing to the trees and bush, no one side of the thickly lined square was visible to the others. Soon men were stumbling over branches and pushing through bush. In the center of the square, exuding confidence, was the general; he was carried shoulder-high on a cane chair, beaming amiably and smoking a large cigar.

Soon all sides of the square came under heavy fire, but nowhere could the enemy be seen. Fortunately the enemy fire was not accurate, but here and there casualties fell to the ground. Communication among the four sides of the square became difficult. In some places it was necessary to hack a way through the undergrowth, in which companies become enmeshed. The air was heavy with the scent of explosive, and smoke billowed up to the treetops and hung overhead like steam from an inferno. The screams of the wounded could be heard through the crescendo of firing.

"The Ashantis stood admirably and kept up one of the heaviest fires I was ever under," wrote one officer. "I was getting very anxious as to the result," he added. Leading the front of the square were the Black Watch. With their pipers playing

"The Campbells Are Coming," they scrambled through the trees in face of a murderous fire. Nearly all their officers were wounded. As they advanced, the Ashanti, using skillful jungle tactics of infiltration, appeared behind them and inside the square. Confusion was considerable.

Wolseley was left in no doubt about the seriousness of the situation when heavy firing burst out all around him. Blandly waving his cigar, he gave instructions. As the Ashanti closed in, newspaper correspondents and staff officers fired away at desperate speed. Surgeons continued extracting bullets while men fought all around them. Still held aloft, an absurdly vulnerable target, Wolseley looked on with interest. He was particularly impressed by the sight of the famous Stanley at work:

> A thoroughly good man [Stanley]. No noise, no danger ruffled his nerve, and he looked as cool and self-possessed as if he had been at target practice. Time after time as I turned in his direction I saw him go down to a kneeling position to steady his rifle as he plied the most daring of the enemy with never-failing aim. . . . I can still see the close-shut lips and determined expression of his manly face which—when he looked in my direction—told plainly that I had near me an Englishman in plain clothes whom no danger could appal. Had I felt inclined to run away, the cool, firm, unflinching manliness of that face would have given me fresh courage. I had previously been somewhat prejudiced by others against him, but all such feelings were slain and buried.

Wolseley came down and strode about, still smoking, and trying, as he said, "to look happy." Gradually the infiltrators were killed off, and resistance at the front began to ease. The noise of battle died away, to reveal the groans of the dying and the excited cackling of alarmed wildlife. The battle had raged with no pause for twelve hours. "Two thousand Ashanti," commented Stanley, "under the leadership of an intelligent British Officer, would soon extend the power of the English from Cape Coast Castle to Timbuktu."

Wolseley decided to make a dash for Kumasi, only 15 miles away, before the Ashanti had time to reorganize another defense. It was a gamble because the main supplies were still lagging far behind the column. Every man would carry two days' supply on his person, and all impedimenta would be left at the camp. Wolseley wanted to dart in and out of Kumasi as quickly as he could. He longed to get out of that dark forest and back to the coast, which suddenly seemed a long way off.

A flying column marched off at dawn. Many of the officers were in bandages, and few of the men were wholly fit. There was little resistance at the head of the column, but the rear guard and flanks were constantly harassed. It was worrying. Were they entering a trap? Then, from far away, came a human call. As it grew nearer, it was clearly heard: "Mercy O! Mercy O!" Two runners appeared, still emitting their musical plea and carrying a white flag. They had a message from Dawson; it explained that the chiefs, independently of the king, were prepared to capitulate. Dawson added a plea of his own: "I humbly beg your Excellency on my knees to let the forces stop, and everything will be settled." Wolseley interpreted this as a ploy to gain time.

Once again the Black Watch led the way, although severely weakened by the fighting of two days before. Each of the villages close to the town held an ambush, but the regiment dashed through them, pipes playing and men cheering. The commander of the attack, a one-armed veteran of the Crimea, declared it "one of the finest spectacles I have ever seen in war." Nearing the town, two hostages, one a woman, were made to walk in front. The Scotsmen rushed the outskirts of Kumasi, but they met no resistance. Another message arrived from the unhappy Dawson: "For heaven's sake, I pray your Excellency halt the forces. . . . If your Excellency do not halt and do not hear from me about twelve tomorrow noon, then all is over with me." It was too late; the British had Kumasi.

The troops, dust-caked, exhausted, and thirsty, gathered in the extensive square of the town. In the dim light of the evening, they were lined up on parade. Wolseley called for three hearty cheers for the queen. The inhabitants of the town looked curiously on; then, with prized belongings, they faded away to join the Ashanti army somewhere in the bush. The only greeting was from Dawson, unharmed, in European clothes and clutching the inevitable umbrella. Up to 40,000 Ashanti evacuated the town that night, leaving it almost deserted except for the British army. With them went the king, with his Golden Stool, the sacred symbol of Ashanti power; Wolseley had no intention of trying to find him.

Because of the many horrific tales about the Ashanti and

their capital which had spread in England, there was a feeling among the troops of awe mingled with extreme unease. Wolseley himself was by no means immune. At the sight of clotted blood and human heads in the royal palace, he not surprisingly hurried off to sleep in the open. The Ashanti did practice hideous sacrifice, although very rarely; other practices, such as murder, rape, adultery, and assault, were not unknown in London and New York.

Wolseley had laid down most strictly that there was to be no looting. That night the air was rent with the cries of those being flogged for disobeying the order. The next day there was an official inspection of the palace, which was much larger than anyone had expected, for the purpose of enforcing the indemnity demanded by the government in London. An amazing and bizarre collection of articles was found, accumulated over the years from periodic contact with traders of the coast: cutlasses, Persian rugs, color supplements of the *Illustrated London News*, gold-studded Arab sandals, children's toys, an engraving of the customhouse on the Thames, damask counterpanes, intricately carved furniture, and a copy of the *Times* for October 18, 1843. The most valuable items appeared to be seven masks of solid gold. Thirty bearers were assigned to carry the selected pieces to the coast. Sappers then mined the palace and blew it up.

Lightning lit up the sky; thunder rumbled over the hills. It began to rain. It was what Wolseley had dreaded. The rains had come early. To the sound of bugles, the column splashed out of Kumasi, beginning what was to be a terrible march. The ground had turned to a morass. On one occasion men struggled through knee-deep mud for nearly a third of a mile.

Eventually, to Wolseley's surprise, Ashanti envoys arrived with about 1,000 ounces of gold. It was considerably less than Wolseley had demanded, but he was glad to accept it. This anxiety to convince the enemy that it was returning in honor and with victory had been practiced on the British in Africa before—3,400 miles away in Basutoland. The Ashanti were also glad to sign a treaty promising "to check" human sacrifice and to pay a further 50,000 ounces of gold. London had always had a false idea of the amount of gold in the Gold Coast area; Wolseley had to admit that the indemnity would "probably" never be seen. The king graciously signed the agreement with two crosses in pencil.

By the time the bedraggled column marched wearily into Cape Coast only one of the staff officers was still walking. Hundreds of soldiers came back swaying in hammocks slung between swarthy Africans. Wolseley himself looked "uncommonly fit." Stanley, too, was little the worse for the experience; he had, of course, been one of the first men back, in order to dispatch his communiqué before his rivals.

Reembarkation was gratefully begun. "The most horrible war I ever took part in," said Wolseley. Nevertheless, he had conducted the campaign, which could easily have been a total catastrophe, with both common sense and dash; of all the many colonial wars in which Britain was engaged during the nineteenth century, the Ashanti War of 1873–74 was one of the few not characterized by blunder.

In his dispatch, Wolseley proudly noted: "The troops refrained, with the most admirable self-control, from spoliation or plunder; and they have left the capital of this kingdom, so famed for its gold, without carrying away as plunder one article of value." The king's ceremonial umbrella was sent home for Queen Victoria, and there was also a souvenir for the Prince of Wales. The articles seized in the palace were auctioned at Cape Coast, where they fetched £5,000; several items of gold and silver were purchased for officers' messes.

Back in London, Wolseley was welcomed as a great hero. He refused a baronetcy on the grounds that one had just been given to the Duke of Devonshire's gardener; "I don't wish to have my name inscribed with such people," he said. He accepted the GCMG and KCB (a knighthood), a sword of honor from the city of London, honorary degrees from Oxford and Cambridge, and a personal grant of £25,000 awarded to him by the government and passed unanimously in the House of Commons. He had, in fact, expected a peerage. Gladstone and Disraeli competed in their eulogies in the House, but privately, Disraeli characterized Wolseley as "an egotist and a braggard—so was Nelson." Balls, banquets, receptions, presentations continued for months. Almost every officer was promoted, many of them decorated—including several Victoria Crosses.

The campaign had cost about £1,000,000. But within a few

years the Ashanti had recovered much of the territory they had relinquished, had rebuilt the palace at Kumasi, had not paid the remaining indemnity, and were again harassing the Gold Coast.

Wolseley was sent out to run the somnolent colony of Natal, where colonization had been proceeding slowly but steadily. British immigrants had struggled to farm the land. The villages of Pietermaritzburg and Durban had grown into towns, with confident public buildings modeled on those in provincial towns at home. The white population, which numbered about 25,000, had established a legislature to conduct local affairs. An order had put the black men into trousers: "Good for trade and necessarily good for morality," said William Butler, serving in Natal. A few years later the ladies were required to cover their breasts. Wolseley's appointment flattered local society to a degree. He was wildly feted. "It is high time I got out of this place," he wrote, "for I seem to live on a female powder magazine. . . . Indeed, I might have had a *rare high time* of it here." Wolseley could afford to resist; his wife, who was with him, always insisted that she had exactly the same proportions as the Venus de Milo. The attentions and intentions of the ladies were increasingly shown "in a very demonstrative manner." Wolseley bashfully escaped to Cyprus as the Chief British military and civil representative—"Lord High Commissioner"—which had recently been acquired by Britain. He was to see Africa again.

When Wolseley left Natal, it was an apparently peaceful colony, quietly growing in prosperity. The Afrikaners to the north were busy with their own fight to keep the Transvaal from economic collapse. The Zulu, now compressed into a fairly well-defined state marked on the maps, were wedged between Natal and Portuguese East Africa; gathered in their kraals, they gloried in their warlike past, under a proud new king, Cetewayo. It was the lull before the storm.

The tremendous interest in Stanley's meeting with Livingstone and in the march to Kumasi delighted the newspapers. Africa equaled India as a source of action and adventure, for which a rapidly expanding reading public, mostly leading dull lives in the great new cities, had an inexhaustible thirst. Two

matters remained to be settled in Central Africa: the controversy of the Nile's source and the outlet of the great river by
which Livingstone had stood. These mysteries were greatly
exaggerated; experts were coming around to Speke against
Burton, and the exit of the Congo into the Atlantic was known.
Stanley was clearly the man to make the most of the remaining
stories in Central Africa. The New York *Herald,* with the
London *Daily Telegraph,* sent him around Africa to Zanzibar.
He had with him a prefabricated boat, in eight sections, and
the most lavish expedition since Mungo Park.

Stanley's impressive train barged through Africa in a way not
seen from white explorers for years. He had with him a large
body of native musketeers and riflemen, three Englishmen, and
hundreds of porters. Men died of disease and starvation almost
daily. Suspicious or angry natives were greeted with blasts of
rifle fire. Under his white sun helmet, gripping his long staff,
always close to the fluttering British and American flags, the
intrepid reporter marched on.

Reaching Lake Victoria, he realized there was only one way
to solve the problem of the Nile's source: a complete circum-
navigation. This he made. He visited Buganda, where he was as
impressed as Speke and Grant had been and where he was well
received: "such a state is not to be found in Africa out of
Egypt." He found that the Kabaka was now "ever anxious to
please white men and to open commerce between Buganda and
Europe." He joined in a war and estimated the Buganda army
and followers to be a quarter of a million strong. While Stanley
was there, a Frenchman reached Buganda, signifying the increased French interest, previously confined to the west, in
Central Africa.

Soon two of the Englishmen were dead; Stanley himself
narrowly escaped with his life in a skirmish after leaving Buganda. He went south to Lake Tanganyika and circumnavi-
gated that also. He found there was no connection between the
two lakes; Burton was therefore wrong. "There remained the
grandest task of all," he wrote. "Is the [river] which Livingstone had traced the Nile, the Niger or the Congo? I crossed
Lake Tanganyika with our expedition, lifted once more my
gallant boat on our shoulders, and after a march of nearly two
hundred and twenty miles arrived at the superb river. . . . My
task was to follow it to the ocean."

Like Livingstone before him, Stanley joined forces with an Arab slaver, but unlike Livingstone, Stanley did not much care for Africans. He was told that the country through which the river went—today's Congo—was inhabited by the most fierce and bloodthirsty people on the continent. But Stanley had 140 guns and 70 spearmen—with porters and camp followers, a column about 700 strong. At first the boat—the *Lady Alice*—was carried, and the party tramped along the bank. Stanley wrote in *Through the Dark Continent:*

> As we struggled on through the mud, the perspiration exuded from every pore; our clothes were soon wet and heavy. Every man had to crawl and scramble as best he could. Sometimes prostrate forest giants barred the road with a mountain of twigs and branches. For ten days we endured it; then the Arabs declared they could go no further. I promised them five hundred pounds if they would escort us twenty marches only. On our way to the river we came to a village whose sole street was adorned with one hundred and eighty-six skulls. . . . [They embarked.] Day after day passed on and we found the natives increasing in wild rancour and unreasoning hate of strangers. At every curve and bend they "telephoned" along the river warning signals; their huge wooden drums sounded the muster for fierce resistance; reed arrows tipped with poison were shot at us from the jungle as we glided by.

Stanley was determined to continue, but some of the Arabs declined to do so. With thirty-three native canoes, the *Lady Alice* led the expedition downriver, flying the Union Jack, the Stars and Stripes, and the flag of Zanzibar. "Armies of parrots screamed overhead as they flew across the river; legions of monkeys and howling baboons alarmed the solitudes; crocodiles haunted the sandy points; hippopotami grunted at our approach; elephants stood by the margin of the river; there was unceasing vibration from millions of insects throughout the livelong day." There were well over thirty river engagements as the expedition paddled furiously to the sea many hundreds of miles away: skirmishes, ambushes, and full-scale battles. On one occasion they were met by 2,000 warriors in large canoes, with two rows of 40 paddlers each, "swaying to a barbarous chorus." On each occasion the natives ("extremely insolent," said Stanley) were greeted with volleys from Stanley and his men. Progress was bloody, tense, and desperate. The natives laughed at the cloth and beads the expedition had brought with it from Zanzibar. As always, Stanley's answer to any native problem was to blast away with his firearms. By this time he must have personally killed more Africans than any other white man in history. The last remaining Englishman was lost in one of the many swirling rapids that had to be negotiated. Stanley hated "this terrible river," and he longed for rest. The danger of famine was almost as great as that from cataracts, wild animals, poison darts, and disease. "Ah, straight for the mouth of the Congo," he wrote. "It widens daily." For whatever doubt he may have had about the identity of Livingstone's river, he now knew it had to be the Congo. Since it had already been penetrated a little from the sea, he left the *Lady Alice* at last and struck straight across the country for the coast. The boat from England had accompanied him across 7,000 miles of Africa.

Of the expedition of 700, only 115 remained to see the Atlantic shore. Literally staggering, half-starved, his hair grown white, diseased, H. M. Stanley arrived at the tiny Portuguese station of Boma on August 9, 1877. It was 999 days since he had left Zanzibar. "A gathering of European merchants met me and, smiling a warm welcome, told me kindly that I had done right well."

Neither Britain nor the United States was particularly interested in the area discovered by Stanley, despite approaches. Stanley accepted a commission to open up the region on behalf of King Leopold of Belgium.

In South Africa the volcano which was Zululand was rumbling. For years there had been deep apprehension among the European settlers, as they contemplated their northern neighbors. Now many were convinced that the Zulu were going to come flooding across the border, and there were 250,000 Zulu, ten times the number of whites in Natal. But it was not only numbers. It was the Zulu reputation—above all, the reputation of its army. In common with other African clans, the Zulu had long been expert at terrifying potential enemies by spreading rumors of terrible but exaggerated practices, studiously cultivating a frightening appearance, and, when at war, leaping and yelling in efforts to unsettle their adversaries further. This was a ploy common to virtually all the indigenous African people, and Zulu militarism was less natural than enforced by their system. Like all African tribes, the Zulu were intensely insecure. Their warlike gestures and acts were as indicative of a basic tribal insecurity as in the age of nuclear missiles, similarly based on fear, only a lifetime later.

Cetewayo, a huge man with kindly face and naked, protruding belly, had become king of the Zulu, and was recognized as such by the British, in 1873. An official British representative, Theophilus Shepstone (a famous expert on African affairs), had attended his coronation. Cetewayo had made a number of promises to the British, who had an interest in his land mixed of prudence, fear, and arrogance; the main promise was that he would rule by trial—and with more regard for human life than his predecessors had shown.

Apart from skirmishes with the Transvaal Boers, the Zulu had known more than thirty years of peace. But they had an army of 40,000 in perpetual readiness, supplied not only with their assegais (spears), but with surplus British army muskets and rifles. Peace had not brought contentment. Their society was founded on superstition and militarism. Witch doctors haunted the land. But of the two it was militarism which was the greatest danger; for frontline soldiers—and there were 25,000 of them—had to remain celibate until they had seen action in war. Not unnaturally, they were anxious for war. When a new king came to power, he was expected to ease the situation by providing a war—a "washing of the spears."

Because of the alarming reports and rumors about the Zulu coming from South Africa, the government decided to send the most successful colonial administrator of the day to Cape Colony and Natal. He rejoiced in the mellifluous name of Sir Henry Bartle Frere. A distinguished-looking man of sixty-two, with hair and mustache of deep gray, he had spent all his career in India. He had a great reputation, not without cause, for he had helped turn Karachi and Bombay into great modern cities. Success in India, where the proconsuls of the raj were treated like royalty, had made him supremely confident. His rule was always basically constructive, and he had definite ideas about South Africa. He wanted to make a United South Africa out of the two impoverished Afrikaner republics and the two impoverished British colonies, with African neighbors under firm "protection." In London it was expected that he would accomplish this task in two years.

Sir Joseph Banks. "The government ought to secure to the British throne, either by conquest or by treaty, the whole of the coast of Africa."

Left: Mungo Park bartering his jacket with a West African chief.

Right: Gordon Laing. "I shall do more than has ever been done before, and shall show myself to be what I have ever considered myself, a man of enterprise and genius."

First British immigrants, landing at Algoa Bay, 1820. "It was a forlorn-looking plight in which we found ourselves."

Treaty being signed with the "King of Iddah," 1842, a Mr. Duncan, formerly a trooper in the Life Guards, wearing full-dress uniform. Duncan perished four years later trying to reach Timbuktu.

Livingstone's last journey, 1873. "Knocked up quite."

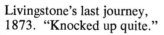

H. M. Stanley after his great expedition from the Indian Ocean to the Atlantic, 1874–77.

Gordon of Khartoum.

Last entry in Gordon's diary, December 14, 1885.

The survivors of Rorke's Drift, Zulu War, 1897; a group photograph taken shortly after the battle.

Rider Haggard, author of *King Solomon's Mines* (1885).

Cecil Rhodes. "The first statesman that modern Africa had produced. He was one of the richest men in the world."

Official British delegation to the Matabele "capital" of Bulawayo, 1888, including three members of the Royal Horse Guards in full dress uniform.

Fort Victoria, Rhodesia, 1893.

The arrival of the telegraph line at Fort Victoria.

Early settlers in Rhodesia, 1891, sans trousers, having crossed the Lundi River.

Kitchener Pasha. "I personally have very little interest in the Sudan and its future."

Sir Frederic and Lady Hodgson arriving at Kumasi before the siege of 1900. "The chiefs politely conveyed their thanks to Sir Frederic for his interest in their affairs, and returned home to prepare for war."

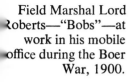

Field Marshal Lord Roberts—"Bobs"—at work in his mobile office during the Boer War, 1900.

Lord Delamere, leader of the white settlers in Kenya, 1903–31.

Lord Delamere

[by H.S.G.]

Frederick Lugard. "I trust that when the time comes it may be said of me that to the extent of my ability I did my duty."

Lord Cranworth, family and servants, in the White Highlands, Kenya, 1909.

Left: Coming ashore at Mombasa, 1906.

Right: Lord Cranworth, Lord Wodehouse, and their trophies; Kenya before the First World War.

A field telephone unit in German East Africa, 19[...]

Nairobi—
the 1930's.

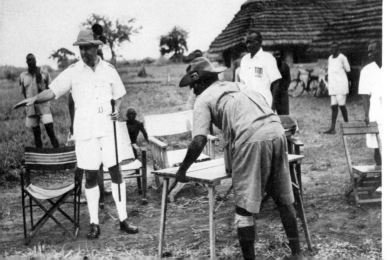

The district commissioner preparing for a court during hi[s] monthly visit t[o] village; he administered a territory the siz[e] of Belgium.

Jomo Kenyatta in England, 1945.

Prince Philip attends Nyasaland independence ceremonies, 1964; Dr. Hastings Banda in dark glasses.

Kwame Nkrumah, the "Redeemer" of Africa; his statue after he was deposed.

Bartle Frere wanted to provide a great new land for the Empire, as Clive had done in India. He had the African dream.

After his arrival he soon became involved in the air of panic in Natal. He saw Cetewayo as his main problem, not so much the Zulu themselves, with whom he said he had no quarrel. He developed an obsession about the Zulu king; he was convinced Cetewayo was an "irresponsible, bloodthirsty and treacherous despot."

The problem of the Transvaal seemed to have solved itself. The twenty-five-year-old republic was in debt, and government had broken down. There was said to be a danger of Zulu and Swazi invasions. Taxes were uncollected. Moreover, the Afrikaners were split among themselves. A party of thirty-six British —including the future writer Henry Rider Haggard, who had arrived in Africa at the age of nineteen—rode to Pretoria; they raised the Union Jack amid a crowd of armed burghers who made no protest. The Afrikaners really had no choice as their country was disintegrating, but those who accepted the British take-over were the townspeople only; whether the "Boers" would ever succumb to British rule (for that was what they considered "union") remained to be seen some later day.

Frere agreed with all he heard from the alarmists in Natal. When missionaries arrived from Zululand, disillusioned and pessimistic, he fastened on them with satisfaction. "It is quite clear the war spirit is abroad," he wrote to the Colonial Secretary. "The sooner the root of the evil, which I consider to be the Zulu power and military organization, is dealt with, the easier our task will be." He began an exchange with Cetewayo about the latter's coronation promises to Britain which the Zulu king had either been unwilling or, more likely, unable to enforce.

Cetewayo tried to be both obliging and firm. He said he wished to be friendly with England. "I do not go to Natal," he said, "and dictate to the governor about his laws. Go back and tell the Governor of Natal that he and I are equal. He is the Governor of Natal, and I am the governor here." Such an attitude was not likely to appeal to those who, like Bartle Frere, belonged to a new generation of Englishmen who believed Britain had a mission overseas, a mission which had to be carried out whether the inhabitants wanted it or not. "The Zulus are quite out of hand," he wrote to London. He suggested "a final end to Zulu pretensions to dictate to Her Majesty's

Government what they may or may not do to protect their colonies in South Africa."

London, hard pressed on other frontiers of the Empire, became alarmed at Bartle Frere's increasingly warlike intentions. It advocated the "exercise of prudence" and "a spirit of forebearance and reasonable compromise." Communications to London took at least three weeks. It was too late.

If the Ashanti War had disquieted some in England, the Zulu War would upset many more. For it was frank imperialist aggression. Did the British want Africa or not? And were they prepared to fight for it? They were questions which few faced as unashamedly as Sir Henry Bartle Frere. "Of the perfect justice of our cause," he wrote to Whitehall at the last minute, "I think you can have no doubt."

One thing was certain: The war would soon be over. The Zulu warriors were a threat to the isolated farmers of Natal, but they would not be a threat to the British army.

The commander in chief in South Africa was Lieutenant General Lord Chelmsford, a slim guardsman with a neat dark beard, an affable, conscientious officer who, so far as is known, had never offended anybody. Under his command he had an army 17,929 strong, of whom 6,000 were Europeans, mainly from regular regiments but also Natal colonists and Afrikaner volunteers. The three large native regiments had been carefully trained in drill and in European-style war, but it was thought wise to arm only one man in ten with a gun, the remainder relying on the traditional spears and shields.

Chelmsford had made a careful study of Zulu methods. He had done so with the greatest thoroughness. "The Zulu," he wrote, "has the advantage of being able to march in one day at least three times as far as the British soldier, and he has no commissariat train to hamper him." Nevertheless, "they are hopelessly inferior to us in fighting power although numerically stronger." Frere was even more confident. A member of the Natal legislature had advised him that "with a hundred redcoats you might march from one end of Zululand to the other."

Chelmsford, fearing that the Zulu might get behind him, invade Natal, and massacre the colonists, decided not to march in one huge column; he split his force into four columns. Three of these were to cross the river border of Zululand, defeat the Zulu, take the capital of Ulundi, and bring back Cetewayo; the fourth was to remain in reserve to protect Natal. Chelmsford himself was to go with the central column, which would cross the Buffalo River and enter Zulu territory at a place called Rorke's Drift.

On January 11, 1879, the central column crossed the river. The troops wore tight red jackets, blue trousers, white belts, and sun helmets. Each man carried seventy rounds, a water bottle, and a haversack. The officers, in red or blue jackets with white or red facings, carried revolvers or swords. With immaculate equipment glistening under the bright sun, the long column marched across the grass plain in perfect order.

A small garrison and base hospital were left at Rorke's Drift.

Progress was slow owing to supply difficulties. By January 20 the whole column was laid out in an extensive camp beside a huge rocky crag, which jutted up from the plain, called Isandhlwana. Despite advice from an Afrikaner, Chelmsford did not laager or encircle the camp with wagons. He was now 10 miles from Rorke's Drift.

Hearing from a patrol that a force of Zulu had been contacted, Chelmsford left camp with half the column. Before leaving, he ordered up some reserves from Rorke's Drift. In the early hours of the morning, his troops in light marching order, Lord Chelmsford left camp to do battle with the Zulu who had been reported.

At Isandhlwana, camp life continued with normal morning routine: Bugles were sounded, breakfasts prepared, horses scrubbed, tents inspected, wagons repaired, companies drilled. At 9:30 A.M. the reinforcements from Rorke's Drift arrived. There were 1,800 men in camp.

Lord Chelmsford, now 12 miles away, acting with his usual care, sent a young officer up a hill to check on the camp through a telescope. The officer reported that he could see nothing unusual; he could just make out men moving around among the tents, and everything seemed in order.

At Isandhlwana, reports began coming in of Zulu activity. About 400 to 600 enemy were said to be in the vicinity. A later report said Zulu were approaching the camp in three columns. There was no alarm. By 11 A.M. it was hot and sultry. Cooks were beginning to prepare dinner. It was not till midday that it was realized a large force of Zulu was massing close to the camp. Companies were hastily called to arms. The infantry were drawn up in a thick red line in front of the tents. A vast mass of Zulu, in battle array, could now be clearly seen flooding down the gentle slopes of the surrounding land toward the camp. There were about 20,000 of them. The two guns of the Royal Artillery began pumping shrapnel into the steadily advancing horde. Soon the frenzied war cries of the warriors could be heard. The sun glinted on the waving spears.

Then the brightness of the sun began to fade. For three hours there was a partial eclipse as the moon passed between earth and sun.

It was soon after 1 P.M. when the British line opened fire. In the line there were 950 whites, 600 of them highly trained and disciplined British redcoats, reputedly the finest infantry in the world. The Zulu continued to advance. Although hundreds fell from rifle and artillery fire, there were always more to fill their places. Clutching their four-foot shields and assegais, in loincloths and ostrich plumes, they came forward. For the first time a feeling of slight unease was felt in the camp.

It all happened very quickly. The supply of ammunition could not keep up with the furious rate of fire in the line. The three lines of the defense were not close enough together. The Zulu, whose firing had been erratic, came within throwing distance. Men began to fall. Here and there Zulu reached the line. For a moment the 600 British bayonets, grappling in ferocious close combat, held their line. Then gaps appeared. There was no question of the line's ever breaking; it was just swamped. Men fought together, back to back, in little groups.

Zulu rushed into the camp, slashing at tents, killing with frenzy. The battle was over. Orders could not be given or carried out. It was every man for himself. Those who could rushed for horses and thundered away out of the camp, through the narrow gap in the ever-enclosing Zulu mass. The Union Jack was run down from its pole and torn to pieces. Cooks, orderlies, and supply men were dragged from beneath wagons or tents and slaughtered. One group of sixty infantry, around their captain, kept fighting, but soon they were killed to the last man. A Zulu warrior later recorded the end of another party: "When

we closed in we came on a mixed party of mounted and infantry-
men . . . they numbered about a hundred. They made a desperate resistance, some firing with pistols and others using
swords. I repeatedly heard the word 'Fire' given by someone,
but we killed them all where they stood. . . . When all was
over, I had a look at these men, and saw an officer with his arm
in a sling and with a big moustache." It was the senior British
officer in the camp.

When the British examined the terrible battlefield months
later, they found the remains of men in small groups around
sergeants and officers.

Those who had escaped fled for the river in a mad rush.
Wagons loaded with screaming natives jostled and crashed in
the anxiety to get away. The Zulu gave chase, and many fugi-
tives were dragged from their horses and slain. Those few who
reached the river were mainly Natal Africans. The Zulu kept
up the pursuit for three miles across the river.

In less than thirty minutes of the assault not a white man was
left alive at Isandhlwana. The Zulu rummaged through the
camp; many of them dressed themselves in red tunics. According to custom, they slit open the stomachs of the dead enemy.
They moved away nearly 1,000 rifles and 400,000 rounds of
ammunition.

Well over 850 whites had been killed in the battle; 471 African troops had lost their lives. Six full companies of the Second
Warwickshire Regiment had been annihilated.

A scout brought news to Lord Chelmsford that he had seen
men in black faces in British red coats back at the camp. The
general and his staff were dumbfounded. What could it mean?
"I shall never forget the scene," a war correspondent wrote.
"The looks of amazement, grief and horror." The general
muttered, "But I left a thousand men there." He had, in fact,
left nearly 2,000 men there.

The column turned and marched back toward Isandhlwana.
Before approaching the camp, Chelmsford addressed the troops:
"There are ten thousand Zulus in our rear and twenty thousand
in our front; we must win back our camp tonight and cut our
way back to Rorke's Drift tomorrow."

But the camp was found empty, save for vultures. Exhausted
after their double march, the men lay down in the dark amid

the signs of carnage. It was a grim night. "How dreadful were those weary hours that followed," wrote one newspaperman. "Discovering, even by that dim light, the bodies of dear friends, brutally massacred, stripped of all clothing, disembowelled, mutilated, and in some cases decapitated."

Chelmsford expected an attack during the night. One of his staff wrote: "A great horror and fear seemed to have taken possession of the general in place of his former cheerful incredulity." The sound of firing could occasionally be heard from the direction of Rorke's Drift. There was a glow in the sky from that direction. He determined to march there in an hour or two, even before first light. In that way he would not only investigate what was happening at Rorke's Drift, but also save his men and himself the sight in broad daylight of the massacre at Isandhlwana.

While the general and his staff pondered on the morrow in their bloody camping ground, the garrison at Rorke's Drift fought for their lives. One large force of Zulu, 4,000 strong, had been in reserve at Isandhlwana. These celibate warriors were determined to engage the white enemy. During the afternoon they had swarmed down on Rorke's Drift.

The station of Rorke's Drift consisted of two thatched buildings, one of which was being used as a hospital. When he saw the Zulu approaching, the young lieutenant in command had hurriedly organized the defense, the main feature of which was a wall between the two buildings. Under him he had about 100 rifles, mostly Welshmen. He made it plain that the post would be defended to the death.

The first assault was beaten off under a terrific blaze of rifle fire. While Zulu riflemen sniped at the barricades from the rocky hill opposite, others rushed back to the defenses in swarm after swarm.

Zulu burst into the hospital building. There was no interior communication between the rooms, and so two riflemen inside hacked through the partitions, from room to room, dragging as many of the wounded as they could through with them, one man holding off the enemy, the other working feverishly with an ax; both men and most of the wounded appeared at the far end of the building which adjoined the perimeter of the defense. (There has never been a more courageous episode in the history of the British army.) By now the roof had been set fire by the Zulu and was blazing. A furious fight took place in the last room as the sick men were pulled out.

At the wall, Zulu were in heaps of dead and wounded. More came on, grappling with the defenders, sometimes jumping over the wall. Then they withdrew in order to concentrate for vast, concerted rushes. Time and again they bore down on the tiny defense, the ground shaking as they came. After dark it still went on. Each time they were beaten off by the defenders, who dared not move an instant from their positions.

It was some time after 2 A.M. when the rushes at last stopped. Through the remaining hours of night the garrison waited anxiously for morning. At last came the first dim light of dawn; the reddened eyes of the defenders made out the rear of the Zulu force returning whence it had come. The only sounds were the groans of the wounded Zulu lying all around. There was a thick musty smell of burned thatch, powder, and drying blood. Seventeen men had been killed, eight wounded.

Chelmsford's column had been marching since 4:30 A.M. It reached the hills above Rorke's Drift about 8 A.M. "I carefully examined the house at Rorke's Drift through my field glass," wrote a correspondent, "and thought I could distinguish the figures of men on parts of the wall and roof of the larger building, and one of them seemed to be waving a flag."

When the column arrived at Rorke's Drift—only half the size it had been when it had left twelve days before—rations were not issued until a strong defense had been arranged. Lord Chelmsford's invasion of Zululand had been obliged to return to Natal, where it had started. The other two columns had halted a few miles inside Zululand and successfully fought off opposition; one of them was virtually cut off. The British army had suffered its most humiliating defeat for generations, and the Zulu had preserved the integrity of their nation.

When the news reached Pietermaritzburg, the capital of Natal, there was considerable alarm. An attack by the Zulu was expected hourly. It was widely accepted that only the defense of Rorke's Drift had prevented an invasion so far. In London the news was received with confusion and anger. The massacre of Isandhlwana was only partly relieved by the gallantry at Rorke's Drift. There were about eighty army survivors of Rorke's Drift; no fewer than eleven of them were awarded the Victoria Cross.

A story came one morning
From a far and distant land,
That savages had massacred
A small but gallant band;
'Gainst twenty thousand savage foes,
'Midst thunder, shot and shell,
Five hundred valiant English fought,
And nobly fighting fell.
Five hundred British soldiers stood,
And nobly fighting fell.

The Cabinet met immediately and decided to send strong reinforcements to Natal. DEFEAT OF THE BRITISH was the *Times'* surprised headline. Some newspapers called for swift retribution. The *Daily News,* describing the war as "of the nation's own deliberate seeking," said the whole affair was "a disgrace" in every way. A petition was organized to stop British "aggression." Disraeli was extremely depressed: "Everyone was congratulating me on being the most fortunate of Ministers, when there comes this horrible disaster." Gladstone said the government should be ashamed of itself, spending lives and taxpayers' money against the Zulu, "who in defence of their own homes offered their naked bodies to the terribly improved artillery and arms of modern science."

No further invasion of Zululand would take place before the reinforcements arrived. Lord Chelmsford left the front, to consult with the unhappy Frere, who found him "many years older." Both knew their careers were in danger. Chelmsford asked to be recalled, but Queen Victoria, who had always admired him, sent him an encouraging message, sympathizing "most sincerely" and expressing her "entire confidence."

Frere fought for his reputation with rare tenacity. He insisted that he had been right, but that only time could prove it. The Colonial Secretary informed him that the Cabinet "have been unable to find in the documents you have placed before them that evidence of urgent necessity for immediate action, which alone could justify you in taking, without their full knowledge and sanction, a course almost certain to result in a war which, as I had previously impressed upon you, every effort should have been made to avoid." There was no doubt that the Cabinet, let alone the Colonial Secretary, did not intend to shoulder the blame.

Desultory but bloody fighting continued with the two remaining columns. A supply convoy and its escort were attacked by the Zulu, with the loss of 62 British soldiers. An attempt by 400 mounted men to take a Zulu stronghold was beaten off; it was led by Redvers Buller, who had a growing reputation for courage and alcohol capacity. More than a quarter of the force was slain; Buller received the Victoria Cross for remaining calm and saving the rest. But Zulu losses, too, were mounting—and in terrible proportion. In one engagement they killed 28 redcoats, but themselves lost well over 1,000, and this particular defeat weakened their morale.

The cut-off column was relieved when Chelmsford returned to Zululand with a force of 5,800, of whom 3,390 were Europeans. When attacked, he was ready, with his camp in laager. Nearly 1,000 Zulu were killed, to the loss of 13 British dead. Firepower had won the war, as in the end it had been bound to.

Bartle Frere was relieved of his responsibilities in Natal but retained his position as governor of Cape Colony, considered a comparatively placid area. This was a resounding insult, but Frere did not resign. His career was in ruins. He heard the news of this snub only a few hours after he had learned of the death in action of the prince imperial, the Bonapartist pretender to the French throne, who had been an observer at the front. The death of the prince reverberated around Europe. Remembering that the Anglican Bishop of Natal had always been pro-Zulu, Disraeli said: "A remarkable people the Zulu—they defeat our generals, they convert our bishops, they have settled the fate of a great European dynasty." When Gladstone returned to power in 1880, Frere was sacked. He died only four years later, at Wimbledon, preparing a full vindication of his policy.

The complete subjugation of Zululand remained. Once again three columns entered the country, in greater strength and with greater care. One of the columns was commanded by a major general who fancied himself as an artist and delighted in wearing a sombrero with a peacock's feather. He insisted on a wagon converted into a mobile hen house so that he could enjoy a fresh egg for his breakfast each morning. There was one more battle; casualties—1,500 Zulu dead, 12 British dead.

To clear up the mess in Natal, the government had sent out the ever-reliable Garnet Wolseley. On arrival, he surveyed the wreckage of several of his rivals' careers with irony and satisfaction. He was just in time to inform Whitehall: "The war is over."

Chelmsford returned home. He received the Knight Grand Cross and was promoted. He was never again granted a command out of the country, and Disraeli refused to see him at his home.

The war had cost British taxpayers £5,230,000. Out of the 32,400 troops who had taken the field, nearly 2,400 had been killed.

Cetewayo was taken to captivity in Durban. His kingdom was split up into thirteen parts, each under a chief appointed by Wolseley. Inevitably, the result was chaos. Cetewayo was then taken to London, where he lived in a rented house in Kensington. Although he had arrived in Durban, the first town he had ever seen, wearing a loincloth and cloak, he was soon walking the streets of London, shopping, in a smart suit; everyone remarked on his regality. Setting the pattern for most African leaders who were to defy the British right to rule in the decades to come, he was now honored. The queen invited him to lunch and found the occasion enjoyable. Cetewayo may have reflected that the British were a curious people. He was sent back to his kingdom, escorted to his old capital in great style by a detachment of the Sixth Dragoon Guards. The result of this was, not unnaturally, some confusion in Zululand. Civil war ensued, and in due course Zululand was annexed to Natal. The Zulu warriors became laborers on Boer and British farms. Sir Henry Bartle Frere had got his way, but it had not been easy.

✦ VI ✦

Defeat at Majuba

For 300 years the word "Africa" had been synonymous with hidden wealth. But it had not realized its potential: The myth of a fabulous Shangri-La at Timbuktu had been exploded at last, the Gold Coast had not brought forth a flood of gold, the commerce of the Niger had not yet fulfilled expectations, and the "black gold" of the slave trade had made only a few men, on both sides of the Atlantic, rich. The economy of South Africa, still the most developed area of the continent, was based on the uncertain market of wool. After the exploding of the legend of Timbuktu, the fact was that Africa seemed a poor prospect when compared to North America or India. Africa had a difficult climate and was evidently underpopulated compared with India. It seemed a land most fit for adventurers, humanitarians, story-tellers, and incurable optimists. But all that was to change. The lobbyists and prophets of the African Association were to be vindicated at last.

The first sight of real wealth in South Africa was glimpsed in a child's hand in 1867. In that year a traveler caught sight of a glistening stone among pebbles in a game being played by a farmer's son. The traveler, whose name in most accounts is John O'Reilly, took the stone to the nearest town, where the opinion was that it was of no value. But farther south, at Grahamstown, it was pronounced to be a diamond; no one had taken much notice of previous rumors of diamonds in Africa. When the governor of Cape Colony bought the stone for £500, the find was accepted as genuine. It caused a sensation. Adventurers flocked to the area, at first investigating the Vaal River and then opening up cavernous diggings near the Orange Free State border. The richest field was on the land of a farmer named Johannes de Beers, who almost accepted an offer of £6,000 for his land but, when a lady's parasol uncovered a diamond during the discussion, demanded an additional £600. Soon afterward the property was sold for £100,000. A large settlement, mostly of tents, grew into an extensive shantytown. Within a very few years of O'Reilly's discovery the town—named Kimberley, after the Colonial Secretary, John Wodehouse Kimberley,—was second only to Cape Town among European towns on the African continent.

To whom did the fields belong? It was a question of obvious importance and one which aroused much bitterness. The diamond fields lay in an area between Cape Colony and the Orange Free State that had become a no-man's-land. It was still nominally under the rule of an African chief. Such European settling as had been done there had been almost entirely by Afrikaners from the Orange Free State. The Free State, with some excitement, realized it had an excellent claim. Britain, however, had no intention of letting such valuable property elude the expanding Empire in Africa. Some 17,800 square miles were annexed to Cape Colony; the British border, which fifty years before had included only the immediate hinterland of Cape Town, was now nearly 400 miles inland from the coast. The chief seems to have had little say in the matter.

The Afrikaners of the Orange Free State were outraged at the blatant disregard for legal niceties, but were partly assuaged by a grant of £90,000. The Transvaalers, however, by tradition more fiery than the Free Staters, were enraged on behalf of their neighbors, and the grievance continued to fester among them. After an expedition under Sir Charles Warren into Bechuanaland, in which the Transvaal had long shown an interest, a further depth of 150 miles was added to British territory in 1885. On that occasion the motive was said to be the restoration of order after native "disturbances."

Whether the Orange Free State authorities could have controlled the diamond fields, peopled mainly by British and American diggers of the most independent and ruffianly sort, is doubtful. Kimberley was a violent town. Shootings were commonplace, gambling ferocious, prostitutes in abundance, suicides frequent, and drunkenness almost universal. At Dodd's Bar there was roulette every night, and whiskey and cigars were free for the players; the famous "Champagne Charlie" was a habitué until he left town suddenly after selling a fake stone. It was estimated that about half the early diamond output was stolen.

It was soon evident that the Kimberley mines were fantastically rich. But it was equally evident that the society which had congregated at Kimberley was fantastically incompetent at tapping the wealth. Very few fortunes were being made; bankruptcies were far more numerous. Small companies, set up efficiently to organize the mining, promised riches but experienced failure. Working the mines proved increasingly costly, and litigation was habitual.

One of the early arrivals at Kimberley, in 1871, was a large, fair-haired youth of eighteen. A vicar's son, he had been sent to Natal for the warm air, being a suspect consumptive. He had trekked the 400 miles from Natal, to make his fortune at the diamond mines, equipped with a bucket, a spade, Plutarch's *Lives,* a Greek lexicon, and a box of lozenges. He was highly enthusiastic about Kimberley—"the richest diamond mine the world has ever produced," he said on arrival. "Fancy an immense plain," he wrote home, "with right in its centre a mass of white tents and iron stores." The remarkable thing about this youth, who was said to be so sickly, was his ability to gain the respect of the exceedingly tough population of the town. While others, disappointed at the lack of quick and easy riches, moved on, he persevered. While some lost as much money as they made, he gradually accumulated capital and claims. A contemporary remembered him at the time as "a tall, fair boy, blue-eyed, and with aquiline features, wearing flannels of the school playing field, somewhat shrunken with strenuous rather than effectual washings." Another recalled: "He was a compound of moody silence and impulsive action. He was hot and even violent at times, but in working towards his ends he laid his plans with care and circumspection."

After two years at Kimberley, Cecil Rhodes had made enough money to send himself to Oxford University. He was ambitious for educational background, as well as for riches. For several years he traveled between the rough tin town of Kimberley and the ancient quadrangles of Oxford. Generations of undergraduates at Oxford knew him as an amiable colonial "character." At Kimberley he was known as a hard, ruthless, and feared young businessman.

Financial failures at Kimberley became worse. Rhodes saw his opportunity. Advised by a friend, Alfred Beit, he began amalgamating the Kimberley claims. Beit supplied the accounting; Rhodes supplied the "persuasion." Beit was instrumental in getting the backing of the London Rothschilds; after that it was merely a matter of time—and not much of that—before Rhodes' De Beers company controlled the South African diamond mines. Rhodes wrote out a check, with the Rothschilds behind him, for "Five Million, Three Hundred and thirty-eight Thousand, Six Hundred and Fifty-eight Pounds, only." To run the mines, Rhodes brought in a leading minerologist, Gardner Williams, of Michigan, who successfully reorganized the mines.* Rhodes said his intention was to make De Beers "the richest, the greatest and the most powerful company the world has ever seen." Cecil Rhodes looked out from Kimberley and saw South Africa, still in confusion, with Afrikaner, British and native all at odds. He looked north and saw an untapped continent. He was rich, and he had power—politics beckoned.

The diamond mines had a dramatic and almost immediate effect on the South African economy: The white population increased, ancillary services and industries accompanied the growth of the mines, money became easier to come by, and trade expanded. Africans were employed in industry at Kimberley for the first time and in large numbers. In twenty years after the discovery, the export of rough diamonds rose from 200 carats to 3,841,837 carats, bringing in a sum of more than £4,000,000 per annum. Kimberley was quickly transformed into a prosperous, planned city; it had electric trams before London. The "Big Hole," in which men had burrowed, gave way to underground mines, but before it was finished, it was a mile around the top, the largest man-made hole in the world.

The promised wealth that had lured men into Africa for so long had arrived. And it had come in British territory.

When Rhodes, aged twenty-eight, took his seat at the colonial Parliament in Cape Town, a leading politician said: "Watch

* Williams was succeeded as general manager of De Beers by his son, Alpheus Williams. These two Americans, father and son, ran South African diamond mining from 1887 to 1932.

that man. He is the future man of South Africa, and possibly of the world." Rhodes himself would have been the last to disagree. But he was worried about his life-span, convinced he would die young. He had already written a will which stipulated that the whole estate was to be used to found a "secret society, the true aim and object whereof shall be the extension of British rule throughout the world." Cecil Rhodes had decided to devote the remainder of his life—and any future riches, power, and influence he might gain—to spreading the British Empire throughout the African continent. And he was a very determined young man.

Trouble with the Transvaal continued to simmer. The ex-citizens of the defunct republic, annexed by Bartle Frere, were not taking kindly to British rule. They looked on the continued independence of the Orange Free State with envy. The leader who rallied support for the reestablishment of the republic was Paul Kruger. Kruger was an untidy-looking man with hunched shoulders, black beard, and a thick, heavy nose; he wore loose black clothes and a large floppy hat. His appearance was utterly foreign to the British people, who were convinced he was a malevolent troublemaker, blinded by obstinacy and cant. To the Afrikaners he was a noble patriot, defending the rights of an oppressed people whose distinct language, customs, and history entitled them to independent status. He was backed by 6,591 burghers, who supported him with their signatures. This out of a total male suffrage of about 8,000 (the total white population was about 40,000). Twice he headed delegations to London. In Whitehall the seriousness of the Afrikaner claim was completely underrated, and communication between Kruger and the Colonial Office was such that the latter considered the Afrikaners would "accept cheerfully the present state of things."

Garnet Wolseley, after the Zulu War, ruled the Transvaal with a firm hand. "So long as the sun shines," he said, "the Transvaal will remain British territory." He gave it the constitution of a crown colony. Kruger waited. British troops, after the Zulu War, began to leave for other parts of the troubled Empire. Gladstone returned to power, and he was known to be opposed to British expansion. He had described the annexation of the Transvaal as "dishonorable," but once in office, he saw things differently. "The Queen cannot be advised," he said reluctantly "to relinquish her sovereignty over the Transvaal." Wolseley assured the government that the Afrikaners would never fight. Impatient for other fields to conquer, he got himself transferred to London.

Wolseley was replaced by Major General Sir George Colley, a forty-five-year-old Dubliner whose reputation was based on a brilliant academic career at the Staff College and at Sandhurst, where he had been a professor. He was delighted at the appointment. "That extraordinary run of luck," he told his wife, "seems to accompany me in everything, and at times almost frightens me."

Disturbances broke out at the country town of Potchefstroom over a matter of £27. It was just such niggardly aspects of administration that had sent the Afrikaners' fathers on the Great Trek a generation before. Shots were fired. Colley was bewildered. "I cannot conceive," he declared, "what can have so suddenly caused the Boers to act as they have." The country rose in arms against the British occupation. There were only three battalions to control an area larger than Britain itself; the scattered garrisons soon found themselves helplessly invested at outposts around the country.

A column of 235 redcoats was sent to Pretoria, the Transvaal capital (which had been founded twenty-five years before). It was Christmas week, 1880, and the men of the Connaught Rangers marched happily up the road, their band to the fore, playing "Kiss Me, Mother, Kiss Your Darling Daughter." A party of Afrikaner insurgents stopped them and, after a brief altercation, shot the column to pieces. Within a few minutes more than half the column were lying dead or wounded in the road; the remainder surrendered without further ado. The Afrikaners had lost two men.

It was war. Colley was not displeased at the chance of putting his military theories into practice. Intending to model himself on Robert E. Lee, he would march his little army of 1,200 men, six guns, and 150 cavalry from Natal into the Transvaal, defeating resistance on the way by superior troops and superior military expertise. It would be an interesting exercise. But Sir George Colley's luck, which had seen him thus far in life, had run out.

Sir George's opponents did not look impressive. The Afrikaner army, organized into commandos, consisted of irregulars, who did not accept much discipline. Major decisions were made only after considerable discussion among all who thought they had a right to be heard—virtually everyone. The men had no uniforms. A British regimental officer described an Afrikaner mounted rifleman with disdain: "A dirty, unkempt-looking fellow, with long hair and beard. The chances are he has one spur on upside down, his head covered with a broad-brimmed felt hat, high in the crown, and a dirty flannel shirt." Unlike the British, they were not a people who saw any glory in war, but they were accustomed to fighting, had been all their history. They considered war a civic duty, were expert shots, and had inherited tactical genius suited to South African terrain, based on many native wars.

Colley decided to advance into the Transvaal on the main route, through the passes of the Drakensberg mountains. The Transvaalers awaited him at a spur overlooking the route, at Laing's Nek. A strong detachment of infantry was ordered up the slope to dislodge them. Reaching the brow, the order was given to fix bayonets. The officers' swords and the bayonets glinted in the bright sun. There was a piercing shout of "Charge."

The redcoats were met by a withering fusillade. Nearly all the officers fell immediately, dead or terribly wounded, one of them shouting *"Floreat Etona"* as he did so. Only a few troops reached the trenches. One of the few remaining officers ordered a withdrawal. The retreat was orderly, and with no signs of panic, but when it was over, 150 of the 480 men who had climbed the hill had not returned.

General Colley was astonished. He was further nonplussed when a supply convoy, guarded by 300 infantry, was set upon and defeated. "It is altogether too sad," he wrote to his wife. His troops were beginning to fear the worst. "A more charming and courteous man you could not meet," wrote a soldier, "but he ought not to be trusted with a corporal's guard on active service."

The British column halted while efforts were made to start negotiations between London and the Transvaal. Colley feared that the government was going to give in to the Afrikaner demands before he could salvage his reputation. His wife, who felt herself humiliated by the reverses, had urged an immediate and impressive victory. But the government had forbidden aggression during its search for a peaceful solution. It was a desperate situation for Sir George Colley. One hill, Majuba, frowned massively over the whole area, dominating not only the British lines but the Afrikaner camp also; the Afrikaners had not occupied it. Colley decided to take it, in the belief that if he could do so without fighting a battle, the enemy might then be forced to retire without a shot being fired. If successful, it would be a master stroke, something of which Lee himself would have been proud, and faith in Sir George's reputation as a military thinker would be restored.

There is little doubt that Colley, goaded by his wife, was in an extremely agitated condition when he made his plan. Rider Haggard, who was ostrich farming not far away, wrote that Colley was "not himself" at this time.

Colley assembled his assault force, about 600 strong, at night. Even most of the officers did not know what he intended. The general went alone to his tent to scribble a message to his wife: "I am going out tonight to try and seize the Majuba Hill, which commands the right of the Boer position, and leave this behind in case I should not return. . . . How I wish I could believe the stories of meeting again hereafter, but it is no good complaining because things are not as one might wish—one must only brace oneself to meet them as they are—think lovingly and sadly, but not too sadly or hopelessly of your affectionate husband." Sir George Colley, it seems, had a premonition that his luck might not return. At 10 P.M. he mounted his horse and led his column out of the camp.

It was a steep climb to the plateau on top of Majuba, and there was a good deal of stumbling and cursing in the dark. But by 4 A.M., just as dawn began to streak the sky, the last of the panting troops had reached the top. Colley himself had ridden much of the way; arriving at the top, he put on a pair of white tennis shoes he had brought with him to rest his feet after the climb. As the light increased, he considered the position with satisfaction. Far below was the Boer camp. "We could stay here forever," he remarked. He sent back a proud message for Whitehall.

No order was given to dig in. The men enjoyed themselves jeering and waving at the enemy below. Some of the Afrikaners alarmed at the possibility of British artillery being hauled up the hill, began to retire. The Transvaal commander believed that "everything was lost to us." But later he decided to call for volunteers to storm the hill. It was Sunday morning, and the Afrikaners did not care to fight on Sundays. Eighty men came forward. The remainder would follow them, covering the climb with a barrage of rifle fire. Most professional soldiers would have considered they were attempting to take an impregnable position.

By 6 A.M. the plateau was under fire. Colley turned down a suggestion that defenses should be dug. "It's only rifle fire," he said. Some of his officers wondered why they were sitting idly on a mountaintop. Was the general not going to follow up his advantage? Where were the guns? Why was not a concerted move being launched on the other flank? No doubt, they consoled themselves, Sir George knew what he was doing. He was, in fact, standing at the crest, quietly staring at the Afrikaner activity below. After that he lay down. Sir George went to sleep.

The Afrikaners advanced slowly. They crept up from hollow to hollow, from boulder to boulder. Arriving at the crest, together and in force, they rushed the thinly spread defense. The redcoats ran back to join the main bulk of their comrades at a corner of the summit. Sir George was awakened by the proximity of the firing. The troops fixed bayonets, and defensive positions were hurriedly arranged by officers. The Afrikaners kept up an incessant fire that was amazingly accurate; man after man fell, shot between the eyes. The British reply was wild; hardly a Boer was hit. Despite the pleas, anger, and exhortations of their officers, the British troops began to withdraw. Some threw away their rifles and ran off down the slope, at its steepest in this sector. They were soon followed by others. As one officer put it: "A general funk had become established." The troops rushed past General Colley, who watched them go without a word. A newspaper reporter who was present wrote: "Within minutes those who survived the following fire were streaming down the hillside. One cannot altogether blame them; they had lost all confidence in their leaders." Men tumbled down the slippery slope, sliding on their backs, falling and slithering; as they were hit, their dead bodies came to rest, splayed out against bushes and stones. Afrikaners stood at the crest and picked off the panic-stricken troops, many of them in the kilts of the Gordon Highlanders, "like buck," as one of them put it.

The survivors of one platoon remained on the plateau with Sir George. It was commanded by Lieutenant Hector Macdonald, who had achieved the rare feat of having risen from obscure parentage and the ranks to a commission. But only two of them were unwounded. Macdonald was at last taken prisoner, after fighting with his bare fists. The last to die was almost certainly Major General Sir George Colley, with a bullet through his head.

Throughout Sunday night the wounded lay on the slopes in heavy rain. The next day there was an armistice to clear the battlefield. Owing to the new cable link, on Monday morning the newsboys were shouting the defeat in Piccadilly and Trafalgar Square. The British public was bewildered. Transvaal farmers had defeated a force of British infantry. British casualties had been 280; Boer casualties had been 6. Of the 120 Gordon Highlanders who had climbed Majuba, only 24 had returned unharmed.

The government was furious. It had been trying to make peace, and this would make it far more difficult. The queen wrote: "I do not like peace before we have retrieved our honour." Most of the country agreed with her. But Gladstone, as usual, was against "shedding more blood." The independence of the Transvaal was recognized, but it was a strange sort of independence, for Britain insisted on control of the republic's foreign relations and its relations with neighboring African tribes. The republic of the Transvaal quickly restored its authority; as for its finances, there were continual rumors of gold in the veld. The antagonisms that had resulted in the Great Trek, nearly half a century before, had not been resolved by the war. Moreover, the British army did not appear to be such a mighty foe in South Africa as might have been expected; the British put it down to a fluke and did not take much notice. The Afrikaners did take notice. As for British ambitions, they were still shadowy—they had conquered Zululand, but they had relinquished their grip on the Transvaal. But the shadow was about to pass over—to reveal territorial acquisitions that would impress even the most ardent of the hundreds of thousands of armchair imperialists at home.

PART THREE

WHITE MAN'S BURDEN

❖ VII ❖

Scramble for Africa

PRIOR to 1880 British expansion in Africa had hardly been conducted at reckless speed. The expansionists had been obliged to fight not only Ashanti, Egyptians, South Africans, and Zulu, but also the anti-imperialists at home, who looked to Gladstone as their leader. In the early 1880's there were only five European nations—excluding the Afrikaner republics—which had possessions in Africa. Turkey, preposterously, still claimed the north from Suez to the Atlas Mountains, but the "Sick Man of Europe" held little or no sway over areas which were virtually autonomous. The Portuguese cultivated their ancient colonies with their customary secrecy and suppression. Spain had a few tiny trading posts of no importance. The two most active powers, as they had been for so long, were France and Britain. And Britain, in view of her firm and extensive holding at the southern tip of the continent, had by far the greatest possessions—a fact which would not have displeased Sir Joseph Banks and his friends.

Britain had been able to proceed in Africa at much her own speed, depending on the actions of her politicians, merchants, and explorers. Disraeli's Foreign Secretary had been Lord Salisbury, whose appearance in the African drama had only just begun. Writing of this period around 1880, Salisbury noted:

> We remained masters of Africa, practically, or the greater part of it, without being put to the inconvenience of protectorates or anything of that sort, by the simple fact that we were

masters of the sea and that we have had considerable experience in dealing with native races. So much was that the case that we left enormous stretches of coast to the native rulers in the full confidence that they would go on under native rulers and in the hope that they would gradually acquire their own proper civilization without any interference on our part. Then, suddenly, we found out that position, however convenient, had no foundation whatever in international law. We had no rights over all these vast stretches of coast, both on the west and east coasts of Africa. We had no power of preventing any other nation from coming in and seizing a portion of them.

Up to 1880 Britain could have had nearly all Africa, without much fuss, if she could have spared her efforts from India and elsewhere. Since the Franco-Prussian War, the greatest power in Europe was Germany, but Germany had shown hardly any official interest at all in Africa; indeed, Germany was considered Britain's natural ally, if she should ever be forced to relinquish her "splendid isolation" from alliances. The only substantial area claimed by France was Senegal on the west coast. There ambitious plans of colonization had been put under way, and the colony had been pacified and "opened up" deep into the interior. Of all the West Africa colonies, only Senegal could realistically claim more than the coastal belt.

But in the early 1880's the situation changed dramatically. Five powers—Britain, France, Germany, Portugal, and Italy— and one king, Leopold II of Belgium, stretched their might to grab great chunks of the continent in which some of them had previously shown no interest at all. There were a number of contributing factors. Gladstonian liberalism was on the decline. The completion of the Suez Canal had made that area more sensitive than ever. The great diamond fields at Kimberley had illustrated beyond doubt that the continent was as rich as legend had always claimed. Then there was the growing rivalry in trade. Britain's industrial lead was disappearing, and other nations needed new markets for their rapidly expanding manufacturing industries, which, in turn, required new reservoirs of raw materials, which they hoped they would find in Africa. Victory in the Franco-Prussian War had welded Germany, and defeat in it had provided a spur to France. Italy took its first tentative step—in Northeast Africa—in 1880 and squabbled with France over Tunis. The pressure in trade was much greater than it had been at the time of Macgregor Laird and the early west coast traders, and competition was more intense. Trade was once again becoming the concern of governments, and it was this in particular which prompted Europe to burst upon Africa with such incredible and irrestible force in the 1880's. It was not so much the desire for new territory and potential markets as the utter determination to prevent others from gaining them.

With these diverse events for fuel, the "scramble for Africa" was begun beside its two greatest rivers: the Congo and the Nile.

For several years H. M. Stanley had been struggling to claim the Congo banks as a trading center for Leopold II. The king seems at first to have seen the Congo purely in terms of trade. But the Portuguese were not uninterested in the area, and when Leopold discovered that the French, too, had ambitions there, a political confrontation was inevitable. Stanley went up the river making treaties with the chiefs and establishing posts. One of the posts he named Léopoldville. He remained in the area from 1879 to 1884 with only one visit to Europe. On one occasion he was visited by an Italian employed by the French, Savorgan de Brazza. Stanley believed they were working together without national rivalry, and it was not till he visited the opposite bank of the Congo that he discovered that De Brazza had founded a post under the flag of France: Brazzaville. Stanley was highly indignant. Leopold was furious. Stanley and De Brazza courted the confused local chieftains, who observed these proceedings with interest but who felt little, if any, loyalty for whichever of the flags flew above their simple villages.

At the Nile, the French and British watched each other with the care of a pair of fighting hawks. The sale of his Suez Canal shares to Britain had not relieved the debts of the Khedive (hereditary ruler of Egypt) for long. Bankruptcy was inevitable. French and British administrators, representing the two most interested creditors, moved in. The French had built the canal; the British had most interest in its operation. They set up a puppet regime, which was not popular.

The Egyptians were different from other peoples on the continent who had come, or were coming, under British control; they had a long history of contact with Europe and an extensive and literate middle class. Foreign traders in Egypt abused the Anglo-French financial control to their own advantage. Rioting was commonplace. A nationalist movement, under Arabi Pasha, grew in strength. Policing became increasingly difficult; the British fleet bombarded Alexandria. The French had seen enough and moved out, thus abandoning an area which had been never far from French influence since Napoleon; they shortly regretted their lack of nerve, but Britain intended to govern alone. The country came more and more under British dominance. The famous obelisk, to be known as Cleopatra's Needle, some 3,500 years old, was shipped off to London, where it was erected on the Embankment (its twin left for New York two years later). The hinterland, the southern Sudan, was governed by Sir Samuel Baker, the erstwhile explorer and discoverer of Lake Albert, and then by Major General Charles George Gordon.

Chaos fed on chaos, and although the Egyptians were accustomed to it, in Whitehall it seemed intolerable. There was not only the canal to consider, but the property of nearly 100,000 non-Egyptians was in jeopardy. The Egyptian army supported Arabi Pasha. Military intervention was inevitable. Once more an expeditionary force was raised for Egypt. There was no need to look further for its command than to Sir Garnet Wolseley, a fact which brought some chagrin not only to his rivals but to everyone who knew him, including the queen, in view of his cheerful but undisguised conceit. It was a considerable force. Some 40,560 officers and men were assembled from England and India. From the home country alone sixty-one steamers plied into the Mediterranean with men, horses, and supplies. Wolseley took with him his usual favorites, including Redvers Buller and William Butler. In 1884 troops embarked at Westminster Pier, virtually in the shadow of the Houses of Parliament, to scenes of great emotion and patriotic fervor cheering crowds lined the embankment for two miles as the ships slowly moved away down the Thames.

As always, Wolseley's strategy was uncomplicated but sensible. He would mislead the Egyptians into thinking he would approach Cairo up the delta of the Nile. In fact, he would cross the narrow strip of desert from the canal. The main Egyptian army was at its huge camp of Tel el Kebir, in the open desert there Wolseley intended to strike, leaving the way open to Cairo.

The first stage succeeded perfectly, and by the time Wolseley had arrived on the banks of the Suez Canal it was too late for the surprised Arabi Pasha to have it destroyed. Wolseley, wearing enormous dark goggles and solar topee, made his arrangements for the advance. A railway ran from the canal to Cairo, via Tel el Kebir, and along this Wolseley marched his force under a cruel and blazing sun. (Rolling stock had been taken by Arabi and destroyed.) Tel el Kebir was 30 miles from the canal, and the great British column was harassed and bombarded all the way. It stopped within sight of the Egyptian camp. Wolseley screwed a telescope to his eye, surveyed the strength of the built-up fortifications facing him, and announced a night attack.

The Egyptian army was far different from the Zulu, the Ashanti, or even the Transvaalers; it had been trained and organized along European lines. There were 20,000 regular troops manning the formidable defenses; against them, Wolseley had 13,000 men in the column that had marched across the sands from the canal. It was essential for Wolseley to inflict a decisive defeat at this place, for otherwise Arabi would have the chance to regroup outside Cairo, where the British supply line would be dangerously stretched.

A night attack was well known to be something of a gamble; there was always the danger of confusion, and the troops had little, if any, experience in night attacks. For this reason, perhaps, Arabi's men were not prepared for such a move. The British force moved silently across the sand, the fires still burning in its deserted camp; out in front was a naval lieutenant, steering by the stars. The gentle desert wind, blowing from west to east, was kind to Wolseley, for it carried away the squeak of the gun wheels as they advanced.

The Highland Brigade was in the vanguard; bayonets clicked into place all down the line. The crisp air of approaching dawn was rent by the pealing of bugles as the Highlanders charged. They clambered up the sandy slopes beneath the trenches and defense bastions while the Egyptian soldiers rushed to their posts. Soon the pipes were wailing, and an artillery duel was in progress. Desperate hand-to-hand fighting occurred all along the line. Although fighting continued, the battle had been decided in the first few minutes. More than 2,000 Egyptians were slain, while British casualties were 480. British troops tore about in the massive camp, slashing at tents and looting. Wolseley smoked six cigars in a row, and he just had time to send off a victorious dispatch for Whitehall before his breakfast, brought up from the rear, was served.

Arabi had fled to Cairo, weeping, in a train. His position was hopeless, for by the setting of the sun British cavalry, led by the famous Bengal Lancers, had clattered into the streets of the capital, beneath its many minarets, having galloped much of the way. When Wolseley arrived, in a more leisurely fashion, he was cordially greeted by an official reception. The dignitaries, said Butler, were "all coffee, cigarette and obsequious courtesy." The Egyptians, who had been under Turkish and foreign domination for so long, were more accustomed to a servile posture than to bold-faced hostility. Wolseley had promised Arabi's nose to his daughter but thought better of it. Arabi was tried, pleaded guilty (by arrangement), and was banished to Ceylon. Wolseley had predicted before leaving London that he would conclude the war on September 16, 1885, exactly. He had missed it by one day and sent a peremptory message to Whitehall: "The war in Egypt is over."

At home it was a tremendous relief. There had been no Isandhlwana, no Majuba Hill. Everything was "All Sir Garnet," a popular expression, in celebration of Wolseley, meaning all was perfect. "Felt unbounded joy and gratitude," said Victoria. Wolseley was welcomed home by the Prime Minister and members of the royal family, before vast crowds at Charing Cross Station. Wolseley's self-satisfaction was finally accepted as reasonable, and even the queen expressed herself delighted with him.

It was Gladstone who had decided to spare Arabi Pasha "frightened of the radicals," his opponents said. Said Wolseley "How different things would have been had Lord Beaconsfield lived." Gladstone promised that as soon as order was restored and a stable regime *in situ*, Britain would leave Egypt. What the Egyptians thought of this British self-sacrifice was no secret but also of no immediate relevance: The security of the route to India was more important. The Egyptian army was to be completely reformed, as an instrument of British power, under Sir Evelyn Wood, a Wolseley man who had spent his career fighting in all parts of Africa. Gladstone meant his promise to depart but few outside Britain believed him. In any event, it was soon apparent that it would be years before Britain could honestly say that Egypt was fully prepared for efficient self-administration. The standards of British administrators were quite different from those of Turkey, which had for long been fairly acceptable in Egypt. Sir Evelyn Baring, later Lord Cromer, was sent to run the country, and he had very high standards indeed. "We must give a little more time to allow the whole machine of government to steady itself," he wrote. "Practically impossible for me to sit still and not advise on all, or nearly all, matters." He considered, always, that Egypt should "be governed in the interests of the Egyptians." He was still in Cairo twenty years later.

Leopold in the Congo. Britain on the Nile. Italy on the Red Sea. It was a situation which the greatest statesman in Europe, who had no innate interest at all in Africa, could no longer ignore.

Prince Otto von Bismarck was at the height of his considerable powers. Born in the year of Waterloo, he had come from modest Junker landowning stock and had not entered politics until he was thirty-two. His training, as lawyer and diplomat, had been apt and his aristocratic background sufficient to give him useful arrogance and confidence, but impecunious enough to give him ambition. As Chancellor of a united Germany, he had become the most formidable figure in Europe. Tall, imposing, with piercing light-gray eyes, he enjoyed making decisions, was quick of wit, fluent in several languages, cultivated in art, literature, and philosophy. His high intellectual quality was ruthlessly applied to one cause: Germany. Obsessed with the power structure of Europe, he had looked on Africa with some lack of interest. "Take Carthage [i.e. Tunis]," he had told the British in 1878, but Britain had not coveted Tunis, so the French took it instead, thus infuriating the Italians, who had been eyeing the pleasant orange-groves of Tunisia. In 1884, Bismarck declared unmistakable interest in acquiring African territory; this came as an unwelcome surprise in many places, especially in the Cape, but as a pleasant one to some Germans, who had been pressing him in that direction for some years. The reasons for this change of policy are obscure. There were probably several factors. Domestic politics, the pressure of growing German commerce, and the recent blatant ambitions of Leopold and Italy stirring the natural competitiveness that is in most statesmen, as in other humans—all probably played their part. Moreover, it was certain that a policy of expansion in Africa would clash with British interests and that a quarrel with England would gain him the confidence of France, and a lasting agreement with France was the linchpin of Bismarck's policy.

Unofficial German action in Africa had been considerable; explorers had been determined, missionaries fervent, and traders persistent—most in comparatively recent years, compared with Portugal, Britain, and France. First signs of official interest were in South-West Africa, where German missionaries had been attempting to convert primitive Hottentot tribesmen. Bartle Frere had foreseen the possibility of this missionary activity leading to annexation, and he had suggested formal British occupation; as usual, his advice had been misconstrued and considered unacceptable. London had shown little concern over the matter or Bismarck's new interest. As the Victorian historian R. Brown wrote, only twelve years later:

> Whitehall dismissed the notion of German competition as a mere bugbear. There was still a traditional idea that the Teutons were an impractical race, devoted to abstract research on the dative case and the evolution of camels from the depth of their inner consciousness; while the idea of such a people searching for colonies was met by a quotation from some obsolete *obiter dictum* of Prince Bismarck regarding the folly of Germany indulging in any such extravagance.

The German missionaries and their secular arm were said to be clamoring for "protection"; Cape Town and Whitehall dithered about whether to provide it. Bismarck sent his son to London, where the difficulty was thrashed out. It was stated that "Germany had no intention to establish state colonies but merely to give protection to her subjects." Whitehall evidently believed that this would calm South African fears. The niceties over, the black, white, and red tricolor was hoisted in South West Africa, the first annexation being 240 square miles. It was not long before it was 250,000 square miles, much of it desert. Despite the missionaries, German administration of the colony was harsh and occasionally ferocious. Cecil Rhodes, viewing the threat to British progress north, grumbled and growled and took poor opinion of British policymaking in Africa; he was a man who seldom changed his opinions.

German traders on the west coast had concentrated on the unclaimed area to the east of the Gold Coast. Bismarck sent Germany's most famous African explorer, his fellow Brandenburger, Gustav Nachtigal, to this stretch of coast. Nachtigal teamed down the coast on the *Möwe,* firing off salutes, signing treaties with careful formality, and hoisting the German flag. Within months of the founding of German South-West Africa, the "protectorates" of Togoland and the Cameroons had also been established. When France claimed some of the German acquisitions, Bismarck gave way with no ado. Nachtigal, as if exhausted by the speed of his efforts on behalf of German imperialism, died before he could return home.

On the east coast, too, which British explorers since Livingstone and Arab merchants had dominated, the Germans were active. A colonization society, founded in Berlin, signed numerous treaties with local chiefs inland from Zanzibar. The company set up to exploit trade with the region was patronized by the German emperor and was thus semiofficial. The area through which Livingstone, Stanley, Burton, Speke, and others had slogged became known as German East Africa.

The distance from Lake Tanganyika to German South-West Africa was about 800 miles. If there were to be British expansion north from the Cape, it would have to go through that gap. In twelve months Bismarck had applied a pincer to British Africa more formidable than any future threat that the Portuguese colonies on opposite sides of the continent might have imposed.

Diplomatists' tempers were getting sufficiently short for Bismarck to consider it a good idea in 1884 to have a conference in Berlin of the leading nations. The topic was to be European claims in Africa. Twenty-four nations were invited, including the United States, which protested in vain that it had no ambitions in Africa. Everyone who could possibly be interested was present, except the Africans and the Boers.

The conference produced a kind of code of conduct for the partition of Africa among the European powers already present in that continent. Every claim would have to be reported to the other powers immediately so that they could have the chance of saying whether they, too, wanted that piece of land. Most important of all, every state which controlled or acquired stretches

of coast could also legitimately claim the hinterland of tha
stretch of coast.

The Berlin Conference did not solve the problems of parti
tion; it merely attempted to provide a set of rules. The clash o
British and German advance in southern and eastern Afric
continued as before. The British sway over the Nile was stil
threatened—not only by the Germans at the river's source, bu
by the natives of the Sudan, for while the statesmen's voices ha
been echoing in the ornate marble halls of Berlin, Gordon an
Wolseley had been directing bloodier aspects of partition unde
the stifling Sudanese sun. And the Afrikaners had not bee
present at the conference at all.

Bismarck was one of the few men in Europe who would hav
realized that not all of Africa's inhabitants might blindly accep
European rule as desirable and beneficial. It was an irony tha
he would have appreciated. "The whole colonial business," h
said, "is a swindle. But we need it for the election."

✤ VIII ✤

Gordon at Khartoum

'OR a moment Africa seemed to be at peace. The voices of the tatesmen droned on in the conference chambers. The lawyers nd the civil servants consulted their maps and drew lines with ulers.

Gladstone hated it. Britain's most famous general, Wolseley,)oked at it all with the indifference of a military man who has one his best and who fully expects politicians to ruin all his fforts. In 1883 he had enjoyed the English countryside—after a rief visit to Paris—and did not expect to see Africa again. He raced himself for finishing his mission of modernizing the rmy, and he lent his energies to fighting against the projected :hannel tunnel. It had been a career more satisfactory than he)uld have hoped, for he was the most famous and successful eneral of his generation. Everything was still "All Sir Garnet."

One day at the War Office, news came from Cairo. A religious :bellion had been simmering in the Sudan for months; now it ad come to the boil, incredibly catching the government nawares. Hordes of fanatical followers of the Mahdi—the Expected One"—were sweeping north, across the desert and up ie Nile. Known as dervishes, they believed that the Mahdi was ie chosen messenger of Allah himself, and all unbelievers, even Ioslems, were to be slaughtered in holy war. The Mahdi was)t a messenger from the Prophet; he was, what was much orse, a ruthless demagogue with a craving for power and rmidable qualities of leadership. He had successfully tapped ie vast reservoir of religious fanaticism in a deeply religious

land and had exploited the hatred of Egyptian rule whose tax
gathering and interference with the lucrative slave trade of
Negroes by Sudanese Arabs had long been a basic factor of the
economy. His followers—and they had grown to number many
thousands—shaved their heads, dressed in long white cotton
garments, and worked themselves into mass hysteria before at
tacking the Egyptian posts which guarded the Nile. Already the
Mahdi had gained southern, equatorial Sudan. A British-led
Egyptian army had been massacred, and Egypt itself was said to
be threatened. Now the "Expected One" was menacing the
capital of the Sudan, Khartoum, 1,000 miles south of Cairo, a
the confluence of the Blue and White Niles.

Gladstone still insisted that Britain was leaving Egypt for
ever, shortly; he did not therefore want to become involved in
the Sudan, for when Britain left Egypt, she would also be
abandoning the Sudan. He was never as fascinated by the rout
to India as Disraeli had been and was more concerned with
domestic affairs, especially his tangling with the Irish question
which had an almost hypnotic effect on him. His view was from
the floor of the House of Commons. He protested that Britain
was neither in Egypt nor out of it. Inevitably this infirmness of
policy of vacillation would bring disaster. The military men
especially, detested Gladstone for committing the army to fight
beside the Nile time and again—but to no purpose. Wolsele
described Gladstone as an "old heartless brute." He had
statuette of the premier ostentatiously placed on his mantel
piece; its face was always turned toward the wall.

Not only had Gladstone lost the support of the military an
the queen, but he was also increasingly out of touch with the
national mood. The press began to call for action in the Sudan
Sir Samuel Baker, the old explorer and once governor general
of the area now conquered by the Mahdi, wrote an important
letter to the *Times;* in it he suggested that Major General
Charles "Chinese" Gordon was the man to settle the Sudan
The idea gained immediate support, and Gladstone detected
way out for himself. He had no wish to send an army—on the
contrary, he wanted Britain out of the Sudan—but one officer
now that was another matter.

Gordon, at fifty-one, was a national figure—a great military
hero. Handsome, with a dark leathery face, graying hair, and
long sideburns, an engineer colonel, he had brought death

nore of the queen's enemies than he had built bridges or miles
of road. He was known particularly as one of the world's
greatest exponents of irregular warfare. The government was
under the impression that during his previous service in the
Sudan he had been widely popular, even loved, by the native
inhabitants; this was not entirely true. Pictures of him in the
extraordinary ceremonial dress of a British pasha—part Oriental, part ambassadorial, topped by a fez—were frequently
reproduced. Gordon had engendered some unexpected and
remarkable victories in the Far East, and his courage under fire
was renowned. It was, in fact, his many miraculous escapes from
death that had convinced Gordon that he had some sort of
special relationship with the Almighty. Probably somewhat
more religious than the Mahdi himself, he was bored by church-
going. Wherever he went, he helped the poor and the destitute,
especially if they were white. When stationed at Gravesend, he
spent most of his time visiting the deprived and sick in that
area; the dying had called for "the colonel" rather than the
clergy. His mind was cluttered up with thousands of ideas on
every subject imaginable, some of them brilliant, others absurd.
He was a latent homosexual. Chain-smoking, he pondered over
the pages of the Bible while consuming liberal measures of
brandy. He had virtually no time at all for authority. Many of
his contemporaries in the army believed he was mad. He was, in
fact, a genuine eccentric.

Gordon had just decided to abandon his army career altogether. He had been on a pilgrimage to Jerusalem, where his
intention to "stay in bed till eleven and have oysters for lunch"
had been distracted by the holy sites. Armed with maps, ruler,
and compass, he came to the conclusion that some of the sites
were inaccurate and pooh-poohing the holy sites of centuries, announced his own. By the time he left Jerusalem the Holy City
was in an uproar.* Returning to Europe, he had accepted an
odd offer from Leopold of the Belgians, who had come to the
conclusion that Gordon was the man to add luster to his African
colony, now established by Stanley. Gordon's task would be to
eliminate slavery in the Congo, and the idea appealed to Gordon. Not only would it be a worthy cause, but it would also very
likely bring the death which had so far eluded him, despite so

* It is a tribute to Gordon's surveying and Biblical knowledge that his theories
are still the subject of heated controversy.

many chances. It was a thought which he by no means detested
First he would have to resign from the British army; he wrote to
Wolseley about it.

Wolseley admired "Charlie" immensely. He had always been
attracted to successful men of action, and Gordon was certainl
that. "Charlie" had never really been one of the select group o
officers which Wolseley had formed around him—the "Wolse
leyites"—he was too independent for that, but the two men had
been friends since serving together in the Crimea. He though
Gordon's departure for the Sudan "desirable." But Gordon
himself was not keen. He took the train for Devon and staye
with Baker. They discussed the situation, and Gordon wa
persuaded to "save" the Sudan; after that he could go t
Leopold. Wolseley completed the conversion. Gordon would g
to Khartoum, "report on the military situation and return.
Wolseley knew that Gladstone would agree to only such a
uncontroversial assignment, but once Gordon got there, h
would no doubt do more than just "report." Gladstone, how
ever, insisted that if Gordon went, he would be going t
extricate the garrisons of the Egyptian army—in fact, to condu
a withdrawal from the Sudan, and leave it to the Mahd
Chinese Gordon agreed to go.

One difficulty remained. Sir Evelyn Baring, ruling Egypt i
Cairo, was unconvinced. He thought Gordon was the last ma
to quench the fire of revolt in the Sudan: "an excellent, simpl
good-hearted and impractical man, about as much fit for th
work he has in hand as the Pope." He thought Gordon "ha
cracked." But the weight of London was too much for Barin
Weakly, he gave way, much against his best instincts. "Gordo
would be the best man," he wrote to London, "if he will pledg
himself to carry out the policy of withdrawal from the Sudan
quickly as is possible. He must also fully understand that h
must take his instructions from the British representative i
Egypt and report to him. . . . I would rather have him tha
anyone else, provided there is a perfectly clear understandir
with him as to what his position is to be and what line of poli
he is to carry out." Baring later admitted this was complete
"against my own judgment and inclination." His main obje
was to get Egypt and Britain out of the Sudan for financi
reasons; he was engaged in the unenviable task of trying
restore order to the Egyptian finances.

Gordon had already made his own view clear. In an interview with the *Pall Mall Gazette* he had declared that an evacuation of the Sudan would not only be extremely difficult, but also unnecessary.

Gordon was summoned to appear before a Cabinet committee for the appointment to be made final. He breakfasted at Wolseley's house in Mayfair, and the two men went to the War Office at noon. Gordon waited in an office, warming himself before a fire and eyeing a civil servant busily working at a desk. Suddenly he broke the silence. "Do you ever tell a lie?" he asked, with interest. Before the secretary could reply, Wolseley appeared. Gordon was ushered into the conference room. Gladstone was absent with a chill. After a discussion, Gordon said he was ready to leave that night on the Indian mail-boat train.

The public was delighted by the appointment. Gordon would fix everything; whether there was evacuation or not, it would be done with honor. The queen was also pleased, but less complacent. "Very dangerous," she noted in her diary.

Gordon was seen off at Charing Cross Station by Wolseley, who carried his bag; by the Foreign Secretary, who saw to his ticket; and by the commander in chief, who opened the carriage door. Wolseley, discovering that Gordon had forgotten to draw any cash (he had a total disregard for money), had been obliged to rush around several clubs in a hansom, managing to raise £200 from friends. There was a shaking of hands, a mumbled "God bless you," and the train pulled out. With Gordon was Colonel J. D. H. Stewart of the Eleventh Hussars. "My wet nurse," said Gordon. He was almost certainly there to keep a watch on the eccentric major general.

On arrival in Egypt, one of Gordon's first acts was to give away £100 to a blind man. He sent off a message to the governor at Khartoum: "Don't be a funk. . . . You are men, not women. I am coming. Tell the inhabitants." He traveled down the Nile and reached Khartoum on February 18, 1884. The town had been founded by the Egyptians about fifty years before as a military camp, near the Sudanese city of Omdurman; it had been an important and profitable center of the slave trade. Gordon evacuated a few troops but lingered in the uneasy town with the remainder. The hot season was just beginning, and temperatures were well over 100 degrees. A barrage of telegrams went back to Baring; diffuse, contradictory, thoughtful, they worried over the problem of whether or not Gordon should retire, like a dog over a bone. "Mahdism must be smashed," he wrote. There was a feeling in London that Gordon was going to pull it off. By now Baring knew in his heart that Gordon and the Nile garrisons would stay in the Sudan. The forces of the Mahdi hovered about in the desert. On February 9, Victoria wrote to Gladstone: "The Queen trembles for Gen. Gordon's safety. If anything befalls *him,* the result will be awful." Gordon showed no signs of completing his mission and returning to Egypt.

Then, on March 13, the telegraph went dead. The line to Khartoum had been cut. Silence.

In Khartoum, Gordon prepared for siege. There was a large civilian population and a small force of Egyptian infantry; altogether there were 34,000 in the city. Apart from himself, the only two Englishmen were Stewart and the correspondent of the *Times.*

Meanwhile, heavy fighting had been in progress near the Red Sea coast, where a small British force from Aden and Egyptian regulars were trying to put down the rebellion in that area because of the danger to the coastal region and consequent threat to India shipping. There was some bloody fighting which left no doubt that the dervishes would provide serious opposition for any reoccupation of the Sudan. The British awaited the full force of the dervish attack, in two squares bristling with rifles, each a brigade strong. Rider Haggard's brother, Andrew, was there as an officer lent to the Egyptian army. "What did it matter to us, then," he wrote, "if the following night should find us dead? Our only wish was to be present in the fight. The only fear we had was, as a matter of fact, lest in the brilliant moonlight we should be attacked, not by Arabs, but by moonstroke." Moonstroke, rumor had it, sent men mad and was almost as much a terror to Victorians in Africa as sunstroke. The prayers for a splendid battle were answered the next morning, after mugs of cocoa. "I never in all my life heard such a hellish din," wrote Haggard. One of the squares was broken and there was "tremendous commotion caused by terrific hand-to-hand combat." As the British troops tried to re-form, the dervishes were "stabbing and hacking with their spears and frightfully sharp long swords like demons. . . . Suddenly I saw two companies of the Royal Marines, with their bayonets flashing in the sun, entirely detached from the rest and away to the right by themselves, repelling in excellent order the thousands of savages around them. I shall never forget the flashing of those bayonets in the bright sun before the rolling smoke in a few minutes hid all from my view." Things looked so critical that the correspondent of the *Standard* galloped back to the coast, to be first to telegraph the news of a reverse; this got him into some trouble, because the huge squares re-formed and the enemy retired; he was killed in the fighting soon afterward. Nothing was achieved by this fighting, as Gladstone's government cautiously ordered the force to reembark. On its way back to the coast, the column, thoroughly shaken by the ferocity of its opponents, panicked late one night after a false alarm, and battle-hardened troops fled en masse for miles.

Gordon was left in the Sudan. The column from the Red Sea could perhaps have rescued him, but now he was alone. All day long, laborers and Egyptian troops worked at the defenses of Khartoum in a temperature of 120 degrees. Everywhere the swarms of flies buzzed. Gordon bought a telescope in Khartoum market for £5 and fixed it on the sandy horizon far away; he spent much time gazing through it from the roof of his magnificent but deserted palace.

In London, tempers were getting short. Gladstone took the view that Gordon had only himself to blame; why had he remained so long in Khartoum? The Prime Minister delayed making a decision, hoping that Gordon would extricate himself. But the public knew that Gordon would never leave his Egyptian troops; it was for their sake that he had gone to the Sudan. Gladstone protested that the Mahdi's followers were only "rightly struggling to be free" and was hissed in the streets. A large and angry demonstration was held in Hyde Park. The queen loathed Gladstone more than ever. Wolseley was furious, as he coldly told the War Minister, Lord Hartington, "I presume the government is not prepared to allow General Gordon and his garrison to fall into the hands of the cruel and barbarous enemy now besieging Khartoum. . . . The English people will force you to [rescue him] whether you like it or not." Gladstone was busy with his efforts to improve the franchise and resented the distraction.

Gordon promised his troops that the British government would save them, but he himself became more and more de-

pressed and disillusioned with politicians. He worked out plans
—or fantasies—for the relief of Khartoum organized by American and British millionaires, by Turkey, even by the Pope.
Occasionally he got a message through, up the Nile, but nothing reached him from Cairo.

"No plans and no preparations," Wolseley said, in despair.
He knew that the level of the Nile fell at Khartoum at the end
of the year, and when that happened, the dervishes would be
able to storm the place. "All the gold in England will not affect
the rise and fall of the Nile," he told the War Minister. "Time
is a most important element in the question, and, indeed, it will
be an indelible disgrace if we allow the most generous, patriotic
and gallant of our public servants to die of want or fall into the
hands of a cruel enemy because we would not hold out our
hands to save him." This sort of thing began to have an effect
The War Minister was won over, and Gladstone became increasingly isolated. "I don't wish to share the responsibility of
leaving Charlie Gordon to his fate," wrote Wolseley. Then a
few messages got through from Gordon; where, he asked, was
the relief column? Fleet Street exploded. It was too much
Gladstone gave way.

It was August; by November the Nile would be falling
Could the army get to Khartoum on time?

A relief ponderously got under way with Wolseley, who had
not expected ever to see the Nile again, in command. An
argument raged about which route to take—from the Red
Sea, across the desert, or down the Nile, from Cairo? Wolseley
favored the Nile, claiming it would be easier for the transport
of supplies. His critics said the Nile could not be navigated all
the way to Khartoum; the army would drown or be slaughtered
on the riverbanks. Wolseley got his way.

Wolseley did not envisage the operation as a "lightning
strike," a dash to Khartoum. The older he got, the greater his
taste for the "grand army." This was to be an operation on a
enormous scale, and so there assembled a great expeditionary
force for the rescue of two English officers, a newspaper reporter, and some Egyptian soldiers.

Probably the best man in the world for the task of relieving
Khartoum was Gordon himself.

Wolseley, as always, pondered on the problems of supply
transport, and preparation. He gathered around him all the

Wolseleyites. Butler was in charge of transport. Boats would
have to be specially designed and constructed—light enough to
be carried, strong enough to withstand whirling cataracts. The
Admiralty, ever cautious, said it could not be done in less than
two months. Butler spread the order among forty-seven firms,
which, working night and day, produced 100 boats in under
four weeks. Nearly 400 rivermen were rushed from Canada,
many of them Red Indians, and 300 boatmen were picked up
by steamer from the Gold Coast.

A camel corps was selected from the finest regiments of
cavalry, from the Guards, and from the Rifle Brigade—the elite
of the British army. Wolseley would use them for his final push,
striking across the desert to Khartoum, thus missing a huge
bend in the Nile's course.

More than a million and a half cans of beef were shipped
from Chicago, along with a thousand bottles of champagne (for
the sick, or so it was said), and tons of jam and marmalade (to
deaden the craving for sweet things of men deprived of drink).
And Wolseley did not forget a stock of cigarettes for Gordon.

The newspapers were not impressed. They spoke of an "un-
floatable flotilla." The commander in chief of the army, the
Duke of Cambridge, grumbled about the "Nile circus." Gladstone insisted that Wolseley's task was to be no more than
"rescue and retire"; he should bring back Gordon, Stewart, and
any Egyptian soldiers or civilians who wanted to leave.

Wolseley went from Cairo to the railhead* down the Nile,
predicting: "I ought to shake hands with Gordon near Khartoum about 31st January next." Gordon, a few weeks later,
wrote in his diary, "If they do not come before November 30
the game is up, and Rule Britannia." From the railhead, Wolseley and his staff boarded a steamer. Aboard, the general sat
alone in his cabin, under the whirring fan, reading *The Life of
Cicero,* whose pandering "to the whims of the mob to gain and
retain power" brought the unwelcome thought of Gladstone to
his mind.

On September 10 Gordon sent Stewart and the *Times* man
down the Nile to run the gauntlet. He did so both for their own
safety and to tell the world of the desperate situation in Khartoum, where food was getting terribly scarce. Their boat struck

---

* At the instigation of the British, railway construction had begun in Egypt as
early as 1852, by order of the pasha. By 1880 there were 944 miles of state railway.

a rock and the travelers, scrambling ashore, were slaughtered. Gordon began a siege journal. On the cover he wrote, "No secrets as far as I am concerned." He unburdened himself at length, not only on the military situation, but also on theology, politics, chance acquaintances ("met him once in the rooms of the Royal Geographical Society"), his own situation ("Personally, I do not care, but I think what a perfect mess we would be in, in an European war"), and the methods of awarding honorary degrees at Oxford. His nearest contact with the outside world was Major Herbert Kitchener, who had helped raise and train the Egyptian army. Kitchener was 300 miles north of Khartoum and 200 miles south of where the British relief force was assembling at Wadi Halfa. He served as Wolseley's forward antenna. A dark, moody, intense man, he was, like Gordon, a sapper. Like Burton, Gordon, and so many English officers abroad, Kitchener loved dressing up in native costume (a taste which accounted for so many stories of respectable men having "gone native"). He wandered around gathering intelligence (of which Gordon did not think much), brilliantly disguised as an Arab and carrying a bottle of poison in case he was captured.

There were three main cataracts to be negotiated by the relief force. Thousands of chanting natives hauled the craft through, while others were carried on the banks. It was a slow business, deadly slow. Meanwhile 8,000 camels were also brought down. Gordon knew practically nothing of all this, and it was just as well. He wrote to Wolseley's chief of staff:

> I cannot too much impress on you that this expedition will not encounter any enemy worth the name in an European sense of the word; the struggle is with the climate and destitution of the country. It is one of time and patience, and of small parties of determined men, backed by native allies, which are got by policy and money. A heavy lumbering column, however strong, is nowhere in this land. Parties of forty or sixty men, swiftly moving about, will do more than any column. If you lose two or three, what of it—it is the chance of war. Native allies above all things, at whatever cost. It is the country of the irregular, not of the regular. If you move in mass you will find no end of difficulties; whereas, if you let detached parties dash out here and there, you will spread dismay in the Arab ranks. The time to attack is the dawn.

Wolseley decided to take himself south, to Kitchener. When he arrived at the palace of the local chief, he was greeted by an "entertainment." Arabs worked themselves up into a frenzy of shrieks and yells, then rushed at the formally attired general, raising their spears inches from him. Wolseley could not resist a wince, but he passed the test. Coffee and sweets were then served.

At Wadi Halfa, the staff was squabbling. Wolseley, disappointed in his old colleagues, thought they had let him down. The army itself was in a wretched state, for getting men and supplies down from Cairo had proved to be a more nightmarish task than even the most pessimistic critic in London had foretold. After Wadi Halfa, there were still more than 300 miles of twisting river to go before Korti was reached, and it was from Korti that the camel corps was to strike across the desert for Khartoum. This final stretch of river was the worst. Men's hands bled at their oars, but there was no time for rest. Sickness was rampant; cholera and typhoid appeared. The army was in tatters; trousers were repaired with bits of socks and rags; some rowed naked—except, of course, for headgear against the bright and pitiless sun. In order "to get the last ounce out of them," Wolseley announced a prize of £100 for the fastest battalion on the last stretch of Nile. (The queen, when she heard of it, was horrified.) It was won by the Royal Irish Rifles. Wolseley was delighted to give the prize to "my own countrymen." Some said the Irish had won only because there was nothing to drink but the warm, smelly Nile water. The prize was used later for adding to the mess silver.

By the time the men reached Korti, in nearly 600 boats, they were in a pretty hardy condition. "Hard as nails," wrote a staff officer, "without an ounce of superfluous flesh upon them, lean, bronzed and muscular, ready and fit to go anywhere and do anything."

It was November. Another message got through from Gordon. He said he could not read Wolseley's messages because Stewart had taken the cipher with him. He seemed more hopeful. "We can hold out for forty days with ease—after that it will be difficult." It had been written thirteen days before. Wolseley knew that Gordon was not a man to exaggerate, and he had been counting on a little more time.

Nearly 10,000 men had sweated and heaved their way down the river to Korti when Wolseley himself arrived before Christmas. The men tried to restore their energies for the task ahead. A great camp of tents, beneath fluttering flags, lay outside the town. Troops relaxed in the shade of clusters of palms or gathered to hear the band of the Royal Sussex Regiment playing the airs that had been popular at home four months before. The staff was in a nervous condition. Every day it was the same thought: would they be too late? Wolseley had given up smoking. Even the birds overhead, the noise of which reminded him of that "old windbag" Gladstone caused irritation. Butler was grousing about incompetence. Buller was not his usual popular self and had displeased the general. When Wolseley heard that Gladstone was unwell, he wrote: "We have anxiously been looking out for Gladstone's death."

A final installment of Gordon's siege journal got through to Korti. It was New Year's Eve. Wolseley read it to a distant chorus of "Auld Lang Syne."

December 12—Small Church Parade. I sincerely hope this will be the last we shall have to witness. We have in hand 1,796,000 rounds Remington ammunition; 540 rounds Krupp; 6,000 rounds mountain gun ammunition; £140 in specie . . . 110,000 okes [a Turkish and Egyptian measure, equal to about 2¾ pounds] of biscuits.

3:30 P.M. The Arabs fired two shells at the Palace; one burst in the air, the other fell in the water in a direct line with the window I was sitting at, distant about a hundred yards.

3:40 P.M. They fired another shell which fell only fifty yards short of the Palace—all these shells are in good line for the west wing, in which the Arabs know I stop.

December 13— . . . *If some effort is not made before ten days' time the town will fall.* It is inexplicable, this delay. If the Expeditionary Force have reached the river and met my steamers, one hundred men are all that we require, just to show themselves. I send this journal, for I have little hopes of saving it if the town falls. . . . All that is absolutely necessary is for fifty of the Expeditionary Force to get on board a steamer and come up to Halfaya, and thus let their presence be felt; this is not asking much, but it must happen *at once;* or it will (as usual) be too late.

December 14— . . . If I was in command of the two hundred men of the Expeditionary Force, which are all that are necessary for the movement, I should stop just below Halfaya and attack the Arabs at that place before I came on here to Khartoum. . . . Now MARK THIS, if the Expeditionary Force, and I ask for no more than two hundred men, does not come in ten days, *the town may fall;* and I have done my best for the honour of our country. Goodbye. C. G. Gordon.

They would have been splendid and imposing last words, but Gordon, typically, could not resist scribbling an irate postscript, thus somewhat spoiling the effect: "You send me no information, though you have lots of money. C. G. G."

The camel corps had already probed into the desert, and a supply depot was being set up halfway across. The main problem was the shortage of camels; not enough had been bought, and those that had were of indifferent quality—British quartermasters had but little experience of purchasing camels. The whole camel corps paraded before Wolseley, a mile long, forty camels abreast. It was a magnificent spectacle, and Wolseley loved it. It was a very different thing from the mere 200 men which Gordon advised. The vast column disappeared across the distant sands. Wolseley, alone on a small hill, watched it go. On the camel corps depended the life of Charles "Chinese" Gordon—and, as he may well have thought, Wolseley's reputation.

In Khartoum the situation was desperate. There was hardly any food left; horses, birds, rats were eaten. Somehow Gordon managed to keep the defense going, mainly by bluffing friend and foe that relief was imminent. He ate alone in the lofty dining hall, waited on by six servants, with a portrait of the khedive looking grimly down on him. At night he slept on the roof, ignoring the governor general's bedroom with its four-poster bed. For hours at a time he scanned the horizon through his telescope.

Wolseley lingered in Korti, in an agony of suspense. How was the camel corps progressing? Had it met the Mahdi's army? Was Gordon still holding out? He told Buller: "This is the first time in my life that I have been chained to the rear in a campaign, and I hope it may be the last. To lead a storming party a day would be child's play to the anxieties of this position."

The commander of the camel corps had underrated the

strength of the opposition. Anticipating a skirmish here and there with the troublesome dervishes, he said: "I don't like unnecessary slaughter." Camels collapsed. Native drivers deserted. Water was forever going short; watches, sovereigns, and other valuables were offered for a drink. With a mixture of foolhardiness, ignorance, and sheer luck, the camel corps continued its advance across one of the most inhospitable deserts in the world.

Not surprisingly, the Mahdi's force was found in front of one of the final wells enroute. The British dismounted, and forming into the traditional square that had served them so well at Waterloo and since, they moved slowly forward across the loose sand toward the precious water. A huge section of the dervishes charged, waving their green banners, throwing pages of the Koran, prancing to drums, and wailing prayers. The British troops fired a tremendous blast, but the horde came remorselessly on. As the front ranks fell, more filled their places. The square was gained, and within minutes it was breached. Spears, swords, and bayonets flashed in savage close fighting. One sheikh, on horseback, reached the center of the square, planted his green banner, and began reading from the Koran, his voice lost in the din and confusion, before he was shot down. The gap was slowly closed, and all the dervishes who had fought their way inside the square were killed. Gradually the enemy drew back. From the British square came three loud, but perhaps somewhat nervous, cheers.

The wells were reached, and men almost dying of thirst eased their parched throats and swollen tongues. None of them would ever forget that drink. Among the many groaning and dying wounded was the commander of the column. He wrote good-bye letters to his wife and mother with firm and steady hand: "I know you are proud of my being hit like this." Command passed to Sir Charles Wilson, a "desk wallah," who had little experience of war. He decided to march on, in square (British four-sided marching formation), to the banks of the Nile not far away. An officer considered it "certain death." But the dervishes charged, instead of picking off the walking British one by one, and were repelled. By nightfall the column had reached the Nile, on which the moon gently glowed. The wounded were lifted to see the longed-for water.

Wilson noticed that the river had considerably fallen.

The suspense had turned Wolseley's hair white. He was suffering from diarrhea. He looked south through his telescope for a cloud on the horizon that would indicate an approaching messenger. "I am nervous," he wrote to his wife, fearing "a national calamity." When news came, it was good: The column had reached the far bend of the Nile, despite heavy loss of life. Congratulatory telegrams poured in from London. There was one from the queen—"rather gushing," said Wolseley.

But Wolseley's fears were uncalmed. It was as if he had known all along that his career had been a little too good, that it was fated to end in catastrophe. He wrote: "Sir C. Wilson, very useful for political work, is no soldier; this is his first dose of fighting." He hurriedly sent Redvers Buller off across the desert to take command. Wilson, meanwhile, ran his command virtually by committee; he received conflicting advice on what to do next. He lingered a day, then another. "Wilson is rather an old woman," one soldier said, "doesn't know anything about drill and funks the responsibility." Reconnaissances were made up and down the Nile. On January 24 Wilson embarked, with a detachment of the Royal Sussex Regiment, on two steamers and headed for Khartoum—four days' journey away.

It was in the early morning of January 26 that the Mahdi at last made his attempt on Khartoum. It was 320 days since the city had been isolated. Gordon was asleep. Up to 40,000 of the Mahdi's followers silently stole across the hard-baked moat behind the town, instead of across the Nile as expected, and then swarmed over the ramparts. A few random shots roused the city. A fierce struggle took place as the Egyptian soldiers fought for their lives. The weak and weary troops had little chance; there was no stopping the wild, fierce charge of the dervishes. Gordon, quickly awake, must have realized the hopelessness of the situation immediately: He nevertheless helped fire a gun from the roof into the advancing mob. The Arabs were all moving toward the palace. Gordon rushed to his room and changed into his governor general's uniform and then went to the top of the marble steps armed with revolver in one hand and sword in the other. The spears of his assailants tore into his body. Gordon was decapitated, the bleeding head carried off in triumph to the Mahdi. His dead body, slashed by hundreds of passing dervishes, was cut to a bloody, unrecognizable mess. Such was the end of the man whom Butler, with some justification, called "the most truthful Englishman of his time."

For six hours the massacre and rape of Khartoum continued. Children were killed in their mothers' arms, men were beheaded, and females from five years of age were selected for harems. The Mahdi, who had inspired more fervor than he could control, stopped it, but by then there were thousands of dead.

Wilson arrived at Khartoum forty-eight hours later. Yelling Arabs on the banks told him he was too late, but he plowed on upstream until he could see for himself that the city had fallen. The green banner of the Mahdi fluttered above the palace in the hot breeze. Wilson's only wish was to get back safely. He just managed it, but not without wrecking his craft and losing many of his men.

Wolseley was desolated: "Utterly knocked out," he wrote. He had admired Gordon almost to the point of love. And he had, for the first time in his career, tasted total failure.

Back home the news was a ghastly shock. No one had really expected Wolseley not to get to Khartoum in time, despite the gloomy predictions of the press. An issue of *Punch* had already appeared celebrating the relief, with a joyful cartoon captioned "At Last!"

The queen was first appalled, then furious. "How shall I attempt to express *what I feel?*" she wrote to Gordon's beloved sister. "To think of your dear, noble, heroic, brother who served his country and his Queen so truly, so heroically. . . . That the promises of support were not fulfilled is grief inexpressible." To Gladstone, "The old Sinner," as she called him, she wrote coldly: "To think that all this might have been prevented and many precious lives saved by earlier action is too frightful." She never forgave him.

There was some bitter infighting before the blame was passed to Sir Charles Wilson, a man who was no match for Wolseley. "I hate to see him," Wolseley wrote. Wolseley himself got away with remarkably little dent to his reputation.

Impressed by public reaction, the vacillating government decided to stay in the Sudan after all, to crush the Mahdi. Wolseley was astonished. It was easier ordered than done, for the Mahdi had 50,000 fanatically courageous troops who had known success and were full of confidence. In order to recoup, the British had to withdraw some distance, anyway. The men were sick, dispirited, and in uniforms which were falling apart. Transport was breaking down. There were failures of supply. Some of the West Indian boatmen mutinied, and the Red Indians packed up and went home. All the excitement had gone out of the campaign. Gordon was dead. Wolseley, in a failure of leadership, could not restore the zest of his army. A successful battle was fought on February 10, when men of the South Staffordshire Regiment changed from the dun-colored uniform of the force into their red coats and the Black Watch into kilts, but it only temporarily restored spirits.

Wolseley said Britain would never desert those Sudanese who remained loyal to her, but it was the Mahdi who gained in support. His victory over the famous Gordon had convinced many doubters that he was indeed the Expected One. One British general, a one-eyed veteran of the Crimea, became so irritated at the miraculous powers credited to the Mahdi that when visited one day by an Arab delegation, he took out his glass eye, tossed it in the air, caught it, and replaced it in its socket. Could the Mahdi do that? he inquired.

In March, 1885, trouble flared in Afghanistan, a land in which Britain took closer interest even than the Sudan. It seemed that Russia was going to force her interests in that area; there was talk of war between Russia and Britain. Press and Parliament fanned the crisis. Like so many nineteenth-century war scares, it was merely a frontier incident which led to nothing. But Gladstone saw his chance for disengagement in the Sudan; by making imperialist faces at Russia, he would be able to distract the nation from its tacit pledge to avenge Gordon.

Wolseley protested and considered resigning, but it was no use. "Chinese" Gordon, the hero of so many, was already forgotten in Westminster. Wolseley wrote to a friend: "I made promises to the Sudan people on the faith of Mr. Gladstone's announcement in Parliament that have *blackened my face* in this land of Egypt and that makes me long to sneak out of it." He went home. Chaos and terror suffused the Sudan.

Wolseley went to see the queen. They spoke of Gordon, for they at least had not forgotten him. It was Wolseley who openly wept. Gordon's sister presented her brother's siege journal to the queen, who displayed it prominently at Windsor Castle as a reproach to all visiting Liberal politicians.

Gladstone's position had been becoming increasingly difficult. The radicals who had supported him were looking elsewhere. The public was moving to the right. He was basically an anti-imperialist leading an increasingly imperialist nation. Khartoum had been not long preceded by Majuba, and to the public it looked as though Gladstone was not the man to run the Empire. On June 10, 1885, his government resigned, ostensibly on an amendment to the budget. He returned briefly the following year, aged seventy-seven, but was defeated over Ireland. Apart from one brief interval, the Conservatives, the party of imperialism, were in for the next twenty years.

The Conservatives were led by Disraeli's successor, Lord Salisbury. The Liberals had lost the confidence of the country, and a vast new electorate, enfranchised, ironically enough, by Gladstone in 1884, had given them an unmistakable rebuff. The Conservative triumph was of great importance. It was not only Ireland; it was also the first real expression of mass public will concerning Africa—south and north. The Empire was no longer a matter for remote official colonization. The British public would have its say.

The new Prime Minister was as interested in Africa and Britain's "responsibilities" there as William Ewart Gladstone had been uninterested.

Only one officer had come out of the Khartoum affair with reputation enhanced—the daring but somber Kitchener. He was promoted to lieutenant colonel. "Since Gordon's death," he wrote, "I personally have very little interest in the Sudan and its future."

While the army had been away in the Sudan, an inventor—Hiram S. Maxim—had been perfecting a new weapon in his London workshop: the automatic machine gun.

✦ IX ✦

Cape to Cairo

NEVER before had Africa so captured the thoughts of men in other continents. In the last twenty years of the century it was the most discussed, argued over, written about, and read about of the continents. England had a Prime Minister who believed in its potential and who wanted to prevent other powers from gaining its territory. The leading politician in Cape Colony was the proudest and most blatant imperialist in the world.

The publication of three novels by Rider Haggard, between 1885 and 1887, presented the idea of an adventurous, mysterious continent to a vast new audience. *King Solomon's Mines, She,* and *Allan Quatermain,* with their bold descriptive power, celebrated an Africa that was still a land for adventurers. It was this Africa of gold, ancient secrets, brave white men, and strange but constant excitement that became fixed in the minds of hundreds of thousands of Haggard's readers. The "Africa man," as Victorian hero, was different from that other stalwart of the Empire, the "India man"; the public pictured him, not without reason, as a much tougher bird, in his striped shirt without collar, his cord trousers and floppy hat—"officer class," really, but not such a good rider as the India hero or as neatly mustached, useless at polo, but perfectly adept at riding bareback.

Every month Haggard's Africa became less real as the coastal regions were developed with sudden speed and railways stretched into regions unknown only a few years previously. A book of a different kind, *The Expansion of England in the*

Eighteenth Century, by John Robert Seeley, published in 1883, also had great influence; it was an apologia for the Empire. Both Haggard and Seeley received knighthoods for their work. Rider Haggard became for the Empire in Africa what Rudyard Kipling was to the raj in India.

The notion of the white man's burden was at its zenith, and there were few, although vociferous, critics. It was a notion favored more by those who stayed at home than by those who actually visited or lived in Africa. The one word which covered so many arrangements and which pleased almost everyone was "protection." Lands won by military conquest, by treaty, by mistake—all were being protected by the British and their gracious queen. It did not entirely displease all the African chiefs or their peoples, who had always suffered chronic feelings of insecurity—until they discovered that "protection" was used rather not to cause offense than to convey a legal definition. Some African people, of course, had no use for it from the start.

Five years after Bismarck's Berlin Conference, very much as an afterthought, the powers met at Brussels in 1890 to discuss the inhabitants of the continent that was being partitioned. This time the gathering met at the instigation of Lord Salisbury. Fine sentiments were aired on the subjects of slavery, traffic in alcohol, gunrunning, and "porterage." It was this conference, rather than the previous one, that the public throughout Europe seized on with gratitude. The reasons for Europe's slow entry into Africa now turning into a flood were several, and there were too many strands for the public to disentangle. They fastened, perhaps in guilt, perhaps in compassion, on the idea of a special humanitarian mission. It was an idea mostly confined to Africa and did not seem to apply to other spheres of colonialism. In England, especially, the idea of a duty in Africa was spreading rapidly. It was an idea which both Tories and Liberals could embrace without embarrassment. The duty was defined by Queen Victoria herself: "To protect the poor natives and advance civilization." Englishmen, it seemed, were not in Africa for their own benefit, but for the benefit of the Africans. It had become not entirely untrue.

By the time of the Brussels Conference Rudyard Kipling was twenty-four years old and was surveying the raj with pleasure. When he turned his gaze on Africa, he wrote:

> Take up the White Man's burden—
> Send forth the best ye breed—
> Go, bind your sons to exile
> To serve your captives' need. . . .

A type of Briton was now at work in the continent who was very different from the drunken "west coasters" of the old days; these were the successors to the missionaries—the surveyors, the doctors, the new administrators. Typical of this new breed was Henry Drummond, a geologist who tramped and boated his way through the old Livingstone country, already known as Nyasaland. He progressed with open-eyed wonder, with a compassionate and unpatronizing view of the Africans, and bewilderment at the conflicting territorial claims which now bedeviled the continent. In 1888 he wrote:

> Nothing could more wildly misrepresent the reality than the idea of one's schooldays that the heart of Africa is a desert. . . . Hidden away in these endless forests, like birds' nests in a wood, in terror of one another, and of their common foe, the slaver, are small native villages; and here in his virgin simplicity dwells primeval man, without clothes, without civilization, without learning, without religion—the genuine child of nature, thoughtless, careless and contented. This man is apparently quite happy; he has practically no wants.

But it was the conviction of the late Victorians that wants were what this African primeval man required. Drummond gives an accurate picture of the white man on his travels at this time:

> At the head of the column I usually walked myself, partly to see the country better, partly to look out for game, and partly, I suppose, because there was no one else to do it. Close behind me came my own special valet, carrying my geological hammer, water-bottle and loaded rifle. The white man, as a rule, carries nothing except himself and a revolver, and possibly a double-awned umbrella, which, with a thick pith helmet, makes sunstroke impossible.

When he returned to the coast, in Portuguese territory, Drummond was asked to pay taxes. He was highly indignant, claiming he had been in British territory. The Portuguese official "went at once to the root of the matter by informing me that the Portuguese definition of the word Interior differed materially from that of England." Drummond asked, "When and where was this claim recognized by England directly or indirectly?" After further argument, he still would not give way. "After much running to and fro among the officials, the representative of John Bull, instead of being dragged to prison, found himself bowed off the premises with a discharge in full of his debt to Portugal, and the unpaid tax-paper still in his pocket." Drummond, not a white man's burden protagonist, commented: "Why Africa should not belong to the Africans I have never quite been able to see, but since this continent is being rapidly partitioned out among the various European states, it is well, even in the African interest, to inquire into the nature and validity of these claims."

Stanley, as irrepressible and evidently as indefatigable as ever in his love-hate relationship with the continent, had returned to the Congo once more. He, more than anyone, kept the public gaze concentrated on Africa. He had come out as an ardent imperialist for Britain and lectured in forthright language on his views, claiming that Britain had been dallying too long. He became engaged on yet another journalistic quest. Emin Pasha, a German whom Cairo had appointed governor general of the remote equatorial Sudan south of Khartoum, had disappeared at the time of the Mahdi uprising. There were many rumors of his whereabouts in Africa. Stanley set out to find him. Although it has been comparatively forgotten by history, this journey turned out to be a far more rigorous and difficult one than the quest for Livingstone sixteen years previously. Stanley traveled 1,400 miles up the Congo, then cut across jungle to Albert Nyanza, with one of the newly invented Maxim machine guns, of which he made some use. His expedition dwindled to a ragged bunch through desertion and death from malaria. He finally found the man he sought, not a ragged fugitive, but "in a well-kept fez and a clean suit of snowy cotton drill, well ironed and of perfect fit." Emin Pasha's first words were: "I owe you a thousand thanks." However, he refused to leave his Egyptian troops and declined an invitation to return with Stanley. He changed his mind after his troops, wearied by months of wandering, mutinied. He arrived at Zanzibar with Stanley, to be greeted by German officials, representatives of the New York *Herald,* and a cable from Queen Victoria. Stanley had been away for two years and had covered more than 6,000 miles.

In Egypt, Baring continued his work with the patience of a martyr. Unlike so many other areas, Britain did not claim Egypt as a protectorate. The legal situation was bizarre. Turkey still claimed suzerainty. The Egyptian hierarchy claimed autonomy from Turkey. France claimed a special relationship. Britain ruled, but her troops were officially "visitors." Authority was exercised by Baring in the form of "advice" to the khedive. The khedive had little option but to accept the advice, for his throne depended on British support. A dozen other nations claimed special privileges in Egypt. Britain was hostile to all pretensions but her own, and especially to those of France. Ostensibly she was there to "restore" Egypt. In reality the situation was more simple. The Suez Canal, in which Britain held nearly half the shares, was emphatically believed to be the vital lifeline of the Empire. Baring was an energetic and dedicated proconsul who took the highest view of his responsibilities and opportunity. He began to improve Egyptian finance, communications, defense, irrigation (and thus the economy), and internal security. It was, indeed, a burden, one which he bore with distinction.

It was at this time that a single event transformed the situation in the Transvaal. For years there had been rumors of gold, but all discoveries had proved disappointing and not really exploitable. The "gold" of South Africa was becoming something of a scandal. However, in 1886 the presence of gold was established on farms in the Witwatersrand. By then Rhodes was a rich man from his holdings in the diamond mines. But hearing of the discovery, he left Kimberley hurriedly on the stagecoach for Pretoria. On arrival in the Witwatersrand, he bought a small farm, which he used as his headquarters. Speculators, many of them Rhodes' rivals from the early Kimberley days, were already on the scene, buying up land fairly indiscriminately. There were Joseph Benjamin Robinson, Alfred Beit, Barney Barnato, and Julius Wernher, all of them exceedingly rich men roughing it on the veld for further wealth. Rhodes' expert, Gardner Williams, was unimpressed. "If I were to ride over these reefs in America," he said, "I would not get off my horse to look at them," a remark for which he had to suffer much ribbing in future years. Some options had been acquired for Rhodes by his colleagues, but he had to return to Kimberley to help nurse a dying friend, and the options ran out (one of them, at £250, was for land valued two years later at more than £3,000,000). However, Rhodes also picked some plums, including land on which Johannesburg was built. In twelve months he had formed the Consolidated Gold Fields of South Africa, Ltd. He arranged its affairs so that the revenues from it, like those from De Beers, could be used for his pet project of opening up the north. He was now tremendously rich—the richest man in Africa and one of the richest in the Western world. But he did not live lavishly, except when traveling at sea or in Europe. He seldom carried any money on his person.

Johannesburg developed with astonishing speed, even more rapidly than Kimberley had done, and it developed into an even rougher town, with whores, professional gamblers, and gunmen. To have such a place within their borders horrified the pious Afrikaners. There were about 25,000 of them in the Transvaal, and they had not forgotten that getting away from the wicked new arrivals in South Africa had been one of their grandfathers' reasons for setting up the republic. Many believed the newcomers had filched them of the land through underhand dealings. They mainly kept away from the bustling, thriving, and vulgar new shantytown. But soon Johannesburg was larger than Pretoria. Fortune hunters poured in from the Cape, Natal, Britain, America, and the Continent. Inevitably a railway was soon being constructed to the gold mines.

The President, Paul Kruger, shared these feelings of distaste but realized that the newfound wealth would eventually bring prosperity to his poor republic. He decided it would be wise to tolerate the *Uitlanders,* as the newcomers were called, but not to grant them the vote; not only were they alien, but they were rapidly outnumbering the Boers in the whole Transvaal. Kruger saw the prospect of the Union Jack flying once more in Pretoria and decided to stand firm on the *Uitlanders.* He was the kind of man who would never change his mind. Since the time of Majuba, the British antipathy towards him had increased. Whichever way Kruger turned, he was bound to lose: If the *Uitlanders* had the vote, they would come to power and very likely invite the British to take over the Transvaal; if the *Uitlanders* did not have the vote, it would provide an excuse for British intervention. Kruger took what he believed was the best and most honorable course for his countrymen, among whom he could never include the brash new gold diggers.

As for the *Uitlanders,* they did not much care about the vote one way or the other. At first, rumbles on the subject were heard in London and Cape Town more often than in Johannesburg.

Rhodes felt involved on two counts: He had financial interests in the Rand and wanted them to be secure, and like other financiers, he complained of maladministration in the Transvaal. However, the Transvaal, like the more amenable Orange Free State, was an irritating gap in the map of South Africa which he wanted colored red. He believed nothing could be done till Kruger left the scene, but Rhodes was impatient; he was still convinced he would meet an early death, and he had much to do in Africa. Rhodes and Kruger met. The solemn President pointed his pipe at Rhodes and said: "Tell him I have heard all these stories before. I am here to protect my burghers as well as the Rand people. I know what I have to do and I will do what I consider is right." He meant it.

The walls of Lord Salisbury's study at his magnificent country home, Hatfield House, and at the Foreign Office (he was his own Foreign Secretary), were covered with maps of Africa. Lord Salisbury was a large, bearded man with an impeccable sense of responsibility and a more than useful brain. He considered his mission to be the maintenance of peace. It has often been written that his greatest work was to preside over the partition of Africa without a single declaration of war among the powers concerned. But it should be remembered that Lord Salisbury and his European contemporaries, while glad of their slices of the African cake, never really considered Africa worth a European war.

Lord Salisbury's favorite policy toward Africa and Africans was one of trusteeship. "They will gradually acquire their own proper civilization," he said in the House of Lords. The duty of the British was meanwhile to provide a just and efficient administration. He laid great stress on the probity of the Colonial Service, and he was not frequently disappointed. One of his biographers has written: "No man ever wanted less to impose his views upon others, even upon the Africans of that day. He had no preconceptions about suitable constitutions for them."

Germany consolidated her position in West and South-West Africa, examining with interest the interior of the coastal strips now under her "protection." The great explorer, Karl Peters, covered immense distances in East Africa and claimed huge chunks of land for Germany, only to find that, while he had been away, Bismarck had recognized the British claims to much of the territory. Nevertheless, Germany's presence in East Africa, joining with the Congo, seemed to end the Rhodes dream of a British Africa from south to north. In East Africa the situation was potentially explosive. Everyone had a different doctrine on the meaning of the "hinterland." Just how far back did it go? The theme of completing a "south-north" strip of British territory had become a popular preoccupation among fireside imperialists, as well as among the pressure group led by Rhodes. Now it seemed that German claims, connecting with Belgian claims from the other side of the continent, would effectively block such a British axis. Relations between the strip claimed by the German company and the adjacent strip to the north claimed by the Imperial British East Africa Company were not good. And each area had its internal problems with Arabs, who had formerly controlled the area. Father north still, the Italians were endeavoring to administer the strategically valuable Horn of Africa, not without opposition from Africans and French. The previous claimant to all these parts had been the Sultan of Zanzibar, whom Salisbury considered an "imbecile." To impress on the Sultan, who was trying to resist pressure from Europe, that his days of power were over Bismarck and the Italians suggested a naval bombardment of Zanzibar. Lord Salisbury considered the suggestion "cynical and arrogant." It was largely due to his cool handling that the crisis died down and that there was no Arab war in East Africa.

German ambitions showed no sign of being satisfied. There were arguments with Britain about Buganda. Buganda controlled the source of the Nile and thus Egypt, as Salisbury was only too well aware. It was worrying. The British feeling about Germany and the Germans changed. Suddenly they began to replace the French as the most disliked of European people. In order to gain concessions from the Germans, Salisbury offered Germany Helgoland. This was a small island in the North Sea which England had gained after the Napoleonic Wars. There had been a press campaign about it in Germany, and the Kaiser was anxious to have it. Salisbury's sop worked, but not before he had faced considerable and keen opposition from the queen ("great uneasiness"), Parliament (especially Sir William Harcourt), and the Cabinet. Salisbury did not get quite everything he had demanded, but the Helgoland barter helped establish Britain beyond all competition as the most powerful nation in Africa. Who got the best of the exchange is arguable.*

British influence over Zanzibar, British East Africa (Kenya), and Buganda was now settled. Under Salisbury, Britain's hold over four of the five most dense centers of population on the continent—the Nile Valley, the interior of the Bight of Benin, South Africa, and around Buganda—was strengthened. At first little was done to consolidate the treaties with Buganda. In West Africa, Lord Salisbury was more inclined to let Britain's rivals get their way, for there was no threat to Egypt from the west. But in the Niger Basin Britain fought her rivals hard. Too many British lives had been lost, too many expeditions, like those of Macgregor Laird, launched, too many treaties signed with local chiefs, for foreign claims to be tolerated. He abhorred the French policy of obtaining exclusive commercial privileges in her protectorates, but much the same practice was maintained in the British areas. For twenty years one of the prime tasks of British and French ambassadors in Paris and London was unraveling African problems, many of them bitter. By 1890 the frontiers of Gambia, Sierra Leone, and the Gold Coast were fairly well defined. The public took a close interest in all these affairs and objected to the vast areas claimed by France, even though they were nearly all desert. On the map, such claims looked formidable. At the Mansion House, the official residence of the lord mayor of London, with a caustic wit that had already lost him many friends in Europe, Salisbury ridiculed the French and himself by admitting they had been engaged in "what perhaps to a satirist may seem the somewhat unprofitable task of drawing lines upon maps where no human foot has ever trod. We have been giving away mountains and rivers and lakes to each other, but we have only been hindered by the small impediment that we never knew exactly where those mountains and rivers and lakes were." Five days later, in the House of

---

* Germany fortified Helgoland and used it as an advanced naval base in both world wars.

Lords, he slapped down the French and his critics. "It is necessary to judge land not merely from extent but also from value. This land is what agriculturalists would call 'light' land—that is to say, it is the desert of Sahara." The French ambassador was most displeased. "No doubt the Sahara is not a garden," he wrote in a note taken to the Prime Minister, "but your public reminder of the fact was hardly necessary."

Statesmen were contemplating the map of Africa, still partly unexplored, as it had never been studied before.

Rhodes, on his visits to London, always urged that Britain should keep the way open north from South Africa. His pressure—as well as that of others—was not unsuccessful. It became a cardinal point of British policy in Africa. After dealing with Germany, there were still the claims of Portugal to be considered. The hinterland theory of the Berlin Conference, if taken at its worth, would join the two old and large Portuguese colonies on both sides of the continent, and maps displaying such a situation were being published in Lisbon. If this were allowed to happen, the way north would be blocked from the Cape. France and Germany naturally gave some support to Portuguese claims.

Salisbury fought hard. A British company had already been set up to exploit Nyasaland, and a junior army officer, Frederick Lugard, was there, fighting the tribes. Salisbury stretched the agreements of the Berlin Conference to their limits or somewhat beyond them. The Portuguese made the mistake of introducing historical claims—"archaeological arguments," sniffed Salisbury. He wrote to the queen that they claimed "half Africa on the supposed cessation to them in 1630 of the Empire of Monomotapa, of which event Lord Salisbury can find no account whatever in this country.* Nor does he consider that the existence of ruined forts proves any claim, but rather the contrary, since it shows the power that built these forts to have abandoned them." Portugal continued to claim, make treaties in, and prepare to administer the area from, and including, Nyasaland westward (later Northern Rhodesia). An ultimatum was delivered from London. To make the situation clear, the Channel fleet was ordered to sail for the coast of

* There was, in fact, truth in Portugal's claim. The Monomotapa Empire had succumbed to the Portuguese in 1629. Portugal had done little except exploit the area for the slave trade, and the Monomotapa had declined.

Portugal under sealed orders. Neither France nor Germany had the slightest intention of going to war over Portuguese claims in Africa. There was rioting in Lisbon, and the British Legation was damaged, but Portugal was not going to war with the most powerful nation in the world. Britain gained the spacious, magnificent land on the African plateau, larger than Britain itself, from the Transvaal to Lake Tanganyika. While Salisbury was fighting to keep the gap open from London, Cecil Rhodes was tenaciously, ruthlessly and resolutely pushing the British presence up into it.

The most powerful people in this area were the Matabele, who had been pushed north from the Transvaal. They claimed some form of sovereignty over the Mashona, to their north, and the Barotse, to their northwest. It was this little-known area which Rider Haggard had enticingly fictionalized as Kukuanaland. The other great tribe in this sector of the continent, the Bamangwato, had already come under British influence (their chief, Khama, was a Christian convert).

Chief of the Matabele was Lobengula, a large man with a useful brain who had been watching the progress of the British with as much alarm as he feared the intentions of the Afrikaners. Since 1870 he had been ruler of his tribe, which was proud and had based its power, as usual in Africa, on fear. Although, like the Zulu, they did everything they could to strike terror into their enemies, including making their appearance as horrific as they could devise, the Matabele were basically a frightened people. Their troubles began with the discovery of gold in Mashonaland by a German explorer. Prospectors and concession seekers arrived at Bulawayo, Lobengula's modest capital (among them was Maurice Heany, a cousin of Edgar Allan Poe). They stalked the countryside, as did hunters like Frederick C. Selous, who oftentimes pleased the Africans by wearing no trousers.

In the north, hunters rivaled missionaries and traders; officers stationed in the Cape had gone north in search of sport, and in 1863 the publication of *African Hunting and Adventure,* by W. C. Baldwin, had brought young men to South Africa for no other purpose than hunting, some for sport, some for ivory and valuable skins, some for both. The most famous hunter was an Afrikaner, Piet Jacobs, who shot more than 400 elephants and

100 lions in his long career. Another was William Finaughty, who, in "the two finest months of my life," had shot 95 elephants. Fred Selous, who had been inspired by Baldwin, was now the leading hunter; he knew Lobengula well but did not care for him. All these travelers wandered about in the lands far north of territory belonging to Britain and the Afrikaners with hardly a man ever being attacked by an African. The most important visitor to Lobengula's country was John Moffat, son of Livingstone's old mentor. Moffat had given up trying to convert Matabeleland, but he took some interest in political matters there. He persuaded Lobengula to sign an unofficial treaty with the great white queen: "That peace and amity shall continue for ever between Her Britannic Majesty, her subjects and the Amandebele people; and the contracting Chief, Lobengula, engages to use his utmost endeavour to prevent any rupture of the same." Lobengula promised not to sell his land to any rival power and got nothing in return. He knew nothing of treaties and had previously devoted his service to his people in quite different matters, notably the collection of women and cattle, but he was not a fool, and he was capable of learning, although there was no one to help him.

Rhodes, of course, had his own emissaries at the primitive native town of Bulawayo: an old Harrovian, a Fellow of All Souls, and an interpreter. Rhodes may have been the greatest man in Africa at that time, and he was certainly the greatest snob, collecting titled ladies as others collect butterflies. He also had a great respect for education, especially for the classics, which he believed to be an essential foundation for all knowledge. He had at last received his pass degree from Oxford, after eight years of intermittent attendance. His men in Bulawayo, graduates of Oxford and Cambridge, argued with Lobengula, but to little effect. Eventually Rhodes sent the Bishop of Bloemfontein up the trail. Lobengula appears to have been impressed, and he at last granted Rhodes a concession—although he was doubtful if, in fact, the great "Rhodes" existed.

The agreement was a remarkable one: Rhodes would pay Lobengula £100 a month and give him 1,000 rifles, 100,000 cartridges, and an armed steamboat for use on the Zambezi— useful for dominating the various lands to which Lobengula laid claim. In action, Rhodes' representatives secured mineral and metal rights in the chief's "kingdoms, principalities and dominions" and all profits from them—"if any." What the dominions were was left undefined, but Mashonaland was certainly understood to be included among them. Other Europeans were at Bulawayo, and to them Lobengula professed some ignorance of what exactly the Rhodes agreement entailed. Very soon Lobengula was denying some of the contractual points. He signed another agreement with a German banker, a cousin of Rhodes' financial wizard Alfred Beit. Two of Lobengula's bewildered henchmen were taken to London by Rhodes' adversaries, under the impression that a plea from them would be heard by the queen herself. They were shown the Army maneuvers at Aldershot and a huge 111-ton gun at Woolwich and, suitably impressed, were sent off home. Lobengula executed one of his advisers, who had urged him to sign Rhodes' agreement. Rhodes' representative left Bulawayo in some haste.

Rhodes, now thirty-six years old, was not disheartened. He had what he wanted, which was a piece of paper with Lobengula's cross on it. He persuaded his Kimberly doctor, Leander Starr Jameson, to rush to Bulawayo. Rhodes, who had a great belief in the ability of doctors to solve all sorts of problems, had been impressed by Jameson's cheerful, persuasive personality. Jameson, who had arrived from London in search of a less humdrum and more lucrative practice than those available to a young graduate in England and had certainly found it, left Kimberley next day. He spent ten days at Bulawayo, after taking the rough old missionaries' "road" (a track sometimes barely discernible in the grass), and calmed Lobengula. He returned to his practice, but six months later he was back again to persuade the chief to allow the digging to start. Rhodes was less interested in Mashonaland gold than in the territory being claimed by Portugal, but it was important to have his concession recognized and in operation. During Jameson's stay at Bulawayo there occurred one of the more remarkable occasions of the British time in Africa. Three members of the Royal Horse Guards, in full regimental dress of plumed helmets, chains and glistening breastplates, arrived at Lobengula's capital of huts. It was January, the hottest month of the year, which was very hot indeed. They bore a message from the great white queen: She had granted a charter to Rhodes' British South Africa Company, the intentions of which were virtually to take over Lobengula's land.

The chief surveyed the strangely attired, perspiring guards-men and listened to all the explanations. The company would be allowed, it seemed, to "make treaties, promulgate laws, preserve the peace, maintain a police force . . . make roads, railways . . . establish banks, make land grants, and carry on any lawful commerce, trade, pursuit," and many other things. Lobengula was under the impression that he had given away only the mineral rights of his land. He was not pleased. Not surprisingly, he was becoming increasingly suspicious: Did Rhodes, even the great queen, really exist? His young warriors were becoming restive at the growing power of the white men. The men who journeyed to him from distant lands he had never seen were to him not only eccentric in the extreme, but frightening.

"Take Rhodes by the hand," Lobengula told Selous, "and bring him here." Rhodes declined the invitation.

Rhodes was exercising all his power to get his way, and he knew that it was not in Bulawayo that it had to be exercised. He had won the support of the *Times'* important correspondent on Africa, Flora Shaw. In Cape Town, Parliament was under his spell. In London, he lobbied furiously. He had met and im-pressed Harry Johnston, explorer, consul general in Portuguese East Africa, and contender for Britain in Nyasaland against Portugal's powerful claims, and after a dinner, still in evening dress, they had talked at Rhodes' hotel till breakfast. Johnston's ambition was to build a railway through Africa, from south to north; he called it the Cape-to-Cairo Railway. Rhodes was enchanted. Lord Salisbury described it as "a curious idea."

North of Matabeleland and west of Mashonaland lay Barotse-land. It was adjacent to the Bamangwata territory of Bechuana-land, ruled by the friendly and obliging Khama, already under British "protection." Rhodes sent an emissary to Barotseland to negotiate a "concession." The chief granted a concession to the British South Africa Company and accepted protection from Queen Victoria for £2,000 a year. "See how things grow," Rhodes commented. This concession brought him in another quarter of a million square miles. The territory of Rhodes was starting to take shape. He had already gained a charter to develop Nyasaland.

There remained Mashonaland. Rhodes talked of the problem of Lobengula one morning to a fellow East Anglian, twenty three-year-old Frank Johnson, over breakfast at the Kimberley Club. "With two hundred and fifty men I would walk through the country," Johnson said. Rhodes, between mouthfuls of bacon and eggs, grunted: "How much?" Johnson went away and made some sums at a desk in the corner. He returned with the cost of taking Mashonaland: £87,500. A few days later Rhodes signed a contract written out by Johnson and gave him a £30,000 advance.

Johnson undertook to clear a track into Mashonaland, bypassing Matabeleland in a semicircle and never less than 150 miles from Bulawayo (Selous later claimed the idea was his). Johnson would pay for everything except arms and ammunition. On arrival in Mashonaland, he would build a fort, as a nucleus for a permanent British settlement. Because of the charter, Rhodes knew that he would not get into trouble with London, only with Bulawayo. The authorities, however, insisted that the 250 pioneers would have to be military-trained, or an official expedition to rescue them could be embarrassing. In the end 200 were prepared—tailors, butchers, farmers, miners, lawyers, doctors, almost everyone, except women, a new country would need—accompanied by 150 Bamangwato attendants and 500 armed police as an escort. Nearly all the whites were British, but there were about a dozen Americans, including Maurice Heany, a pioneer in Rhodesia and previously a leading figure in Johannesburg. Dr. Jameson was to go along as Rhodes' personal representative.

The great column, with its vast convoy of wagons, assembled for depature. An extraordinary adventure, one of the greatest of the Victorian Age, was about to begin. Ahead, hundreds of miles away, lay a vast unexploited country, which might bring wealth or might offer massacre. No men have ever deserved the title "pioneers" more than those of Frank Johnson's column. They were inspected by the commanding officer of the Cape, Major General Lord Methuen. "Gentlemen," he said, "have you got your maps?" Everyone consulted his map, which claimed to show the nature of the north. "And your pencils?" They had their pencils. After a few more words, the general said: "Good morning, gentlemen." The project was under way.

The ninety wagons stretched for two miles as they trundled across the veld. The expedition was well equipped. The pioneers had been issued brown uniforms, yellow leggings, and

hats. Food supplies, building and engineering tools, medica
equipment, and other necessities were lavish. Even a huge nava
searchlight was included.

The bush country of southern Africa consists of grassy plain
dotted with millions of low, stubby trees. For the convoy to pas
through, a way had to be hacked through the trees, or bush
Men went ahead clearing a road through the obstacles for th
wagons which followed. It was a laborious process. The Baman
gwato returned to their villages. The pioneers and the polic
were on their own. A message arrived from Lobengula: "G
back at once."

At last the column rolled into Mashonaland. It was a splendi
country. "Must ultimately become a very valuable possession,
commented Selous. They stopped at the foot of a hill and bega
building a community, which they aptly called Fort Salisbur
The column had traveled 400 miles in two and a half month
"without the loss of a single life, and without the necessity c
firing a shot." The task had been done at about £5,000 le
than Johnson's estimate at the Kimberley Club. The whol
thing had been a magnificent success. On September 13, 189(
the Union Jack was hoisted on a crooked, ungainly pole. "Ma
nificent," said Johnson, looking around. He read out a procl
mation claiming all the land, the rights of which had bee
granted to Rhodes by Lobengula, for the British Empire.

Small forts had been built on the way up to keep open th
road, and through them a message went back to Kimberle
announcing the success. "I do not think there was a happi
man," Rhodes wrote. He had brought a vast tract of countr
into the Empire, and he envisaged a great new country, lik
Canada or Australia, for the future. Soon the road was bus
with second-line pioneers. Within six weeks of the founding c
Salisbury 150 wagons entered the country.

The British South Africa Company was virtual dictator in th
land, and it ruled efficiently, if not always wisely. Jameson s
off for the Portuguese-held coast to consider another line c
communication to the outside world. The Portuguese were f
from friendly about the pioneers, and fighting ensued betwee
Portuguese and British. Jameson reached the coast. With Sali
bury's work in London, bullying the Portuguese governmen
and Rhodes' *fait accompli* in Africa, the Portuguese reluctant
abandoned the idea of joining their two colonies on the east ar

west coasts—a concept that could have easily been put into practice during the several centuries when no other country would have shown the slightest interest in the union.

Cecil Rhodes had become an international figure, the first great statesman that modern Africa had produced. In the same year as the founding of Salisbury, he had become Prime Minister of the Cape, after nine years in Parliament. He was also one of the richest men in the world.

Within two years there were 1,500 settlers, including women. Salisbury, a hardy, extrovert settlement of wooden shacks, was in telegraphic communication with the rest of the world, and a railway was under construction from the Portuguese port of Beira. Still, it was 1,700 miles from the coast, and outside food supplies cost £70 a ton. The first important visitor was Lord Randolph Churchill, slowly dying of syphilis, in 1891. He found it "vigorous, confident and full of enterprise," although he was disconcerted to find English ale and stout selling at 6s.6d. (at the time $1.66 in U.S. currency) a bottle. While Lord Randolph was here, Rhodes himself arrived on a mule cart to have a look at Salisbury. What should the new country be called? At that time it was known as Southern Zambezia. A Cape Town newspaper, controlled by Rhodes, suggested another name: Rhodesia.

At Bulawayo, Lobengula brooded on the rape of his lands and the snub to his authority over Mashonaland. He was less outraged than worried; it was his young advisers who were outraged, for they saw their inheritance being whittled away by the advancing white man. From time to time Matabele hordes raided Mashonaland, the sovereignty of which was still claimed by Lobengula. There was a widespread and dangerous feeling of insecurity among both Africans and the newcomers.

Rhodes thought he had already fixed the answer to Lobengula. All men had a price, and the chief had named his price. "We are on the most friendly terms with Lobengula," Rhodes told the company shareholders. "He receives a globular sum of a hundred pounds a month in sovereigns and he looks forward with great satisfaction to the day of the month when he will receive them. I have not the least fear of any trouble in the future from Lobengula."

Dr. Jameson had been appointed administrator of the company's territory, in an effort to maintain law and order among the rowdy and murderous pioneers. When a Matabele army, which had been punishing the Mashona, appeared at Fort Victoria, he hurried from Salisbury to the spot. Forty police issued from the fort, fired on the Matabele, and began what has absurdly been called the Matabele War. The Matabele, who had never been under disciplined rifle fire, turned and fled, leaving 50 dead behind.

Jameson telegraphed for help, asking for 1,000 men. Rhodes, caught up perhaps in the drama of the moment, counseled caution, replying with the customary Biblical reference beloved of British commanders as an unbreakable code. Even if the Matabele could read, about the only book available to them in Bulawayo was the Bible (although very few had been converted). Always the optimist, Jameson ignored the advice. Two detachments were raised from the settlers: the Salisbury Horse and the Victoria Horse. The company was not attracting much capital in its effort to open up Mashonaland, and there was no pay for the troopers;* instead, they were promised Matabele land and cattle. This act caused an outcry at home, where it was suspected that the "war" had been engineered for the purpose of looting, but it was exactly the same terms of war as had existed in Africa for many centuries.

The imperial government now thought it wise to enter the arena, and a force of Bechuanaland border police was sent up toward Matabeleland. The government wondered if perhaps it rather than the British South Africa Company's shareholders should not get Lobengula's land.

Three years after the founding of Salisbury, Jameson's force nearly 700 strong, rode into Matabeleland. They were met by the Matabele army, more than 10,000 strong, some armed with the rifles obtained from Rhodes. Discarding the traditional modes of battle, which had proved initially successful to their Zulu cousins, they relied on their firearms, fumbled with bolt and sights, and fired wildly. British rifle fire, supported by machine guns and artillery, mowed them down. The Matabele stood again outside Bulawayo, where the result of their courage was an appalling massacre in less than an hour. "Cannot speak too highly of the pluck of these regiments," commented S

---

* Shareholders received no dividends for the first thirty-five years.

John Willoughby. "I believe that no civilized troops could have withstood the terrific fire." Willoughby had been on the original pioneer column.

On November 4, 1893, the British force entered the smoking ruins of Bulawayo to the sound of bagpipes, as some conquering force of old. Two British traders who had been caught in the town at the outbreak of the fighting had been left unharmed by Lobengula. Eleven days later the official force from Bechuanaland arrived. The Union Jack was already flying, and Rhodes had claimed Matabeleland for the company. Rhodes said he considered the interests of Cape Colony and the company in the newly won territory "identical" and claimed there was no need for friction.

A column was sent after Lobengula and his army, fleeing towards the Zambezi. It was clumsily led, and discipline was poor. An advance guard of thirty-six men was surrounded by the Matabele. Three escaped, and the remainder, after fighting for about twelve hours and running out of ammunition, shook hands and awaited their death. This action became known as the Shangani Patrol, and provided a convenient heroic touch for the settlement of Rhodesia, which had up till then noticeably lacked the heroic legends of so many other pioneering movements the world over. Jameson, who heard of the scene via a native, wrote to Rhodes about it: "They fought all day, killing a great number of the Matabele, but finished their ammunition, then the Matabele fired at them from close quarters, killing, as they thought, those still alive. After a time they approached nearer and found there were still some alive, all seriously wounded, writing on pieces of paper. As soon as the Matabele came close to them, they drew their revolvers, but the whole thing was very soon finished, and not one of the whole party was left alive."

The Matabele War had consisted of three brief engagements, causing about half a dozen British casualties and the fatal Shangani Patrol. At Bulawayo, land was parceled out to the new white lords. "It is your right," Rhodes told them, "for you have conquered the country." Complaining of the continued government interest in Matabeleland, Rhodes explained to a friend: We must watch them carefully, we know the predatory instincts of our race, their present position is entirely due to

plunder, and when not plundering a foreigner, sooner than do
nothing, they plunder each other." Rhodes, as was his custom,
won. Matabeleland became part of Rhodesia, not of the Cape.

Lobengula died a few weeks later, some said of smallpox,
some of shame. His army had suffered decimation and lurked
far away in the bush. The white man was not a friend, but a
terrible enemy. This lesson they would not forget.

The surface of Africa seemed to erupt like a simmering stew
as chiefs and their tribes objected to the requirements of British
protection. No sooner had the Matabele bubble been pricked,
at least temporarily, than another bubble emerged, in 1895, far
away on the west coast. The Ashanti kingdom, ruled now by the
proud Prempeh, showed as much desire for independence as
ever. They had still not paid the indemnity demanded of them
after Wolseley's expedition twenty years before, and they had
no hope of ever being able to do so. This seemed to put the
British in some power over them. Tales of hideous practices
continued to reach England, causing the Ashanti to be con
sidered as abominable as ever. When a deputation from Kumasi
arrived in London at its own expense, utterly bewildered and
astonished by all its members saw, their attempts to overcome
prejudice and to come to a lasting agreement were met by a
series of snubs.

A new campaign for the Gold Coast and Ashanti was an
nounced. It was remembered that Wolseley's expedition had
brought glory to many, and now officers connived in every way
to be included. Competition was intense. One lucky office
wrote that when selected, an officer "treads on air, the envy o
his non-selected fellow-aspirants." As always when an expedi
tion abroad was announced, the morning post of selected officer
brought in invitations, congratulations, and circulars from ou
fitters, insurance agents, moneylenders, "and others anxious t
utilize such a chance of sucking money. . . . Kind friends pres
on him presents of varied utility from hip-baths to tea-cosies."

Once more a force of British troops was landed at Cape Coast
with all its accouterments, supplies and "basewallahs." A
special service corps had been picked from various regiments t
strengthen the force, which mainly consisted of the West York
shire Regiment. As in the Zulu War, use was made of African
against Africans; Hausa troops were brought up the coast from

the Niger. An enormous train of bearers, some 10,000 strong, was assembled for carrying the supplies, which ranged from necessities like tea, canned beef, and quinine to delicacies and musical instruments. Old friends met again in this outpost of empire. "We have seen that eye and brow before," wrote one, "although the beard and solar topee do much to disguise the man. His necktie of faded Old Carthusian colours makes suspicion a certainty, and once again old schoolfellows are flung together for an hour to talk in an African swamp of old times on English playing-fields."

The column set off for Kumasi with every confidence. Sickness was already rampant. Two men died on the road after less than five miles. Men fell like "rotten sheep"—thirty fell out in one day. But excitement at the prospect of facing the Ashanti army was great. In camp they sang:

Oh Prempeh! Prempeh! Prempeh: You had better mind
    your eye.
You'd better far be civil or, by Jove, you'll have to die.
And your kingdom of Ashanti, you'll never see it more,
If you fight the old West Yorkshire and the Special
    Service Corps.

Among the staff officers was Major Robert Stephenson Smyth Baden-Powell, of the Thirteenth Hussars, one of the latest of Wolseley's "bright young men," a churpy, ambitious little man, who enjoyed dressing up at concert parties and singing in a falsetto voice. One of his special tasks was scouting. "That the Ashantis will fight is the great hope of those who toil through the long hot hours in this steaming, fetid atmosphere," he said. But the Ashanti did not fight. The column wound its way along the road, to a chorus of false alarms and rifle-firing into empty forest, preparing for attack and ambush against an enemy which was not there. Prempeh and his chiefs had decided there was no point in fighting a war they could not win; they had resolved to accept British "protection."

The column marched into Kumasi, having faced only imaginary opposition all the way from the coast. Once more a major task was to bring back gold and to destroy the practices of the Ashanti, especially human sacrifice, about which there had been so much talk but so little evidence. The unhappy Prempeh was asked to produce 50,000 ounces of gold forthwith, but he could find only 680 ounces. It was decided that the king and his mother would have to be taken to the coast in default; this, it was hoped, would finally end the pretensions of the Ashanti. The queen mother, as with many African peoples, was an extremely important figure in the hierarchy. As for the fetishes, Baden-Powell was given the task of searching for loot, smashing down doors, battering through temples, opening sacred mausoleums, breaking ornaments, and collecting the few valuables in an orgy of destruction that horrified the Ashanti who witnessed it. Baden-Powell did the job well, finally setting fire to the holiest buildings in the town. "Like a flock of sheep without a leader," he noted.

Leaving Kumasi partly in flames and completely in despair, the column began the long, hot, feverish march back to the coast. Prempeh's mother made her feelings plain, for "she was rather given to spit at any white man who approached." It was a ghastly march; a large proportion of the force endured nearly every mile of it vomiting and sweating in swinging hammocks. Noble officers were carried piggyback style on the shoulders of native bearers. Almost 50 percent of the expedition came down with malaria. It was little or no better than Wolseley's expedition.

Eventually the little army, sick and exhausted, but every man entitled to a campaign ribbon he would treasure all his life, embarked for Europe and the Thames. At the dock in London their ship almost collided with another just arrived from South Africa, on which were Dr. Jameson and some friends coming home to face an investigation about a raid into the Transvaal which had brought South Africa right back into the news. The Ashanti, it seemed, were broken. The British colony of the Gold Coast had been doubled in size. Prempeh and his mother, who had never before seen the sea, were shipped away to exile in the Seychelles Islands. Their miserable condition evoked some pity from the sailors. The Ashanti would also not forget

Britain's control of her various colonies was remarkably tenuous. Those at home loved reading of Africa, but few wished to settle there. The government had no wish to spend the immense sums necessary if the new colonies were to be fully developed. Only in South Africa was progress more than steady

From nothing only twenty-five years previously, Kimberley, in 1895, had grown to quite a large European-style town, with two suburbs (Gladstone and Beaconsfield), several churches, two cemeteries, a racecourse, a club, a hospital and "native camps" set discreetly apart. Johannesburg continued to thrive and expand. A writer described it in 1895:

> Like all such cities, the mining metropolis of South Africa is not a thing of beauty; no, it is a cheap place to live in and perhaps, from a moral point of view, Johannesburg is not quite the town for a deacon. Men make money quickly and spend it recklessly. The beggar of today may be the millionaire of tomorrow. Naturally all class distinctions are effaced. Ignorance flaunts in silks and diamonds, and learning is valued in an exact ratio to the power it gives the possessor of finding reefs or developing them.

There was a weekly and well-patronized shipping service from Southampton to Cape Town. There were two cables to England, down each side of the continent. Coastal settlements had developed into towns at Durban, East London, and Port Elizabeth, and railways went inland from each. The speed of development was astonishing. Only five years after Lobengula left his smoking, primitive capital of huts, Bulawayo boasted streets, buildings, telegraph, a railway station (with trains to Cape Town), and a massive City Hall reminiscent of one of the larger English provincial cities.

The intransigence of the Transvaal under Kruger was the only shadow, and few took it seriously.

Research in tropical medicine had made West Africa slightly more tolerable. More "old coasters" survived their tours of duty than in the old days and even lived to argue loyally over the respective merits of the colonies. In 1895 there were about sixty whites in the swampy Gambia colony, nearly all of them French; at the tiny capital of Bathurst practically all commerce was still in the hands of Frenchmen.

In Sierra Leone there was some friction between the native Africans and the descendants of the freed slaves for whom the colony had been founded. Freetown, after a hundred years, had a cable to Europe, a cathedral, water supply and drainage, bewigged and begowned African magistrates (before whom Europeans appeared), and slums which seemed more than acceptable to Africans from the interior but appalling to visiting English people; a railway line was begun in 1896.

On the Gold Coast the capital was moved from Cape Coast to Accra in a search for health. About 150 whites were resident, administrating and overseeing the trade in ivory, gum, skins, cotton, grains, timber and palm oil. Gold still appeared at the coast, but the efforts of several European mining companies had not done much to increase production or fulfill the promises of centuries. By 1892 the value of exports from the Gold Coast was £665,000, nearly double what it had been only five years before, producing a small surplus.

Farther east, toward the Niger Delta, the small colony of Lagos, once a great slaving entrepôt, languished in steamy heat; it had been established, separate from the Gold Coast, in 1886. The neighboring delta area had been the scene of bitter rivalry between British and French traders, but the British had won, and their claim had been ratified after the Berlin Conference. The Royal Niger Company, under Sir George Goldie, an ambitious Manxman, was developing the area, and a protectorate had been proclaimed. Goldie was dedicating his life to obtaining the Niger region for the Empire, just as Rhodes was doing in the south. It was he who had reintroduced the idea of the powerful chartered company, which could rule territory, an idea supposedly dead since the end of the East India Company. The company, which he personally directed, had more than thirty river steamers and its own police of 1,000 men. The interior was ruled by Moslem leaders, and they were proving jealous of their rights. The many trade treaties (more than 400) that had been signed had not given Britain her expected domination in the Niger interior. Lagos had a population of some 40,000 in 1895, with about 110 Europeans.

Compared to the French, the British appeared to be neglecting their West African possessions. France took great pride in her African colonies, which were mainly confined to the west. There a real effort had been made to colonize the Senegal, not without bloodshed. A railway already linked the two chief towns of Dakar and St.-Louis, both of which had been planned. There were lights by the 1890's. Africans mixed freely in cafés and hotels with whites, and a fortunate few received higher education.

The most eccentric British territory in Africa was Cape Juby

This trading post, protected by an impressive castle, was in the most desolate sector of the entire African coast, where the Sahara met the Atlantic. It had been founded in 1879 by one of the last of the great Scottish pioneers in Africa, Donald Mackenzie. The idea was to divert the desert caravans to the post and direct their trade to England rather than, as for many centuries, to Morocco. It was not a success. In 1895 a leading historian of Africa said of Cape Juby: "It would be a national loss were it to be abandoned to any foreign power." This was a reference to Spain, which had expressed more than an interest in Cape Juby. Lord Salisbury was undismayed. Mackenzie had already made a name for himself by suggesting the irrigation of the Sahara, a project which was to fascinate many after him.

In East Africa, the foundations of British colonies were also being laid. In Zanzibar, which, as a result of the Helgoland barter, had become a protectorate, slavery was abolished in 1897 (an occasion of some moment inasmuch as the island had lived on slavery for centuries). In Uganda, Captain Frederick Lugard tried to establish the British claim. For some years there was chaos, with French and British native factions at war and absurd difficulties between Protestant and Roman Catholic missionaries which also led to bloody native wars. Lugard enlisted the remnants of Emin Pasha's army, and some order was obtained by the mid-1890's, at which point European traders began to arrive. The British East Africa Company, because of lack of capital, had said it would have to abandon further attempts to open up Uganda. There had been a public outcry, led by the *Times,* and the company had been deterred. Chief advocate for withdrawal had been Sir William Harcourt, the most dedicated of the Liberal anti-imperialists.

In British East Africa (Kenya) a handful of Britons endeavored to develop the country. The government took over administration from the company in 1895. In the same year a revolt on the coast failed, and Arab power declined. Lord Salisbury encouraged the construction of a railway to Victoria Nyanza, mainly to make contact with the populous area of Uganda. It was to be paid for by the British taxpayer. Work began from Mombasa in 1896. Soon the track was snaking up in the direction of the peak of Kilimanjaro. Among normal hazards, laborers and engineers had to contend with man-eating lions, but they were not always successful. One of the engineers,

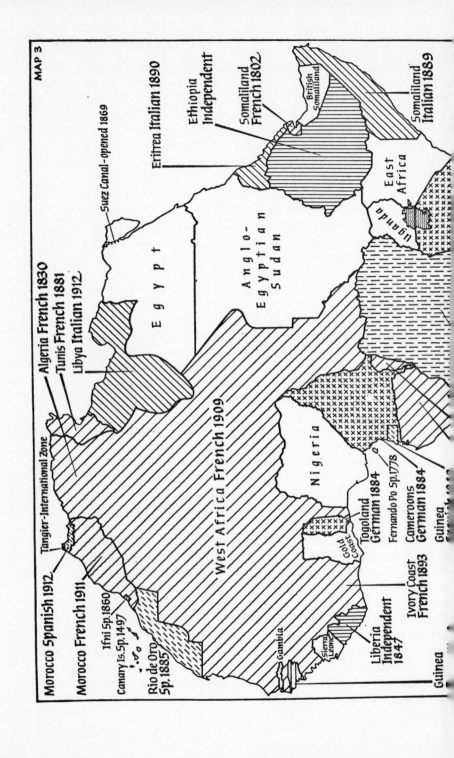

MAP 3

Morocco Spanish 1912
Morocco French 1911

Tangier-International Zone
Algeria French 1830
Tunis French 1881
Libya Italian 1912
Suez Canal - opened 1869
Eritrea Italian 1890
Ethiopia Independent
Somaliland French 1802
British Somaliland
Somaliland Italian 1889

Ifni Sp.1860
Canary Is. Sp.1497
Rio de Oro Sp. 1885

E g y p t

Anglo-Egyptian Sudan

East Africa

Uganda

West Africa French 1909

Nigeria

Togoland German 1884
Fernando Po Sp.1778
Cameroons German 1884
Guinea

Gold Coast

Liberia Independent 1847
Ivory Coast French 1893

Gambia
Sierra Leone

Guinea

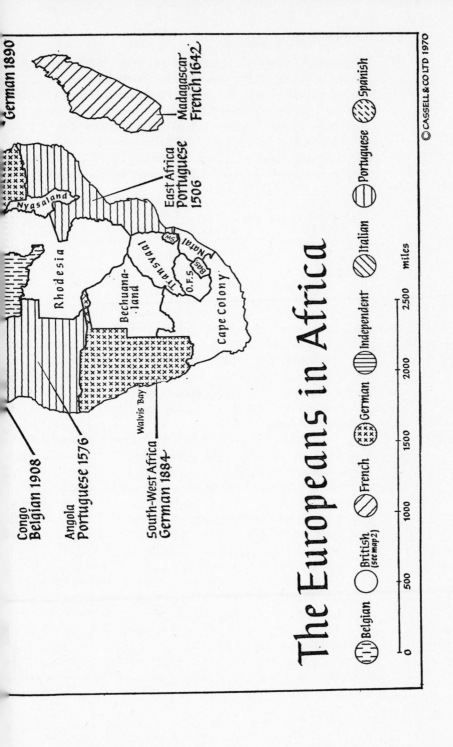

The Europeans in Africa

German 1890

Madagascar
French 1642

East Africa
Portuguese
1506

Nyasaland

Rhodesia

Bechuana-
land

Transvaal

SW

Natal

BAS

O.F.S.

Cape Colony

Congo
Belgian 1908

Angola
Portuguese 1576

Walvis Bay

South-West Africa
German 1884

Belgian | French | German | Independent | Italian | Portuguese | Spanish
British (see map 2)

0   500   1000   1500   2000   2500   miles

© CASSELL & CO LTD 1970

J. H. Patterson, wrote a clever and readable book about his adventures building the railway, *The Man-Eaters of Tsavo* ("two most voracious and insatiable man-eating lions appeared on the scene") ; it was an immediate and tremendous success.

Everywhere British territory had grown since the Berlin Conference and the advent of Lord Salisbury. By 1895, of the 11,500,000 square miles of Africa, only about 3,300,000 did not belong to European powers. The claims were split as follows:

France	..	..	2,750,000 square miles
Britain	..	..	1,828,000 " "
Portugal	..	..	841,000 " "
Germany	..	..	822,000 " "
Italy	..	..	603,000 " "
Spain	..	..	214,000 " "
The Congo State	..	900,000 " "

The map grew more red, as an expanding blush. Railways, telegraph lines, roads were constructed in every part. Education was left to the missionaries, but a rail network connected the thriving Johannesburg with Cape Colony and Natal. The remote, mysterious, dangerous interior contracted every week. All this had happened in the lifetimes of those who could still remember when Britain had nothing but the freed slaves of Freetown in all Africa.

On June 22, 1897, Victoria, Queen of Britain and Empress of India, celebrated the diamond jubilee of her accession. Her possessions amounted to the largest empire in the history of the world: about a quarter of the earth's land surface and a quarter of its population. It was a very great occasion. The procession through a gloriously sunny London was the most wonderful that had ever been seen, with 50,000 immaculately presented troops, among them carabineers from Natal and Hausas from West Africa clumping in boots for the first time, and with representatives of the Empire from all corners of the globe. Said the London *Times,* proudly: "History may be searched, and searched in vain, to discover so wonderful an exhibition of allegiance and brotherhood amongst so many myriads of men. . . . The mightiest and most beneficial Empire ever known in the annals of mankind." On that day few wanted to be excluded from this "family," as it was so often described. "We are a part," said the New York *Times,* "and a great part, of the Greater

Britain which seems so plainly destined to dominate this planet." Even the unloved President Kruger of the Transvaal released two Englishmen from jail. The Sultan of Zanzibar held a special dinner. Gunboats fired salvos in Table Bay.

"Indescribable," the queen noted of her diamond jubilee, "deeply touching." The British, it seemed, were in a position of such power that their Empire must last for centuries, as that of their Roman predecessors had done. It all had seemed to happen so quickly. It was a thrilling, magnificent dream that filled every Englishman with pride. But in the Empire itself the jubilee was merely a punctuation, for the fighting among the brotherhood continued.

✤ X ✤

Omdurman

By 1893 Sir Herbert Kitchener had served queen and country in the Near East and Egypt for nearly a quarter of a century. He was more familiar with the sound of the muezzin than he was with the cabs of St. James's. Like other heroes who had found fame in the scattered Empire rather than at home, he was a bit of a legend. There was something distinctly glamorous about the handsome, unmarried, distant soldier, with his enormous black mustache, who had tried to keep contact with Gordon till the last. When the post of sirdar, or commander in chief, of the Egyptian army became vacant, the authorities did not have far to look, but the appointment of Major General Kitchener was greeted with some disgust by the Egyptian army—officers and men.

Kitchener was a lonely figure, with no real friends. He had not curried favor, either above or beneath him. In Cairo, which had been his base for so long, he was inclined to favor solitary work or the company of wealthy Egyptians, Turks, and Jews to the social round of his fellow officers and their families. To the troops he was a stickler for discipline, unloved and unloving. His biographer says of him at this time:

Tall, straight, lean as a lance, Kitchener gazed out imperiously over most men's heads, wearing a harsh mask against the world. He spoke with a soft and almost self-deprecatory drawl, and he remained aloof and self-contained. He often dined in mess, and occasionally demanded a rubber of bridge afterwards; but he generally went home immediately after dinner, either to work indefatigably into the small hours of the morning or to entertain a few of his oriental friends and acquaintances.

For years the government had resisted pressure to regain the Sudan. Attempts by the Mahdists to move down the Nile into Egypt had easily been pushed back. The only really worried people were the Italians, who saw a permanent threat to their colony on the Red Sea. Under the Mahdi's lieutenant and successor, the Khalifa, the religious fervor and revolutionary spirit of the movement seemed to be disintegrating. The Khalifa managed to distract his people from time to time by ambitious but fairly empty threats to the surrounding foreigners. Such an occasion occurred in January, 1898. Kitchener saw his chance, and wrote to Baring (now Lord Cromer): "Reports confirming news of a dervish advance . . . reinforcements should be sent to Egypt." Despite the protests of that dedicated anti-imperialist Sir William Harcourt, they were. Salisbury, who was concerned at French ambitions in the area, had been planning to reenter the Sudan for some time.

By the end of the month the Egyptian army, reinforced by a brigade of British infantry, had concentrated at Atbara, on the Nile, some 200 miles northeast of Khartoum. The column was more than 12,000 strong. The great army, its khaki uniforms almost the color of the surrounding desert, accompanied by gunboats and hundreds of craft plying up river with its supplies, marched toward Khartoum and its great twin city of Omdurman to seek revenge for Gordon at last.

From Omdurman, the Khalifa sent an army of 18,000 men. They entrenched themselves across Kitchener's path and awaited the arrival of the British force. Kitchener continued till he was 13 miles from the enemy, then stopped. What should he do? He wrote to Cromer, waiting anxiously in Cairo, pondering on the cost of the expedition. "Rather perplexed by the situation here," Kitchener wrote. "I should be glad to learn your views on the subject." Cromer, who was not a military man, referred the problem to Lord Salisbury. The Prime Minister passed it on to the War Office. Cromer was advised that Kitchener would be supported whether he attacked or whether he did not attack. This was not much help, so Cromer telegraphed Kitchener: BETTER NOT ATTACK FOR THE PRESENT, BUT

WAIT YOUR OPPORTUNITY FOR ACTION AND ALLOW EVENTS TO DEVELOP. Too late. Kitchener had already decided to attack. Wolseley, who had never been a man to avoid a decision in the field, was somewhat startled. He wrote to Kitchener sharply: "Were I in your place, I would not ask such a question."

During the night of April 7 the British force concentrated in huge squares, each a brigade strong. They were about three miles from the dervish army. Soon after midnight they began to march steadily forward. After a bombardment of nearly an hour and a half, the infantry made its assault, to the accompaniment of suitable martial music from bands and pipes. The dervishes put up a surprising resistance, considering the barrage they had been subjected to (which, although doing little more than disturbing quantities of sand, had been demanding enough for men never subjected to one before). There was some hand-to-hand fighting, and then the dervish army gave way and fled. Kitchener picked for himself the best of the loot from the evacuated camp. He was infuriated by the shooting of prisoners, complaining of the waste of ammunition. He rode about on a magnificent white charger, while the enemy commander, shackled in chains, a halter around his neck, was made to run behind a horse.

By July reinforcements had arrived from England. There was now a whole division of British troops at Kitchener's command. A regiment of British cavalry, the Twenty-first Lancers, had been sent out, and with it was a twenty-three-year-old British officer named Winston Churchill. Young Churchill was impressed by Kitchener's appearance: "Heavy moustaches, the queer rolling look of the eyes, the sunburnt and almost purple cheeks and jowl." Among the commanders of the six infantry brigades in the force were such national heroes as Major General Arthur Grenfell "Andy" Wauchope and Major General Hector Macdonald, who had fought the Boers with his fists at Majuba. Kitchener's army was nearly 25,000 strong and, with its brigade of artillery, the most formidable ever seen in Africa; about a third of the personnel was British. This great army on the march toward Khartoum, down the west bank of the Nile, was a noble sight: In front were the clusters of cavalry and clattering horse artillery; then came two lines of infantry squares, each of brigade strength, accompanied by gunboats on the river, followed by batteries of field artillery, and behind was the great mass of supply columns and boats.

The Khalifa had brought his main army, about 60,000 strong, out of Omdurman. The two armies closed together with remorseless inevitability. About six miles from Omdurman, Kitchener halted. The dervish horde came on. At 6:40 A.M., September 2, Kitchener had deployed his infantry in line, one rank kneeling, one standing. The shouts of the advancing enemy could be plainly heard. Then, banners waving, they came into view. The British artillery opened up, followed by rifle and machine-gun fire. The mass of dervishes kept surging forward; there seemed no end to them. The British line kept up a rapid, ceaseless fire, for there was little need to aim. The London *Daily Mail* correspondent wrote: "They could never get near and they refused to hold back. By now the ground before us was all white with dead men's drapery. Rifles grew red-hot; the soldiers seized them by the slings and dragged them back to the reserve to change for cool ones. It was not a battle, but an execution." After about an hour, the surviving Arabs withdrew, leaving some 2,000 dead behind and many more wounded, singly, and in writhing, groaning piles. This success was followed up by a bombardment from the gunboats and skirmishing from the Egyptian cavalry.

Kitchener decided to march on Omdurman before the Khalifa had time to recover. The Khalifa had foreseen this and had 20,000 men lying in wait. It was at this juncture that the Twenty-first Lancers were ordered to reconnoiter the route to Omdurman. They encountered a body of dervishes hidden in a dip and trotted in to their celebrated charge. "The collision was prodigious," wrote Churchill. "The shock was stunning to both sides, and for perhaps ten wonderful seconds no man heeded his enemy. . . . The general battle was forgotten, as it was unseen. This was a private quarrel. The other might have been a massacre; but here the fight was fair, for we, too, fought with sword and spear." Of the approximately 30 lancers unhorsed, all were killed or terribly slashed. The remainder rode through and re-formed on the other side of the enemy. Some were hideously wounded. Churchill wrote of one sergeant, collecting his troop: "His face was cut to pieces, and as he called on his men to rally, the whole of his nose, cheeks and lips flapped amid red bubbles." The charge had hardly been necessary, but it had added some glory to the scene: Three Victoria Crosses were awarded.

The Khalifa made his attack on the marching column, but to little effect except the loss of many more of his troops. Hector Macdonald kept his head, while Kitchener sent out a stream of orders direct to brigades, ignoring divisions. The *Daily Mail* man wrote of the redoubtable "Fighting Mac": "So sturdily built that you might imagine him to be armour-plated under his clothes. He has been known to have fever, but never to be unfit for duty." The dervishes' assault was flung back, and the column renewed its interrupted march on Omdurman. Putting away his binoculars, Kitchener observed that the enemy had received a "thorough dusting." Churchill described the day's proceedings as "slaughter." Some 12,000 Arabs had lost their lives. The British force had suffered fewer than 50 killed.

The keys of the city were brought out to the British general, who accepted them brusquely. Omdurman was occupied. Churchill found Kitchener, on a native bed, "in well-deserved repose." A staff officer was stretched out on the ground, composing the telegram to London announcing victory. In the background stood a European, with a sergeant at his feet, clinking away with a hammer; he was having the fetters knocked off that had shackled him for thirteen years. The coupling irons were broken, but the rings had to wait till morning. "He talked volubly," noted Churchill. "The remark that seems most worthy of record was this—'I have forgotten how to walk.' " (None of the Mahdi's and Khalifa's European captives was ever killed.)

Kitchener entered Khartoum, across the Nile from Omdurman. "The troops formed up before the palace in three sides of a rectangle," wrote a reporter. "The Sirdar raised his hand. A pull on the halliards: up ran, out flew, the Union Jack, tugging eagerly at its reins, dazzling gloriously in the sun—*Bang!* went the 12½-pounder, and the gunboat quivered to her backbone. 'God Save Our Gracious Queen' hymned the Guards' band—*bang!* from the gun—and Sirdar and private staff stood stiff—*bang!*—to attention, every hand at the helmet peak in—*bang!*" It was a great moment, nearly fourteen years after the flag had been brought down by the Mahdi. A church service followed, with the singing of Gordon's favorite hymn, "Abide with Me."

Kitchener was overcome with emotion, and his staff was astonished to see tears streaming down his cheeks.

The next day Kitchener wrote an account to the queen, who was also moved. "Surely he is avenged," she said. But the Khalifa had evaded the occupying troops. He fled down the Nile, pursued by gunboats and troops and always supported by emirs and men of fanatical devotion and loyalty. He continued his opposition till finally hunted down fourteen months later.

Kitchener was on the peak of tremendous popularity, but suddenly he got himself into trouble. Some newspaper reports began to appear commenting on the nature of the fight for Omdurman. Kitchener was not popular with the press; he thought they were a nuisance, did not hide his opinion, and gave them little of his time. "Drunken swabs," he called them. He ordered that the Mahdi should be disinterred from his impressive tomb and his bones flung into the Nile. Gordon's nephew, a major in the force, carried out the order. The Mahdi's skull, however, was saved and presented to Kitchener as a souvenir. There was talk that Kitchener intended using it as an inkwell. It was the sort of thing that had long been said of the Ashanti. The press saw its chance and struck.

Kitchener announced that he intended giving the skull to the College of Surgeons, but it was too late. The queen was horrified and spoke to the Prime Minister. Salisbury wrote to Cromer: "The Queen is shocked by the treatment the Mahdi's body has received, and thinks the head ought to be buried."

Cromer, seeing trouble, stepped aside adroitly. He replied to Salisbury:

> Apart from the natural reaction, he has not the faculty of making friends. . . . He has his faults. No one is more aware of them than myself. . . . He was quite right in destroying the Mahdi's tomb, but details of the destruction were obviously open to objection. . . . Kitchener is himself responsible for the rather unwise course of sending the skull to the College of Surgeons.

Kitchener wrote to the queen. After explaining that the remains had been thrown away in order to dispel a belief, which he claimed existed among the Arabs, that the Mahdi had been "translated bodily to heaven," he continued: "The Mahdi's skull, in a box, was brought to me and I did not know what to do with it. I had thought of sending it to the College of Surgeons where, I believe, such things are kept. It has now been buried in a Moslem cemetery." Despite the explanations and the delicate mention of the box, the queen was not entirely mollified. She replied: "The destruction of the poor body of a man who, whether he was very bad and cruel, after all was a *man* of a *certain* importance . . . savours in the Queen's opinion too much of the Middle Ages. . . . The graves of our own people have been respected, and those of our foes should, in her opinion, also be." The matter was closed. Kitchener was a hero once more, but the public never again felt as completely comfortable about him as it was with its other heroes. When he received a grant of £30,000, fifty-one MP's voted against it. He was also awarded a peerage; he wanted to be Lord Khartoum, but became Lord Kitchener.

Under Kitchener's guidance—he was, after all, an engineer—the reconstruction of Khartoum took place. Roads and streets were neatly laid out, trees planted, and government buildings restored. A lengthening railway stretched down from Egypt. Perhaps, one day, it would meet with Rhodes' railway advancing north. Kitchener was a man who believed in taking, as well as in giving. "Loot like blazes," he ordered. "I want any quantity of marble stairs, marble pavings, iron railings, looking-glasses and fittings. . . ." He ruled the Sudan, as well as the Egyptian army, with an iron hand.

At home there was a slight but perceptible feeling of guilt about Britain's continued presence in Egypt and about the Sudan campaign. The *Daily Mail*'s correspondent wrote:

> Egypt alone could by no miracle have saved herself from utter destruction by Mahdist invasion. We have saved her—and therewith we have paid off the purblind, sincere undertakings of Mr. Gladstone. We undertook to leave Egypt; we have redeemed the promise in an unforeseen manner, but we have redeemed it amply. If we undertook to evacuate the old Egypt, we have fathered a new one, saved from imminent extinction by our gold and our sword. Without us there would have been no Egypt today; what we made we shall keep.

It did not sound convincing.

Immediately after the return to Khartoum, there was a singularly bitter disagreement between France and England, bitter even by the standards of disagreements between those two nations. It was described in the ambiguous diplomatic language of the time as an "incident," and an incident was an extremely serious matter, even implying the possibility of war.

Two years previously a French expedition, under Major Jean Baptiste Marchand, a veteran of campaigns in Senegal, had left the Atlantic for the Nile. For the last six months nothing had been heard of him. Then, after a massive journey across the breadth of Africa, he had arrived at Fashoda, on the Nile, 400 miles south of Khartoum. The threat to Egypt and the Sudan was obvious. To make matters worse, a twin expedition was planned by the French from the Red Sea. This would meet Marchand, thus attempting to cut the British south-north axis at the neck rather than in the legs, as the Portuguese had attempted in the south. The British government had already declared that an expedition such as Marchand's would be considered "an unfriendly act," which was strong language. Now the tricolor, of all hated flags, was flying on the Nile.

Kitchener left Khartoum for Fashoda on September 10. He took with him five gunboats, two battalions of local troops, a company of Cameron Highlanders, and supporting artillery.

Marchand, meanwhile, had concluded a treaty with an emir, placing a large part of the Upper Nile under French "protection." He had with him 7 French officers and 120 native soldiers.

The general and the major met cordially enough, although Kitchener was excited by the sight of the French flag flying over the old British administration building. Kitchener handled his end of the affair with more diplomatic skill than the diplomats in Europe. He made a real effort to get on with Marchand and sympathized with his position. "I knew he was a gentleman," he said. He congratulated the Frenchman on his remarkable journey and acknowledged gracefully the congratulations offered him in turn for his victory over the Khalifa. He agreed to the French flag's continuing to fly but insisted on the Egyptian flag's flying alongside it. Marchand, for his part, explained that he would have to await orders from Paris; he could not move without them and respectfully pointed out that while Kitchener had an overwhelming superiority in arms, any attempt to remove him by force would undoubtedly result in a war between their two countries. The situation was electric, to say the least. The fact that it was saved was due mainly to the good sense of the two men on the spot. The two forces were kept carefully apart. Kitchener accompanied his formal written protest with a present of a bottle of wine.

In London and Paris, both sides believed the other was bluffing. Russia indicated she was reluctant to support her ally France and did not wish to go to war with Britain. Jingoism was at its zenith, and newspapers fanned the affair into a dangerous blaze. Lord Salisbury was utterly firm in demanding French withdrawal but did little to supply an escape with honor for the French government. He told the French ambassador that the sovereignty of the upper Sudan "was, of course, a question which could practically only be settled, as it was settled, on the field of battle." In case that was not clear enough, he informed the French government: "No title of occupation could be created by a secret expedition across unknown and unexplored wastes, at a distance from the French border, by Monsieur Marchand and a scanty escort." The French, it seemed, had made a grave error of judgment. Perhaps, after all, the British were prepared for a European war over Africa—when it concerned Egypt and thus the Suez Canal and the way to India. Or perhaps Lord Salisbury was just better at bluffing.

Marchand withdrew via Ethiopia, the first European to cross North Africa from west to east, despite a break in the journey.* Kitchener easily persuaded the local emir to declare that he had never really intended a treaty with France at all. The French public took it as a national humiliation. On March 21, 1899, a treaty was concluded giving Britain the Upper Nile and France yet more useless desert area to the west as spheres of influence.

In West Africa there was war again. The strange, bloody saga of the Ashanti continued. Its final episode was one of the most dramatic, bizarre, and heroic in African history.

After the previous campaign, the British had remained in Ashanti country, where attempts were made to consolidate their position. About a dozen white men were considered sufficient to control a populous and hostile country—a revelation of the usual British attitudes toward colonization in Africa: parsimony

---

* He became a general in the First World War and lived to 1934. The difficulty of finding Fashoda on the map is because Cromer renamed the place Kodok in an effort to appease the French.

and overconfidence. A substantial fort had been constructed at Kumasi with a garrison of African troops. The Hausa people from Nigeria had proved good soldiers, loyal and amenable to discipline. They were used throughout West Africa, and by the 1890's some had risen from the ranks to be officers. Roads were improved, with the help of forced labor. Disobliging chiefs were heavily fined.

Indignation at the deportation of Prempeh continued unabated. As the years went by and he still did not return, bitterness and discontent increased. "Protection" by the British was not an entirely uncomfortable prospect for an African people, but like so many others, they found that protection was not the end of the matter.

Then there was the affair of the Golden Stool. This was the symbol of Ashanti national integrity, and as such it was virtually sacred. At the time of the sacking of Kumasi it had been carried off into the forest and buried. The British, gathering that it was an important element in Ashanti nationalism, were anxious to have the stool. An armed expedition to find it was unsuccessful and aroused fury and fear among the people. When the governor of the Gold Coast announced a visit to Kumasi, it was widely assumed that he was going to supervise a search for the stool.

The governor, Sir Frederic Hodgson, took with him his wife. They were courteously received; Lady Hodgson was handed a bouquet as a chorus of drums welcomed them. Later in the day Sir Frederic emerged from the fort to meet the assembled chiefs officially. His Excellency was in full-dress uniform as the queen's representative, proudly displaying his row of medals. After a fanfare of bugles, he mounted a wooden chair and addressed the gathering.

Sir Frederic explained how glad he was to be in Kumasi at last. Prempeh, he said, would not be returning to Ashanti, and his powers would be vested in the British representative. The matter of the indemnity must not be forgotten. With interest, the chiefs were now required to pay the British government £160,000 a year. There was also the matter of the Golden Stool. The queen was "entitled" to the stool, and she ought to receive it. The chiefs were distressed to hear Sir Frederic's next remarks. "Where is the Golden Stool?" he asked. "Why am I not sitting on the Golden Stool at this moment? I am the representative of the paramount power; why have you relegated me to this chair? Why did you not take the opportunity of my coming to Kumasi to bring the Golden Stool and give it to me to sit upon? However, you may be quite sure that although the government has not yet received the Golden Stool at your hands, it will rule over you with the same impartiality and with the same firmness as if you had produced it." The governor was not dissatisfied with his stern approach to the situation. He believed he knew what he was doing. The Ashanti would respect firm authority, and there should be no sign of weakness. But since even the Ashanti kings did not sit on the stool, his audience had heard his suggestions with some repugnance.

The chiefs politely conveyed their thanks to Sir Frederic for his interest in their affairs, expressed their regret that they would be unable to pay the indemnity that he had mentioned, and returned home to prepare for war.

With his handful of troops, the governor was a long way from the coast, but he did not feel in any way alarmed. Three days later an expedition set off to make another search for the Golden Stool. Once in the "deepest recesses of the forest," as a member of the party said, they were faced by a shouting mob of armed Ashanti. The officer in charge realized that he and his party were in danger of annihilation. He decided the only hope was a casual display of nonchalance. He ordered afternoon tea. A traveling table was opened and carefully laid. The potential enemy grew increasingly infuriated, but they waited until preparations for tea were complete before blasting table and surrounding officers with a burst of hectic fire. "As we looked, the tin of condensed milk leapt wildly into the air and disappeared into the undergrowth by the roadside, closely followed by the butter tin, while the enamelled cups and saucers kept up a continuous chatter until they, in their turn, dived from the table." Having given up all hope of survival, the British party was saved by a heavy storm, made its escape, and reached Kumasi with considerable relief.

Sir Frederic, facing realities, sent off a cable asking for reinforcements to be sent to him with the greatest urgency. The telegraph line was cut shortly afterward. The acting director of telegraphs for the Gold Coast calmly set off from the coast to find the break. He was caught by Ashanti, flogged on the soles of his feet with his own wire, and left to hobble to the nearest village, his feet bandaged with strips from his shirt. The line remained cut.

The Kumasi garrison huddled in the fort, with the gates slammed closed. Some 3,000 pro-British Ashanti gathered around its walls, hoping for the "protection" which had so often been promised. It was April 25, 1899. The remarkable siege of Kumasi had begun.

While the government began collecting troops from all over West Africa, two small columns struggled toward Kumasi from the Gold Coast. They found that they were up against a redoubtable enemy who, although mostly armed only with muskets, used the prevailing conditions with great skill, as they always had. The British, because of their supply problems, were forced to follow the tracks and roads. The Ashanti blocked the roads with massive barricades of tree trunks and hid in the surrounding forest.

The first "relief" column arrived at Kumasi, after tremendous fighting, with more than half its 250 men wounded. It did not receive a rapturous welcome, for it brought no supplies with it and practically no ammunition. In fact, there were now extra mouths to feed, and a great strain was put on the precious medical supplies.

The Ashanti had given up attempts to storm the fort, with its well-placed machine guns, and settled down to starve the garrison out. Nerves among the defenders were tautly stretched. There was no doubt of their fate if they became too enfeebled to defend. There was no sign of a major relief column. At night the drums of the Ashanti beat out fearsome and ominous messages; some British officers attempted to keep up their spirits by retaliating with a record of "Rule Britannia" on a gramophone. Rations inexorably diminished. After a month most were living on a small portion of canned beef and one biscuit a day. The refugees huddling round the walls were in a pitiable condition. Negotiations were opened with the besiegers, who demanded the departure of all the white men to the coast and a promise to leave the Ashanti alone forever—an argument that got nowhere.

Another "relief" column arrived. It brought no supplies either and was even more disastrous than the previous "relief." After six weeks, deaths from malnutrition and disease numbered more than twenty a day. Survivors fought for scraps of

rotting food and roots. Sir Frederic and Lady Hodgson gave
whist parties for the officers, but on occasion Lady Hodgson's
attempts at gay unconcern ended in outbursts of tears. Rumors
of impending relief occurred almost daily. Ears were attuned all
day for the sound of distant gunfire. Rockets were sent up, guns
fired almost vertically, messengers sent out to run the gauntlet
with promises of vast rewards if successful, but there were no
replies. Would relief never come?

In fact, the main relief column, under Colonel James Willcocks, had only just left the coast.

Hodgson and the officers decided there was only one thing
that remained: a breakout. Ninety troops, more sick than the
others, were to be left at the fort with twenty-five soldiers in
better condition, a doctor, and two English officers. They would
have enough rations to eke out their lives for perhaps another
three weeks; after that they were to destroy everything of value
and await their end.

After two months of siege, the escaping column formed at
dawn. Weak, terrified, driven by despair, they walked out
through the gates: some 600 troops, a dozen civilians, porters
and servants, and the governor and his wife. At first they were
successful. Only the early-morning calls of the forest greeted
them. But when they were discovered, a force of 1,500 Ashanti
was sent rushing down the track behind them. Progress, with
barricades in front and fighting in the rear, was a desperate
business. A way forward was forced only by deadly rushes. Occasionally, panic sent the rear charging through the column.
Despite confusion and heavy fighting, progress was somehow
made.

Lady Hodgson rocked about in a hammock, listening to the
sound of battle. "Sheer exhaustion gave me fitful dozes, but
always with dreams that the Ashanti were pursuing me. I woke
up to know that they were not without foundation, for could I
not hear the incessant beating of their drums." Her exhausted
carriers had to be changed every half hour, and eventually she
was obliged to walk. "How I managed to stumble along I cannot now understand." Supplies were virtually nonexistent. An
officer had saved a bottle of Bovril, a beverage, and shared it
with the Hodgsons. Two men died after drinking a bottle of
ammonia found in the luggage.

At last the column staggered into friendly territory. Hodgson took the salute of survivors of the march in a village square, then collapsed to the ground unconscious.

Colonel Willcocks' relief column was still pushing forward, on a different route, to Kumasi. Ambushed and halted by formidable obstructions, it was learning of the fighting qualities of the Ashanti. There was great anxiety about the fate of the remaining defenders of the fort. That they should be rescued was a point of honor, a matter of loyalty which impressed the Ashanti. A message got back at last: "Governor broke out seventeen days ago. Remaining garrison rapidly diminishing, disease, etc. Can only last out few more days on very reduced rations. Help us."

Willcocks telegraphed Whitehall: "I will personally relieve Kumasi . . . under any circumstances." With 64 white officers and NCO's, 1,000 troops and 1,600 porters, he plunged into the thick belt of forest before Kumasi, where the main enemy army was known to be lying in wait.

In the fort, men lay at their emplacements, never raising themselves from their machine guns or rifles. Almost every day someone died. There was no strength for proper burial, so the gates were carefully eased open at dusk and bodies were rolled outside. The officers had given up hope of relief, "but we kept up an appearance of cheerfulness for the sake of the men, who bore their sufferings with the greatest fortitude." They heard that the escaping column had been annihilated. Smallpox broke out. It was decided that they would make a dash for safety, every man for himself, and the officers equipped themselves with poison. When distant firing was heard, it was not at first believed to be the relief; so many previous hopes had been unfulfilled. Then, "at 4:30 in the afternoon we heard terrific firing, which removed any doubt we had, and after opening a pint bottle of champagne—one of our few remaining medical comforts—we mounted the look-out, field-glasses in hand." Willcocks' force, utterly exhausted from forced marches, had reached the surrounding stockades and forced a way through them. Two buglers stood on the walls of the fort and announced that the relief was not too late.

It was the end of the siege of Kumasi, but not of the fighting. Sporadic ambushes and battles occurred as British columns penetrated the country. When peace moves were made, there was no mention of the Golden Stool. Willcocks received the

KCMG and was given the freedom of the City of London (by the First World War he was a general but resigned after a row with Douglas Haig).

Before returning to England, Sir Frederic Hodgson held a garden party at his official residence in Accra. Kings and chiefs, with a restricted number of their ministers and families, who had remained friendly during the war were entertained on the lawn with European delicacies. Africans watched curiously as the British played tennis and croquet. Trays of claret were served; one of the kings politely remarked it was a splendid drink for a hot day. "It was a great success and quite an interesting event," said Lady Hodgson. "A number of interpreters were also present so that the guests could converse easily with the Europeans and others. The kings and chiefs wore their most gaudy robes." A group picture was taken by a local photographer.

It was, perhaps, the last official photograph to be taken in that era of British rule in Africa. For a greater war had broken out in the south. The confidence of the British, which had marked the last half century in Africa, was being rudely shaken. And things in British Africa were never to be the same again.

✤ XI ✤

On to Pretoria

THE gold mines of the Witwatersrand, in operation now for a decade, had brought much wealth to a few people; they had brought discontent to many. Kruger was as adamant as ever: The *Uitlanders* were too many and too foreign to have the franchise. Rhodes and the Consolidated Gold Fields of South Africa Ltd. were as adamant as ever: The mines were too rich to be left to the mercies of an ill-run rural state. The pioneers in Mashonaland and Matebeleland were finding the promised fields of gold in those areas disappointing. Kruger had watched Rhodes' expansion north with alarm, for his Transvaal was being almost encircled by British territory. Seeing the danger, he arranged for an independent railway line to be built to the coast—through Portuguese territory.

The *Uitlanders* in thriving Johannesburg were busy making money and contriving fortunes. They had little time for politics, but there are always some politically minded men in any community. A reform committee was organized, consisting of fifty-one British or South Africans, eight Americans, two Germans, one Australian, one Swiss, one Dutch, one Turk, and one Afrikaner. They complained of judicial, religious, language, and civil service matters. Kruger and the vast majority of his countrymen were not impressed, for they and their forefathers had carved out the country against British, Zulu, Swazi, and Matabele, while the others were newcomers—"outlanders"— who could not and should not expect full rights. Only a few Afrikaner burghers, depressed by an influx of Dutch and German immigrants taking the best posts, were dissatisfied with Kruger's firm, fundamental, Biblical approach to politics.

In numbers, the *Uitlanders* of Johannesburg were powerful. Perhaps an armed rising, with help from Rhodesia, was the answer.

The Colonial Secretary was the monocled Joseph Chamberlain. The onetime radical mayor of Birmingham, he had become obsessed by the mystique of Empire. He believed a close-knit Empire would keep Britain predominant in the world and ensure peace. Lord Salisbury had given Chamberlain complete freedom of choice in his Cabinet and had rather expected him to take the Home Office, for which he seemed ideally suited. Chamberlain had asked for the Colonial Office, not one of the major positions of power, "in the hope of furthering closer union between them and the United Kingdom." When he heard of a possible rising in the Transvaal, it did not appear to him a bad thing, as he concluded that it might bring South Africa and Britain closer together. What he did not seem to know was that the agitators in Johannesburg were more interested in founding a new republic than in providing a new colony. "If the rising is successful," he wrote, "it ought to turn to our advantage."

Some of the initial plans had been hatched in Rhodes' house at Cape Town. Rhodes was still Prime Minister of the Cape and in a delicate position. His judgment, always courageous, had never been faultless. Realizing he could not take a leading part, he delegated authority to various men, none of whom had much influence over the others. Jameson raised a force from Rhodesia and Mafeking to ride into the Transvaal to support the *Uitlanders,* who received cases of arms and ammunition with which they planned to seize the arsenal in Pretoria and to declare a republic loosely attached to Britain. Rhodes' brother Frank was one of the leaders. Did he have enough men? "Lots, my dear fellow." But as the day drew near, the *Uitlanders'* nerve seemed to desert them. Frank Rhodes telegraphed Jameson asking him to postpone "the polo tournament." But Jameson could not keep his men or the secret indefinitely. He was supremely confident that all would be well. Then he received a telegram from his brother Sam, in Johannesburg: ABSOLUTELY NECESSARY TO POSTPONE FLOTATION. The rebel leaders were not getting the expected support in Johannesburg.

Soon after sunset on December 29, 1895, Jameson, the peren-
nial optimist, crossed the Bechuanaland-Transvaal frontier with
mounted force of 356 men. They were joined by 122 men
rom Mafeking. The column had one field gun and half a dozen
machine guns, and it was under the nominal command of Sir
ohn Willoughby. Johannesburg was 180 miles away. The at-
empt to take the Transvaal from Kruger and his stolid Boers
nd burghers had begun with quite unusual inefficiency and
muddle and ridiculous overconfidence. Only one man could
ave stopped it. Rhodes, hearing that the *Uitlanders* were
osing their nerve, had wired Jameson: ON NO ACCOUNT WHAT-
VER MUST YOU MOVE. It was too late; the line was cut.

Hearing that Jameson's force had entered the Transvaal,
Rhodes immediately realized the catastrophe in which he had
nmeshed himself. "I will take the blame," he said, "but I am
uined." To another visitor that day, he said: "Yes, yes, it is
rue. Old Jameson has upset my apple-cart. . . . Poor old
ameson. Twenty years we have been friends, and now he goes
1 and ruins me."

Still trotting in to the Transvaal, Jameson's column was met
y several messages begging it to return: from the Prime Minis-
er of the Orange Free State, from the high commissioner in
!ape Town, from the British agent in Pretoria. Soon it was
red on from a distance, and one man was wounded. The in-
aders started to drink from the liberal quantities of liquor in
heir saddlebags. No force came from Johannesburg to meet
hem, only two bicyclists. Then they came to a strong line of
.frikaner defenses under Piet Cronje. Willoughby gave orders
or a frontal attack, was easily repulsed, then tried a flanking
movement and got the column cut off in the rear. Jameson sent
message into the town: "I am getting on all right, but you
ust send out some men to meet me." Frank Rhodes said later:
I do not think we were in a position to send them anything
hat would have been of very much service to them."

Having been maneuvered into a hopeless position by Wil-
oughby and nearly run out of ammunition, the raiders had no
hoice but to surrender. At 9:15 A.M. on January 2 someone
aised a white cloth overhead.

All raiders and leading rebels were imprisoned in Pretoria.
'he sixty-three rebels, worth about £50,000,000 among them,
ound themselves sleeping on straw in a corrugated-iron build-

ing. Thirty-five of them were in one cell 22 feet by 14½ feet
and one committed suicide. They were visited by Mark Twain
who happened to be in Pretoria. He told them that prison life
was "in many respects an ideal existence—healthy, undisturbed
plenty of repose, no fatigue, no distraction." Despite this com
fort, all were glad to be eventually released. Jameson and th
raiders were transferred to the British and sent to London fo
trial, for Kruger realized that nothing would be achieved b
twisting the lion's tail to the point of violent anger. There wa
much sympathy in Britain for the raiders, and there was ever
more when the Kaiser, the current ogre in English eyes, cor
veyed to Kruger "my sincere congratulation." The *Times* le
opinion in favor of Jameson and Rhodes.

Rhodes resigned as Prime Minister. To get away from vis
tors, he wandered alone on Table Mountain. The fiasco ha
cost him about £400,000 and spelled the end of his politic;
career. His only hope was to save his precious chartered con
pany in the north. "Now that I am down," he said, "I shall se
who are my real friends." He found he had none. A committe
of the Cape Parliament denounced him. Jameson and Wi
loughby were sentenced to short terms of imprisonment. Char
berlain, who laid on much whitewash for others, as well
himself, was later cleared. Rhodes decided to go to London, to
to face the music, but he did not, after all, shoulder the blam
Jameson, he said, had left without his "knowledge or consent
Rhodes burst onto the scene in London in a masterful moo
Existing on a diet of porter and sandwiches, he salvaged f
himself as much as could be expected. At a parliamentary sele
committee he was haughty, cultivating a picture of a coloss
above the petty riffraff, but this façade sometimes gave way ar
all accounts agree, that he was a man who was ill at ease. Wh
about written evidence? "I never write letters," he said, lofti
To the most persistent member of the inquiry, Sir Willia
Harcourt, he said: "Anyway, no one will ever name a count
after you."

Rhodes showed admirable loyalty to all those involved in t
raid. He found jobs for many and paid their bills. "Inundat
with claims for damages," he said. Jameson was given an imp
tant job on the telegraph with which Rhodes planned to cr
Africa from south to north. But from now on Rhodes was

private individual whose power once again rested on his wealth
alone, which, although damaged, was still considerable. By the
time he rejoined the chartered company board, its powers were
restricted.

The damage done by the raid was tremendous. All hopes of
an understanding between the Afrikaners and British were
dashed. For years Rhodes had been courting the Afrikaners in
all South Africa, and his efforts were now wasted. The Afrikaners had lost all trust in him they might have had. The
British had been shamed, and that, too, was dangerous. Reconciliation would have been a difficult task for the new high
commissioner, Sir Alfred Milner—if Sir Alfred had believed
reconciliation was the suitable attitude. Milner, an Aglo-
German from Hesse-Darmstadt, was considered something of a
genius by his contemporaries. At Oxford he had been "the
finest flower of culture that had been reared in the university of
that generation." He had worked well under Cromer in Egypt
and had later been head of the Inland Revenue in London; he
had been a very good tax collector, a fact which would have
impressed the Afrikaners less than the British. He was conscientious. He learned Afrikaans so that he could read the Pretoria
newspapers and studied the recent history of South Africa with
intelligence. A great believer in the Empire, he came to the
conclusion that the sooner Britain was master of all South
Africa, the better it would be for the inhabitants of whatever
nationality or color. Chamberlain was much inclined to agree.

The question was: Could Milner's policy be conducted peacefully? Since the Jameson Raid the answer was not difficult to
find. One young Cape Afrikaner, recently returned from a
brilliant career at Cambridge, a lawyer and a politician, wrote
of "that fatal and perfidious venture." He declared: "It became
so clear to me that the British connexion was harmful to S.A.'s
interests that I feared my future position as a Cape politician
would be a false one. I therefore left the old Colony for good."
He traveled to the Transvaal, where he soon offered his services
to Paul Kruger. His name was Jan Smuts.

When Rhodes returned to Africa, while waiting for the
inquiry, he went straight to Salisbury. The Matabele had risen.
With the Germans blocking the route north, in German East

Africa, it seemed as if fate had decided that he was to los₊
everything, even his precious Rhodesia.

Since the defeat of Lobengula, about 1,500 white people
about 600 of them women and children, had settled in Mata
beleland. The Matabele, who did not consider themselves de
feated, attacked outlying homesteads in February and March
1896. They had heard of the defeat of the British in th
Jameson Raid and were well aware that, because of the de
mands of the raid, the police force had been depleted. Hun₊
dreds of lonely families were overwhelmed and beaten an₊
chopped to death with sticks, axes, and spears. Two doctoᵣ
were among the first to be slain; one had just arrived froɴ
home with his bride, who when attacked fled into the bush bu₊
was caught and stoned to death. Soon 190 whites were dea₊
The people who had rebuilt Bulawayo into a European outpos
left the comparative safety of the town in armed parties t
rescue miners and farmers and their families still holding ou
Many were brought back to Bulawayo in that way.

Relief columns left from Salisbury with Rhodes and froᵣ
Bechuanaland led by regular British officers, among theᵣ
Major General Sir Frederick Carrington, Lieutenant Colon₊
Herbert Plumer, and Lieutenant Colonel Baden-Powell. Bade
Powell, who was chief of staff but who managed to get in som
scouting, described the campaign as "the happiest days of m
life." Once again the Matabele showed themselves no match f₊
the white men and were unable to use their firearms to muc
advantage. Rhodes, fearing the collapse of his life's work, foug
like a tiger. The Matabele retired to the rocky, almost impre₊
nable Matopo hills.

Then the Mashona people, hearing of the Matabele risin₊
also rose in revolt, taking the opportunity which they kne
might be their last to rid themselves of the busy intruders. Th₊
slaughtered well over 100 Europeans. But their effort, to₊
faded out against marksmanship and the machine gun.

Dressed, as always, in his old white trousers and his soft bus
hat, Rhodes himself conducted the peace talks with the Mat
bele. The chiefs were no match for him and had little to do b₊
yield. Rhodes' relief was tremendous. "One of those moments i
life that make it worth living," he said.

But the terror of the rising, the horror of the isolated mass

:res, left a legacy of distrust between the races and an intense
feeling of insecurity among the Europeans that would take
generations before it was erased.

The crisis in South Africa drew with appalling inevitability
oward war. Kruger, inspired by Majuba and confident of
German support, believed there might never be a better time to
establish independence from the British once and for all. Milner believed that "absolute downright determination plus a
large temporary increase of force will ensure a climb down"; if
not, "it would be better to fight now than five or ten years
hence." On June 8, 1899, Wolseley, commander in chief in
London, sent a secret memorandum to the Secretary of State for
War: "We should prepare for war." He had lost much of his
influence, carried absentmindedness to ridiculous lengths and
was physically frail. Wolseley had become a bit of an embarrassment, and his advice that war would require a much larger
army in South Africa went unheeded.

The commander in chief in the Cape was Wolseley's old
protégé, now General Sir William Butler. Butler was sixty-one,
tall, striking, genial man who still bore an Irish brogue. He
was one of the few in authority who believed that war in South
Africa was not only unnecessary but also avoidable. He made
his views known with considerable courage. There was, he said,
a plot to force war on the Transvaal," and for his pains he was
severely censured" by Milner. But Butler continued his warn-
ings. Africa, he said, did not need "a surgical operation." It was
no use. Butler resigned his command in protest at what he
believed was a calculated policy to wage cynical war against the
Transvaal.

The news of Butler's resignation was received with some joy
in the small outpost of Mafeking, on the vast, lonely length of
railway between Kimberley and Bulawayo. In command at
Mafeking was Baden-Powell. He had been sent by Wolseley to
patrol the Transvaal-Rhodesia border with a locally raised
force; the War Office, in its written orders, had only referred to
Mafeking as the place with "the nearest friendly force." Leaving Herbert Plumer to look after Rhodesia, Baden-Powell had
made straight for Mafeking. There he had prepared for siege
and filled the town with stores, despite explicit orders not to do

so from Butler, who foresaw the likelihood of having to mount a relief column. Money for the stores (£500,000) was provided by a note of hand from one of Baden-Powell's staff, Lord Edward Cecil, the Prime Minister's son. Cecil told the contractor: "I place this order with you without the authority of my superiors. I may have to pay for it myself, but I will take the responsibility on my own shoulders." Goods wagons chugged up the line from Cape Town and Kimberley loaded with supplies, stores, essentials, and luxuries of all kinds. Newspaper reporters sniffing news, also arrived. Africa had completely overtaken India in public interest.

On October 5 an Afrikaner force began concentrating in a number of camps on the Natal border near Kimberley and near Mafeking (both just across the border from the republics) Kruger, who was no fool, saw that the key to the coming campaign would be the railways. In the south, the important junction was Ladysmith; in the west, the long haul north began at Kimberley. Three days later Kruger issued an ultimatum demanding, among other things, the withdrawal of British forces, like Baden-Powell's, from near the border.

The jolting old black mail coach made its last journey from Mafeking to Johannesburg, baggage strapped on top, clattering out of the town in a cloud of dust. It did not return. Jameson headed for Ladysmith. Rhodes went up the line to Kimberley where the alarmed population, headed by the mayor, begged him to leave in fear his presence would act as bait to the Boers. On October 11, at five o'clock in the afternoon, Kruger's ultimatum became effective. The next day the telegraph line from Mafeking went dead. Two days later the line from Kimberley went suddenly silent while the commander of the small garrison, Lieutenant Colonel Robert G. Kekewich, was talking to GHQ in Cape Town. The Transvaal and the Orange Free State bound to it by treaty were at war with the British Empire—fewer than 100,000 people against nearly 500,000,000; 160,000 square miles against 15,000,000 square miles. It hardly seemed fair. It certainly would not take long.

Sir William Butler had predicted it all. In one of his last dispatches he had said: "Present policy, in my opinion, can only end, if persisted in, in producing a war of races—a conflict the ultimate consequences of which no one could adequately estimate. . . . I believe war between white races would be the

ON TO PRETORIA · 193

greatest calamity that ever occurred in South Africa." But no
one had wanted to hear.

The largest part of the Transvaal army had been assembling
near the Natal border. It seemed that the main Boer effort was
to be in the east. On the night of October 11 the Transvaal
army, 14,000 men under Commandant General Piet Joubert,
rode into Natal. "As far as the eye could see the plain was alive
with horsemen, guns and cattle, all steadily going forward to the
frontier." In the bitter cold they rode over the mountains that
formed a natural barrier between Natal and the Transvaal, then
down into the plains, past the looming presence of Majuba Hill.
To their astonishment, there was no opposition. Passes were
unmined; bridges were still standing; the railway was unsabo-
taged.

The British commander in Natal was yet another Anglo-
Irishman, General Sir George White, who had won the Victoria
Cross in the Second Afghan War. He had only just arrived in
Africa and knew little of the Afrikaners or of the conditions.
After two weeks of skirmishing and fierce little engagements,
about a quarter of the colony of Natal and 100 miles of railway
were in Afrikaner hands. Five small actions had been fought; in
none of them had the British been able to inflict a decisive
defeat, and in one of them they had suffered a humiliating
reverse. White had concentrated his force, about 12,000 strong,
at Ladysmith. There he was soon besieged.

A great army corps was hurriedly assembled in England. The
thought of Ladysmith, Kimberley, or Mafeking actually falling
to the enemy irregulars, who did not even wear uniforms, was
appalling. Grimy stokers sweated away in the transports speeding the arrival to South Africa of the invincible "Soldiers of the
Queen," who would soon correct the situation. In one of them
was the old "Wolseleyite," General Sir Redvers Buller, who was
to take up the South Africa command; he would explain the
real business of war to the cheeky Afrikaners. A cartoon in
Punch depicted one urchin confiding to another, "The Boers'll
up it now. Farver's gone to South Africa, *an' tooken 'is strap.*"

While the British ponderously brought their military machine into operation, the enemy forces continued to laze around
Ladysmith, Kimberley, and Mafeking without doing anything
particularly offensive. It was as if they were hypnotized by their

potential prizes. Natal and Cape Colony, virtually defenseless, waited to be raped. Afrikaner sympathizers in the Cape waited to rise. Every day the British reinforcements got nearer. And still the Boers did nothing.

The ships that the government had chartered to transport the troops were old and slow. The crowded soldiers, some of whom had never before been out of England, suffered agonies of seasickness. Of the 50,000 men being sent out, only 5,600 were cavalry, although it was well known that virtually all the Afrikaners were mounted. But the army was felt to be of such quality that it would overcome all. One observer of the embarkation commented: "The troops were of splendid physique a large proportion being reservists; their conduct was sober steady and irreproachable." As the world-famous Brigade of Guards marched through the London streets to Waterloo Station, it was cheered all the way, according to the *Daily Mail*' report:

> The Guards were literally fighting their way through. Women hung sobbing to the arms of husbands and sweethearts; relatives and even total strangers, carried away by the enthusiasm, broke into the ranks and insisted on carrying rifles, kitbags. . . . The chorus of cheers seemed never-ending, and at Waterloo all semblance of military order had disappeared. The police were swept aside and the men were borne, in many cases shoulder high, to the entraining platform, while others struggled through in single file.

Said the queen of her departing soldiers: "Quite a lump in my throat." Jingoism was at its height, and the war had given it an outlet through which it burst. The country was drunk with the idea of empire; the word "imperial" was uttered with pride and frequency, mingled with constant comparisons with the Romans. The British had not had their Empire long, and they were not going to let a lot of killjoy Boers upset it. It would not do in other places—especially India—if the word got about that few thousand armed farmers could shake the British lion.

On arrival at South Africa, the forces split. The majority under Buller, went to Natal to relieve White at Ladysmith. The remainder, under Lieutenant General Lord Methuen, disembarked at Cape Town. Their task was the relief of Kimberley and Mafeking. When this was done, the two armies would converge on Pretoria and the war would be over.

The relief of Kimberley seemed an urgent matter. Rhodes had been getting messages out of the town indicating that it was on the verge of surrender or being taken. These conflicted with the ambiguous reports from Kekewich, but after all, Rhodes was the most famous man on the continent, an ex-Prime Minister, a member of the privy council, and he presumably knew what he was talking about. "Boers oozing around on every side," Rhodes told Milner. He urged an immediate relief, "otherwise terrible disaster." By contacting the Rothschilds in London, he was able to exert pressure on the Cabinet. There was genuine alarm, for it was rumored that if Rhodes was captured, the Boers were going to parade him through the streets of Pretoria in a lion's cage. Moreover, Kimberley was the richest few square miles in the world. The capture of so famous an imperialist as Rhodes and the loss of the mines would be an almost unthinkable humiliation.

In fact, Rhodes had grossly exaggerated the situation, evidently in an attempt to get the route from the Cape reopened to his beloved Rhodesia, for which he feared. Enemy bombardment of Kimberley had done little damage, there were few shortages, and no attempt had been made to rush the town. Rhodes detested the restrictions of siege life, was in very bad humor, and blandly ignored all military regulations imposed by Kekewich. He managed to get a message through to Baden-Powell, at Mafeking, urging him to make use of similar exaggerations: "Do not be foolhardy and pretend you can hold out for months. My theory is, if you make out you are all right they will not bother." Baden-Powell ignored the advice. He sent back cheery reports about the real state of affairs, which were almost farcical. As at Kimberley, the Afrikaner gunners were so reluctant to get their guns to close range and their ammunition was so faulty that bombardment was a kind of game. There, too, they waited for the town to surrender itself, without rushing it, and with Cecil's huge stocks of food, they would have a long wait. Baden-Powell got messages out fairly easily. The first read: "All well. Four hours' bombardment. One dog killed. Baden-Powell." The public loved it. It was so obviously a masterpiece of the understatement and "pluck" and "grit" for which the British believed, with some justification, they were so renowned. Who was this man Baden-Powell? Soon he was the hero of the war.

Baden-Powell was not a bellicose kind of soldier. He was a gentle man and no mean artist. He designed currency for use in the town and issued stamps with his own portrait. His advice to the civilians was: "Sit tight and wait for them to go." For the troops, he said: "We only have to sit it out." (After the siege, however, he declared: "We acted as much as possible on the principle that aggression is the soul of defence.") It could have been worse. Food was in plentiful supply except for the Africans. Baden-Powell was glad to entertain the captive audience with his sketches and party songs, including his favorite, a fluttering soprano and a frenetic concert pianist.

Lord Methuen was forty-four years old, and for one of his high rank, his experience of war was minimal. He was schooled in traditional methods, and he relied implicitly on the invincibility of British infantry. He had assembled his force, about 8,000 men, some 65 miles south of Kimberley. His plan was to march up the railway; in fact, he could do little else because a deviation would require a vast convoy of wagons and mounted men. The Boers appreciated his difficulties and selected advantageous ridges on the way, at which they intended to delay him.

Under a hot sun, Methuen's column covered the first 20 miles in two days. On far-off hills, Afrikaner scouts shadowed the column as it progressed across the grassy veld. The shrill shrieks of command drifted across the plain, and sometimes whistling and singing could be heard. It was a magnificent spectacle: the row upon row of dun-colored helmets steadily advancing, rifles and brasswork gleaming through the risen dust. "The pure, invigorating air," said one account, "and the absence of all obstacles except an occasional wire fence, with the consequent width of front available, contributed alike to compactness of column and to steady brisk progress. The men stepped out well." A steep escarpment soon blocked the way, and the enemy was seen on top. Lord Methuen was asked whether he would go around it. "My dear fellow," he said, "I intend to put the fear of God into these people." The ridge was taken by a frontal rush—but not before 291 had been killed or wounded.

Lord Methuen allowed his troops only twenty-four hours rest. If Kimberley was to be relieved in time, there was not a moment to wait. At the next considerable ridge of hills the Afrikaners were in position again. The troops and Lord Methuen were undismayed. When told they were to lead the assault next morning, the officers of one detachment rejoiced. "Is it really true, sir?" asked a company sergeant, who was "radiant with anticipation. . . . Everyone felt a sense of subdued joy and satisfaction." The next morning the leading troops were terribly mauled as they crossed the open plain in full view of the enemy sharpshooters above, and as they stumbled up the slopes, nearly 50 percent were either killed or wounded. The queen sent her "congratulations on their gallant conduct" and expressed her "regret" at the losses sustained. The column, not surprisingly, had lost some confidence in both itself and in its leader. Although both battles had been successful, they had been singularly bloody and "close run." That night a finger of light, far away, was seen to be stabbing the sky. It was the searchlight at Kimberley, beckoning the relief on.

The next barrier was the Modder River. There Methuen at last tried a turning movement, left his command post, and splashed about in the water directing his troops. He lost control of the battle, but the next morning the Afrikaners, who had experienced a bayonet charge from Scottish infantry, were discovered to have left the field. On this occasion the casualties were 483. Methuen had now lost about one-seventh of his original strength.

Chastened and battered, the column plodded on, marching indomitably across the plain, stumbling through warfare it did not really understand, but still convinced of its invincibility. It had been reinforced. The Highland Brigade, perhaps the most famous in the British army, had arrived, and it contained such regiments as the Black Watch, the Gordon Highlanders, the Seaforth Highlanders, and the Highland Light Infantry. Two of the most illustrious brigades in the world, the Guards and the Highland, were now combined in the attempt to relieve "the diamond city."

Methuen studied the land before him. Five miles ahead the railway disappeared among the Magersfontein Hills. There, as Kekewich had warned, the Boers would stand. Methuen decided to soften the ridge with a great artillery barrage and then advance at night. This time there was to be no mistake. The Highland Brigade would storm the heights.

The brigade formed up in light drizzle at about midnight. To cracks of lightning and the mumble of thunder, it advanced slowly, kept in close formation by men on the outside holding ropes. Its commander was Major General Andy Wauchope, a Scottish hero with political ambitions (at one election he had challenged Gladstone himself and had surprised the nation by the size of his vote. At another he had nearly caused an upset at a supposedly safe Liberal seat). At about 4 A.M. the heights of Magersfontein could be made out, looming ahead. There was a shattering roar of rifle fire. The Highlanders fell, turned about or charged blindly ahead. There was consternation, which quickly turned to panic. The enemy were not on the top of the hill at all. Under the direction of a brilliant amateur, Koos de la Rey, they had entrenched at the foot of the hill. De la Rey had realized that, apart from the surprise, it was more effective to shoot straight than downhill. Wauchope was one of the few who kept his head. "Gather round, Black Watch," he shouted, "it's not my fault." But it was no use; the stampede for the rear had begun. It was worse than Majuba. Wauchope fell dying, muttering: "What a pity." The colonel of the Highland Light Infantry was trampled underfoot by his own men. The terror grew. The Highland Brigade, as one of them later put it, was "like a flock of sheep running for dear life."

The sun rose, the sky cleared, and the rain ceased. The British column lay out all day under a remorseless sun, under heavy fire. Methuen, nonplussed, did nothing effective. The next day the column, mumbling, wretched, angry, streamed back to the Modder River in considerable disorder. They are among the most ignominious hours in British military history.

In Natal, Buller had also been defeated. A young Afrikaner commander, Louis Botha, had successfully disputed the crossing of the Tugela River at Colenso. Buller had shown his usual personal bravery, but his army had been bloodily repulsed. "A very trying day," he said.

These defeats were known as Black Week. Back home, there was a feeling of deep national humiliation. Something had gone terribly wrong. How could the imperial might of Britain, all those proud and fine young men, be so casually thrust aside by the bearded, untidy-looking Boers? The prestige of the government was at stake. Buller was replaced as commander in chief by Field Marshal Lord Roberts of Kandahar. Kitchener was to dash from Cairo, via Gibraltar, to be chief of staff (he joined a Cape ship at "Gib" eight days after leaving his Cairo residency). The dispatch of this formidable pair was what Queen

Victoria had urged from the start. Also bound for South Africa was Hector Macdonald, the redoubtable "Fighting Mac." Roberts—an Irishman, it goes almost without saying—was the most respected and loved soldier in the army. For years he had been Wolseley's great rival. Whereas Wolseley was an "Africa man," Roberts had spent nearly his entire career in India. "Bobs," as he was known, received his appointment in London on the same day as he heard of the death of his only son at Colenso. The Secretary of State for War himself conveyed the news: "The blow was almost more than he could bear, and for a moment I thought he would break down, but he pulled himself together." Roberts was seen off at Southampton by a large, silent crowd, many dressed in mourning. Unsmiling, dwarfed by the many dignitaries around him, the little man with the dark, leathery face raised his hat and walked briskly up the gangway. It was a cold, gray winter's day. As the ship moved off, the trim field marshal, a piercingly unhappy figure, could be seen pacing the deck on his own. With him went the hopes and reputation of all those who cherished the British Empire.

It was the Christmas season, and the British had a traditional need for finishing their wars in time for Christmas, with all its protestations of peace and goodwill. On the Modder River, Lord Methuen's men, waiting for "Bobs," enjoyed extra rations and energetically pursued the traditional celebrations. At Ladysmith, where White's 13,496 men were being placidly invested by less than half that number, there was considerable disease. On Christmas Day the Boers thoughtfully fired plum puddings into the town. In Mafeking, Baden-Powell ordered that Christmas would be celebrated on the nearest Sunday, since the enemy never fired on that day. In the same order, a native was sentenced to death for stealing food. So far casualties from bombardment in Mafeking had been fewer than a dozen. Rationing was still something of a joke. At the Mafeking Hotel there was a Christmas menu of twenty-eight items. At another hotel, "we [the guests] had quite a royal Christmas dinner. It included everything conceivable; we revelled in plenty." Baden-Powell himself partook of turkey, plum pudding, wine, and brandy and afterwards—a group photograph. In his official report of the siege, Baden-Powell wrote of "the entire absence of all luxuries." It was certainly very different from what the public at home imagined. Only the Africans, in their quarter of the town, were suffering. The local magistrate wrote: "I am considerably worried during all hours of the day by hungry Natives, who lean against the garden wall and stare at me, exclaiming at intervals—*Baaje hongore Baas;* at the same time the fact is demonstrated by the supplicant smiting with his hand the black, empty leather bag which represents his stomach. These people will soon be a source of anxiety to us. . . ."

At Kimberley, "numerous" plum puddings were distributed, the gifts of Rhodes. As in Ladysmith, the main trouble was sickness, especially among the Africans. Rationing was becoming somewhat more serious, although hardly severe; meat, sometimes horse, was down to 4 ounces a day, bread to 12 ounces. Rhodes was as restless as ever. The failure of Methuen to relieve the town, when having been only a few miles away (the battle at Magersfontein had been heard in Kimberley), had infuriated him. Explosive rows with Kekewich were frequent, and on one occasion Rhodes had attempted to strike the colonel in the face, missing him only through the intervention of the mayor. Rhodes' mind, however, was not confined to Kimberley, for he kept up business messages, with his private system of brave dispatch riders who broke through the loosely held enemy lines—"Pay De Beers debentures by first January"—and, of course, he never forgot his beloved railway and cable through Africa: GERMAN EMPEROR HAVING SIGNED AGREEMENT WITH ME CABLE HOME THEY MUST PROCEED TANGANYIKA WITH ALL DISPATCH. IF NOT WE SHALL BE IN OUR GRAVES BEFORE TELEGRAPH REACHES EGYPT.

When the Afrikaners began shelling more seriously, Rhodes exploded with rage. "Military men may make maps at the War Office; they may continue to evolve the most wonderful schemes and plans. . . . [But] is it unreasonable, when our women and children are being slaughtered and our buildings fired, to expect something better than that a large British Army should remain inactive in the presence of eight or ten thousand peasant soldiers?" Rhodes threatened that if something were not done soon, the town might surrender. His bluff worked. Kekewich, Methuen, and Roberts were horrified. Preparations to force the relief were hurried up. In fact, however, the shelling continued to do little damage, and there was no "slaughter." But infant mortality among the Africans was up to 93.5 percent and scurvy was rampant among them.

While Roberts and Kitchener prepared for the final push to Kimberley and to Bloemfontein, the capital of the Orange Free State, Buller was battering away at the approach to Ladysmith, when not doling out horns of champagne to his staff. The fall of Ladysmith, said the queen, was "too awful to contemplate." At the hill called Spion Kop, the British infantry, with unflinching courage, had reached the top, only to be ordered down again. This useless operation had cost 1,733 casualties—"a military crime," said Churchill. Redvers Buller was no match for Louis Botha, and the failures were due mostly to deficiencies in command. Buller tried again, and again he failed. In Ladysmith there were 708 enteric cases in hospital, and rations had become intolerably low. When at last Buller bludgeoned his way into Ladysmith, he left behind him, lying dead on the battlefields, some of the best troops in the British army; his casualties had been more than the entire enemy force opposing him. The first officer to ride into the town was Captain Hubert Gough. General Sir George White greeted him with controlled imperturbability in the main street: "Hello, Hubert, how are you?"

Roberts sent his cavalry on a vast flanking movement, rounding the Afrikaner army and relieving Kimberley. Poor Methuen watched the ease with which it was done with some discomfort, but he'd had hardly any cavalry. Rhodes held a fairly sumptuous reception for the relieving officers, including "all manner of luxuries" and, of course, plenty of champagne. Kekewich was not invited and was snubbed by Rhodes, and the colonel found himself on the carpet from his superiors.

"I have borne with this man as long as I could," he said.

"Yes, but you should remember that Mr. Rhodes, or this man, as you call him, owns the place and that he is a power not only in the Empire but in Europe, and you should have tried to work with him."

"I thought I was in supreme command."

Rhodes, who had detested the constraints Kekewich had tried to place on him, particularly censorship, had sworn he would ruin Kekewich's career. He had some success, for when Kekewich shot himself, in 1914, he had advanced only one more step in rank.*

---

* "Fighting Mac" also committed suicide, in 1903, when faced with allegations of homosexuality. After an interview with Edward VII, he blew his brains out in a Paris hotel.

After Kimberley, a force of 1,149 was sent north to relieve Mafeking, together with a posse of newspaper correspondents anxious to interview the by now world-famous Baden-Powell and see for themselves the plight of the town. Plumer, who had successfully defended Rhodesia, joined in the relief of the man who was meant to have done the task Plumer had carried out. When the relievers arrived, they entered the town at night with little difficulty and woke Baden-Powell in bed.

The relief of Mafeking was the most sensationally received item of news in the history of London. The whole metropolis went wild. There was an outbreak of mass hysteria never equaled before or since by the British people. Said the London *Times*: "From the Mansion House as far as the War Office there was a continuous roar of more or less articulate applause and an unbroken array of waving flags." The *Daily Telegraph* noted that "total strangers shook each other heartily by the hand." Theaters announced the news and audiences stood in uproar. Restaurants were in chaos. Women took shelter on the steps of gentlemen's clubs. The parks were crowded with fornicators. Trains progressed through the country with the whistles in constant shrill acclaim, waking villages with the news. The sky of Britain was alight with rockets and bonfires. The party, the greatest in British history, lasted for five days. Baden-Powell's picture was everywhere. He was the greatest British hero since Wellington and Nelson. Somehow he seemed to sum up the successful British defiance of the insufferably cheeky Boers: a strong, calm soldier with superb understatement. Frank Rhodes had got himself a place in the relief column, and he too was tremendously impressed at the sight of the famous "B-P": "I should say he is the best man the country has produced. He is very plucky, very quick, very slim."

Baden-Powell, surprised but gratified, wrote his report. He said he had been ordered to defend Mafeking and claimed he had been surrounded by 8,000 Boers (in his general orders at the start of the siege he had said "5,000 to 6,000"—the figure went up nearly every time he wrote of the siege, which was not infrequently, and eventually finished at "12,000"). It was too late for anyone to explain that the siege had been the most comfortable in all history. If Baden-Powell had tried to correct the misconception, no one would have believed him. Everyone was so grateful. The Boers would be beaten. Everything would be all right, after all.

Up till the relief of Mafeking, the great hero of the war had been a young newspaper correspondent, Winston Churchill, who had left the army and was being paid one of the highest rates in journalistic history. Churchill had been captured by the Afrikaners but had made a sensational escape, reaching Portuguese territory after a number of very genuinely daring and courageous adventures. "My name had resounded at home," he wrote. Now it was all Baden-Powell.

Kitchener and Roberts found the army that had been battering Methuen, now under Piet Cronje, the victor of the Jameson Raid, who had come from the investment of Mafeking. With 4,000 men, Cronje capitulated to Roberts on the anniversary of Majuba. "Glad to see you," the field marshal said. "You have made a gallant defense, sir." The somber, ponderous Cronje, in black coat and hat, looked down on the little Britisher and said nothing. He was transported to exile in St. Helena.

Roberts pushed his army hard as it plodded on to Bloemfontein. Three newspaper correspondents were first to enter the city, where they found the leading citizens in the town club and suggested that the mayor go out to meet Roberts. A few hours later "Bobs" rode into the capital at the head of his cavalry. He was greeted with flags and cheering, but the Free Staters had never been as anti-British as the Transvaalers. Lord Roberts produced a silk Union Jack that his wife had given him as a parting gift, with a small shamrock appropriately in one corner, and it was run up the flagpole. It was a strange war.

Pretoria remained. There was no lingering, for the enemy had 5,000 British prisoners of war around Pretoria. "Bobs" showed just how tough and demanding a commander he was. Soon 38,000 men were pushing unremittingly up the road for the Transvaal. Roberts dealt with attempts to stop him by flanking movements coupled with thrusts at the center, forcing the enemy to withdraw each time. He was warned about the length of his supply line, now 500 miles long, much of it thinly guarded. He pressed on.

Johannesburg welcomed him. Then his army set out over the rolling hills to Pretoria, while the enemy fled from the town eastward down the railway. Botha decided to evacuate and fight another day. Only De la Rey was left, with a small rear guard. Having marched the 300 miles from Bloemfontein in thirty-four days, advance parties of the British army moved into Pretoria on the evening of June 4, 1900. The next day a great parade was held in the city square, before the government buildings. Roberts and Kitchener saluted as Lady Roberts' flag was once more run up, followed by a two-hour march-past. Pretoria was the seat of power. The Afrikaners were surely finished for ever. Little "Bobs" had not let his country down.

Two months of battling and skirmishing down the railway to Portuguese East Africa remained, but Lord Roberts declared that the war was virtually over. The Transvaal was annexed to the crown. Kruger fled for Holland. The troops could begin to go home. "Lord Roberts telegraphs that war is over," Chamberlain told his wife. "Bobs" returned to England, where he received greater honors than any commander in chief since Wellington: the Garter (the most prized of all British awards) an earldom, and £100,000.

Kitchener took up command. When he had arrived in South Africa, he had said: "People here do not seem to look upon the war sufficiently seriously; they consider it too much like a game of polo with intervals for afternoon tea." He had been changing all that. He began work punctually each morning at six and had no leave and no recreation apart from riding and an occasional game of billiards after dinner. Once Roberts had gone, Kitchener concentrated on the problem of subduing the enemy, with complete dedication. But Kitchener had been fighting Europeans for the first time in his life, and he had not been making a thorough success of it. Botha, De la Rey, Smuts, and especially Christian De Wet, a brilliant field commander, were still free and roamed the country with Boer commandos, inflicting embarrassing defeats in skirmishes. Kitchener was a practical man who saw that the only way to combat the guerrillas was by cutting up the country into sections, using wire fences guarded by some 8,000 blockhouses, and then sweeping across each section. To this end he caused more than 3,000 miles of wire to be erected. Conscious of the enormous expense, Kitchener did his best to keep costs down, but his policy was partly responsible for an increase in the income tax at home. Innocent people caught in the net were herded into what were called concentration camps. Farms were burned, cattle moved away. "It is no longer real war," Kitchener said, with disgust, "but police operations of considerable magnitude to catch various bands of men who resist. . . . Like wild animals they have to be got into enclosures before they can be captured."

The policy was not entirely successful. Large groups of commandos kept on escaping. "Fighting Mac" himself let one commando escape. The principal leaders were not among those captured. De Wet and Smuts (with Kant's *Critique of Pure Reason* in his saddlebag) even turned up in Cape Colony. And the policy of burning and the concentration camps brought about much feeling against Kitchener, the army, the government, and in the end against the British (even though a large proportion of the population at home was vociferous in denouncing the strategy). Sir Henry Campbell-Bannerman, who had become leader of the Liberal Party in the year Gladstone had died, described the policy as one of "barbarism." The forty-six camps were hideous, and at one time the death rate in them averaged 34 percent. An Australian reporter wrote of "death through criminal neglect of the most simple laws of sanitation. . . . In some camps no latrines were dug, no supervision was exercised." Kitchener, who never saw one, said they were "very well run." He also said the death rate was due to the dirty habits of the Boers, a protestation which was not well received, as habits, in some circumstances, among a people not used to living close together, appear very different in totally different circumstances. The government pointed out that many Afrikaner children were for the first time receiving formal education; critics claimed that the education was being used for indoctrination.

In March, 1902, sporadic fighting still continued. Lord Methuen returned to the news, much to everyone's chagrin. His column was surprised. They panicked and fled, and Methuen was mercifully taken prisoner. Kitchener was appalled at the disgrace of a severe defeat and the capture of a general when the war was meant to be over. He collapsed and went to bed for thirty-six hours: "Gone all to pieces," he said.

But the Afrikaners could not continue much longer. All idea of outside help had faded. The bitter-enders, as they were called, had lost support among their own people. South Africa was sick of the war. Conscious of the unpopularity of the war, the government was anxious to conclude it. In April, Kruger's successor, Schalk Burger, met Kitchener, with President Martinus T. Steyn of the Orange Free State (who was still free), Botha, De Wet and De la Rey. The Afrikaners said they would grant concessions to the *Uitlanders,* but the republics must remain independent. A month later the parties met at Vereeniging. But Kitchener and Milner would not budge. Kitchener explained that in a few years a Liberal government was certain to be elected in Britain, and then the Afrikaners would surely get all, or nearly all, they wished. It seemed sensible advice. At the last election, the first and last to be fought primarily over the Empire in Africa, known as the khaki election, pro-Boer feeling had been loudly expressed, but The Conservatives had increased their majority by three seats. One young politician, David Lloyd George, had made his name by his support of the enemy, while another, Winston Churchill, twenty-six, just back from Africa, had been elected to the House of Commons as a Conservative. The main Afrikaner worry, as always, concerned the Africans. "They are much afraid of a native rising," Kitchener noted. The peace treaty was signed on May 31, 1902, at 10:30 P.M., on Kitchener's dining-room table in Pretoria. The Transvaal and the Orange Free State were incorporated in the British Empire, with a promise of eventual self-government. A grant of £2,000,000 was made toward the recovery of the wasted lands.

In less than four weeks Kitchener was on his way to Southampton. Thus ended one of the most unnecessary, tragic and useless wars in history—which is saying a great deal. About 400,000 British troops had been employed to fight far less than a quarter of that number. Loss of life might have been greater, but as Butler had predicted, ill effects could not.

The South African War has often been seen as a watershed in the history of the British Empire, and so it was. It showed conclusively that the British, despite attempts to prove otherwise, were hopelessly divided about their Empire. Disunited, they did not have sufficient strength for successful imperialism, and the patches of the imperial garment were starting to show.

But the British were by no means done for yet. Botha, De la Rey, and De Wet landed in England. A considerable crowd greeted them in London with streamers, flags, and cheers. Banners proclaimed GOOD OLD BOTHA and BRAVE SOLDIERS ALL.

The Afrikaner leaders looked out at the enthusiasm and friendliness with bemused expressions. They were, said a historian, "surprised."

The war had seen two other watersheds in the history of the Empire. The great queen had begun to weaken at last. Appropriately enough, Lord Roberts was the last commander she saw, and Joseph Chamberlain the last politician. Almost her last words had been: "What news is there from Lord Kitchener?" She had died, after thirty-eight years of pining widowhood and sixty-three years of a most conscientious reign. At her bedside had been her beloved grandson, Wilhelm, the Kaiser.

A year later, in March, 1902, Cecil Rhodes met the death he had so long been expecting. Forty-nine years old, he had, as he often pointed out, a country named after him, a suitably impressive will (which he had rewritten many times till finally perfected), and £4,000,000. His funeral was held in Cape Town Cathedral. His remains were then taken north on the railway he had cherished. For 750 miles the progress of the special train was "accompanied by all the outward and visible signs of mourning which as a rule are only to be witnessed on the burial days of kings." Groups of farmers stood bareheaded as the train steamed slowly past. At guardhouses, troops stood rigidly at present arms. At towns, local dignitaries stood on platforms as the train went by. It was not out of a sense of loss, for he was a man who had never been loved, but out of respect for the first man that Africa had produced who gained world renown. From Bulawayo, Rhodes was taken in an awed and silent procession to the resting place he had chosen, among the Matabele chiefs who had detested him, in the Matopo Hills.

With the end of the Victorian Age, the shock of defeats in the Boer War, and the death of the prime mover in the Cape-to-Cairo dream, the British Empire in Africa would never again have the same force and the same confidence.

Till the last, Rhodes had remained the spokesman of unrepentant imperialism. Near the end, he had said: "The world is nearly all parcelled out, and what there is left of it is being divided up, conquered and colonized. To think of these stars that you see overhead at night. . . . I would annex the planets if I could. I often think of that."

✦ XII ✦

The Proconsuls

THE twelve years between the South African War and the First World War were peaceful years of careful consolidation in British Africa. The worst of the colonial fighting was over, and from that time forward the great battles of the future were to be offshoots of conflicts in Europe. These were the years when the roads, the bridges, many of the railways, and the public buildings appeared—monuments to British rule—in what had been the "Dark Continent," some in places where white men had never been only a few years before. Natives of East Africa, who had never seen a white man till they were youths, were now porters at railway stations hundreds of miles inland. They were the years when Britain sent out its public servants to rule over vast areas and peoples, with great responsibilities and little encouragement—the years of the modern proconsuls. India had known such figures for years, and now an equally fine breed gave their careers to Africa. First of the modern school had been Milner and Cromer, but perhaps the greatest was Lugard.

Before the First World War, the European possessions in Africa were divided as follows:

France	..	..	3,867,000	square miles
Britain	..	..	3,701,000	" "
Germany	..	..	910,000	" "
Belgium	..	..	900,000	" "
Portugal	..	..	788,000	" "
Italy	..	..	200,000	" "
Spain	..	..	80,000	" "

Compared with the "claims" of the 1890's the three great powers had expanded at the expense of the lesser powers. But the map of Africa, which showed so much red at the end of the South African War, was not a little misleading. West Africa had lagged behind the south and Egypt and was being overtaken by the east. In areas claimed by Britain, few British ever visited, some were virtually unexplored, slavery was rampant, and in large tracts there was no British administration whatsoever. Nowhere did this apply more than in Nigeria.

It was Flora Shaw, the influential colonial editor of the London *Times,* who had first pressed for the word "Nigeria" to apply to the area (in an article in 1897). Mercifully the idea was adopted, in preference to "Goldesia"—after George Goldie. Goldie's Royal Niger Company had done much to open up the interior to trade, but it had found difficulty in warding off the attentions of the French, of whom the British government was still as perennially suspicious as were, say, the Ibo of the Yoruba. The government bought the company's administrative, territorial, and mineral rights and property for £865,000. Goldie said it was like a highwayman stripping his victim, as well as robbing him. The government gained a million square miles. Goldie could not be too displeased, for he had always said he had acted in Britain's name. Joseph Chamberlain, Colonial Secretary, was also somewhat constrained: He held £3,000 worth of the company's shares.

Nigeria now became three areas: two on the coast and the hinterland of Northern Nigeria. The split of responsibilities and esoteric differences in administration were as complicated and as finely drawn as only British civil servants could have devised. The governor of Northern Nigeria was to be Frederick Lugard, who had already been responsible for the deaths of many Africans in that area and also in Uganda and Nyasaland, on behalf of the chartered companies and in the quest for Empire.

Lugard was a gruff, gloomy little man of forty-one who sported an enormous walrus mustache on a small face. He was dedicated to the ideal of Empire and accepted the notion of the white man's burden. His appointment was virtually the end for Goldie, who had been trading with and developing the area for over twenty years, against considerable hostility from French and Germans. He boarded a slow boat to China.

Lugard knew that his new domain looked better on the map than it was in reality. Often acting on his own initiative, he set out to conquer the land that was nominally Britain's or being "protected" by Britain. At his little capital of Lokoja, a post near the confluence of the Benue and the Niger rivers, he read the royal proclamation. The company's flag was run down, the Union Jack run up. The governor spoke to the small assembly in the clearing that had been hacked from the bush: "Gentlemen, I do assure you that I enter on this task with a deep sense of responsibility, and of doubt of my worthiness for it, and though (as our greatest poet has said) it is not in us to command success, I shall at least endeavour to deserve it. . . . I trust that when the time comes for me to 'hand in my cheques' and look back on my tenure of this office, it may be said of me that to the extent of my ability I did my duty." The next morning he went to his humble wooden office and noted of his territory: "The greater part quite unexplored." It took vision to see such an expanse of "undeveloped" country as a great modern nation. This was the vision which men like Rhodes, Goldie, and Lugard had.

Economy was much in the government's mind, and Lugard had little money for his enormous task; his force of white soldiers and administrators was puny—fewer than 100 among 20,000,000 people. The climate was as notorious as ever. After fifteen months, Lugard went home for seven, at which time he got married. Flora Shaw, a close friend of Rhodes' and probably more than that to Goldie, had hoped to marry Goldie when his wife had died. Goldie had, in fact, received a letter from "an intimate woman friend" proposing marriage. Goldie, whose affairs were well known in society, had, rather surprisingly, not married Miss Shaw, who was one of the most talented and most intelligent women in London and who, at forty-six, was by no means ill-looking. She had many influential friends, including the Colonial Secretary. Miss Shaw settled for Lugard. Her ambition was "to endeavour to bring all the influences which I believe to be working for good in Africa into harmony with each other." She wrote to Lugard: "I hope you look upon our marriage as I look on it—and I think you do—that is, as a loyal friendship made absolute for life by the public tie with which we bind it." And later: "You once said you would win my *love*.

I, too, hope to win yours. . . . Let us be content to marry as friends."

When the couple left for the Niger, Flora had with her forty-six trunks and cases and a lady's maid. She found the life of a remote governor's lady, of which she gives a splendid picture, somewhat in contrast with the salons of London. It was a far cry from the busy social life, the receptions and local committees of the next generation of governors' ladies:

> The days as they pass at present are absolutely without incident. I wake between four and five. Early tea is brought at six. I send round to Fred's room to let him know that it has come. He comes in very sleepy to have a cup and then goes away to his office, where piles of papers await him. . . . At six Fred stops work. The sun then is just on the edge of setting and we go for a tearing walk in the dark, which gives us exercise. . . . After dinner there is an hour on the veranda and between ten and eleven we usually separate for the night. I have not yet managed to get myself really interested in local affairs and Fred's time and thoughts are necessarily almost wholly involved in them, so that for the moment I feel somewhat dull and depressed and have lots of time to miss you all very badly. But I have no doubt that will pass. I shall gradually be able to feel that all these strange things are my concern and to settle down to some sort of enjoyment of the life itself. I have begun today to organize some little improvements in Government House garden, which is at present merely a cleared enclosure. The black labourers are absurd, just like a crowd of children. . . . Some of the civilian staff are hardly perhaps what we would call gentlemen. . . . Books will, I expect, give me my principal companionship.

With Flora at his side, Lugard's approach became more vigorous. The two great cities of his province were Kano and Sokoto. Hardly a white man had visited them since Clapperton three-quarters of a century before. Lugard resolved to establish British claims to "protection." The ruler of Sokoto did not think Lugard's intention was a good idea: "From us to you. I do not consent that any one from you should ever dwell with us. I will never agree with you. I will have nothing whatever to do with you." It could hardly have been more clear. Lugard believed that treaty obligations overrode all other considerations, that they were a matter of honor; the emirs believed that

treaties were white men's nonsense and, anyway, virtually in-
comprehensible. Slavery continued in Sokoto. France wanted to
establish where *exactly* the borders were, but no one could tell
until the places had been seen. The government expressed its
"regret" at the impending action, and Lugard went ahead. His
force of 722 African troops, 36 British, and four machine guns
went off to do battle with some thousands. There might have
been a disaster, but, as Hilaire Belloc pointed out:

> Whatever happens we have got
> The maxim-gun and they have not.

The Nigerian War was a nasty one, but it was quickly over.
The African troops displayed the loyalty and endurance that
had already impressed the British officers in Ashanti campaigns.
"Never served with finer fellows," said one officer. "How I love
them! Rippers!!" It was all over in less than two months.
Lugard did not enjoy it, but he did his duty as he saw it. "What
idiots we little mortals are," he wrote to Flora from camp. "As
though life were not short enough but we must hack each other
to death as well." The dying Africans would doubtless have
agreed. After the occupation of Kano, only one death was reported. A soldier had killed a civilian and was later court-mar-
tialed and condemned to death. "I directed," said Lugard, "that
some of the chiefs of Kano should witness this vindication of
British justice." The offending soldier was machine-gunned to
death sitting on an empty crate. Sokoto fell soon afterward, and
British officers walked around the battlefield chopping off legs
and arms with gold bracelets.

Four years of hard administrative work followed, and gradually Nigeria's three sectors became developed. Lugard evolved
the system of indirect rule—typical of the British Empire—
which became a characteristic of British rule in Africa. By it,
Britain ruled through the native chiefs and kings, who were
"advised" by residents and commissioners from Edinburgh to
Tunbridge Wells, from Bath to Felixstowe—instead of ruling
directly. It was little more than an adjustment of the system
already existing in much of India under the raj. It was a system
which was critized then and since as having corrupted or un-
necessarily prolonged systems, but in fact, it came about as

much from necessity as from design. Britain was either unwilling or unable to provide anything like enough administrators for direct rule. It may not have been entirely in the best interests of the Africans in the long run, but it was practical, and by and large it did not work badly.

In 1907 Lugard was succeeded by the Canadian Sir Percy Gitouard, son of a Quebec judge. In the same year it was decided to build a railway from Kano to the coast, a colossal undertaking. Sir Percy, who had started his career in the Royal Engineers, had built the railway to Khartoum and had extended the South African network. The inhabitants of Southern Nigeria had been influenced longer by Europe, and Christianity had gained much ground. In the north the influence had been Arab and Moslem. There was strong tribal distrust in all areas. But it was hoped that the railway would weld together this country which had been cut out of Africa irrespective of natural barriers of race and terrain. In 1914 the areas of Nigeria were united under one government, ten years after the union had been first proposed. It was a fateful decision. Lugard was recalled to run the new colony.

In the Gold Coast, the crushing of the Ashanti had begun a new era. A railway was begun to Kumasi. Engineers and laborers sweated up the route along which Wolseley's and successive armies had fought only a few years before. In 1903, only three years after the siege, trains from Kumasi Station were rumbling down to the coast. Trade with Ashanti revived immediately, and soon it was greater than ever before. Under a succession of governors, progress was made in sanitation, education, and health.

The main African crisis of this period concerned Morocco. The so-called Moroccan Empire had been collapsing, and France, Britain, and Spain had agreed on a dissection as soon as death ensued. The Kaiser, objecting to Anglo-French collusion, stepped in, thus strengthening the new Anglo-French Entente. Germany next tried a show of strength, in 1911, and sent a gunboat to the Moroccan port of Agadir. The British government was outraged by this flaunting of her naval superiority, so near to Gibraltar and her trade routes. There was much foolish talk of war. The matter was settled when the French gave up some land to Germany elsewhere. France remained in control of most of Morocco, and Germany was more than ever the potential enemy instead of the old friend.

In Egypt, as in West Africa, these were years of progress. In 1901 Cromer was able to report to the Foreign Office: "The foundations on which the well-being and material prosperity of a civilized community should rest have been laid. . . . The institution of slavery is virtually defunct. . . . Law and order everywhere reign supreme." This situation was largely due to Cromer's unglamorous but patient and dedicated hard work over many years. Arabi Pasha, whom Wolseley had defeated at Tel el Kebir in 1882, was allowed to return from Ceylon, where he had been in exile. The Sudan was being firmly controlled by Sir Francis Reginald Wingate (governor general, 1899–1916). Things were not as perfect as Cromer had indicated, and there was always an undercurrent of fervent nationalism, but by and large Egypt was enjoying greater prosperity than it had known for centuries. Cromer's greatest achievements were in finance (he had found the country bankrupt), in improving the lot of the peasantry, and in fighting corruption. His long term of office ended when he resigned in 1907, after twenty-four years in Egypt. He had done more for that unfortuante country than any man since the pharaohs. The Foreign Secretary said of the occasion: "The greatest personal loss which the public service of this country could suffer." One of his successors was that old Nile man Herbert Kitchener, who ruled Egypt from 1911 to 1914.

Cromer retired in a haze of glory, for Egypt not only was fairly peaceful, but was also paying its way. The ideal colony or protectorate to London was one which was self-supporting. The leading question about any territory was always: How soon can it pay for itself? The white man's burden was best when it did not cost too much. The administrators had to show a flair for finance. Cromer had come from a famous banking family, but not all were so fortunate. One difficulty was that the Europe of the time had little use for the available African exports, and this problem had dogged all efforts since the end of the slave trade. Sir Harry Johnston had been running Nyasaland on £10,000 a year plus his own salary. He could just afford seventy-five African soldiers and one British officer (even this had been thanks to Rhodes). But at the beginning of the century Nyasaland's grant had increased to £100,000. Nigeria was getting a great deal more, while Uganda received a grant of £400,000. But by 1914 the grants were tapering off again. There was great rivalry between the European powers to see whose colonies were paying their way; the least successful—*i.e.*, the most expensive—by 1914 were said to be Germany's.

The most quickly developing colony in Africa, in the early years of the century, was British East Africa (Kenya). The completion of the railway to Victoria Nyanza, at a cost of £5,-331,000 to the British taxpayers, transformed the country. When the railway had reached the high plateaus, it was discovered that there were large areas of pleasant, cultivable land, in an equable climate, ideally suited to European colonization. There were few whites in the colony other than railway engineers, administrators, and missionaries. News of the Mount Kenya highlands reached Britain, and in 1903 settlers began to arrive. Among the first on the scene were impoverished farmers from South Africa, who were soon followed by a group of aristocrats from England, led by Lord Delamere. He was followed by Lord Cardross, Lord and Lady Cranworth, Lord Francis Scott, the Earl of Portsmouth (350,000 acres), and Lord Wodehouse. There was a hard core of men who had known one another at Eton. From these earliest days the settlement of Kenya took on a character quite different from any other colony in Africa: exclusive, snobbish, gay, upper-class. Blue blood, however, did not necessarily imply a balance at the bank. Typical was Lord Cranworth: "There were two prime objects impressed in my mind—sport and the adding to a most exiguous income, and I pursued the former just as far as the demands of the latter would permit."

By 1906 there were about 600 whites in British East Africa. They found they could live in greater style on their small incomes than at home. Soon the highlands were dotted with houses, built with Tudor-style beams and with leaded windows. Settlers carved out large chunks of land at good prices. The Masai, whose cattle had previously grazed on the land, were persuaded to move elsewhere. Tribes (and game) were herded into reserves. Most of the chiefs were amenable, but long-lasting bitterness and misunderstanding between settlers and liberal opinion at home began at this time, as it had decades earlier concerning South Africa. The home government, to the consternation of the settlers, offered 6,000 square miles to Jews, but the Zionists turned the offer down. In 1907 the settlers established their own legislature.

Nairobi developed into a primarily European-style town, with a large percentage of the population made up of Indians, who had been brought in as labor for the railway and were now running much of the commercial and trading activity. The white railway employees kept boredom at bay by trading in the handsome young Masai women. By 1911 there were 3,175 Europeans and 11,886 Indians in the colony. Racial relationships were uncomfortable. The Kikuyu people seemed as contented as any and worked on the farms and estates. The locally raised King's African Rifles—which immediately became the smartest regiment in Africa for British officers—kept order. The least well-off whites were the administrators. The salary for the district commissioners at the time began at £250 per annum, rising through promotion to £650. Fortunately the service attracted excellent men, despite its low financial reward. The travel, the service, the sport, the adventure provided their own rewards, although for some they began to pall. For those who persevered, a pension of £300 was waiting. Education was still mainly in the hands of the missionary societies. An official budget of £7,000 for the education of more than 2,000,000 people was not excessive. The seeds of racial discontent, based mainly on the holding of land, were being well sown. Winston Churchill visited the colony and reported, in 1908: "There are in miniature all the elements of keen political and racial discord, all the materials for hot and acrimonious debate. The white man versus the black; the Indian versus both. . . . Colour is already the dominant question at Nairobi." He warned against the "fierce self-interest of the small white population."

For the whites there were the fairly luxurious Nairobi Club and Turf Club. The *East African Standard* reported gossip and social news, as well as controversy with the UK. One of the greatest features of Nairobi life was the Masara Hounds. There were two joint masters; they and the whips used to hunt in the traditional "pink." As Cranworth said: "Their arrival with the hounds at the meet as the sun rose used to bring poignant memories of the covert side at home." There were no foxes; a crowd of straight-faced Africans watched as the Englishmen streaked away, horns sounding, after jackal and buck.

The first automobile arrived about 1906. By 1912 there were seven cricket clubs, a football league, and six golf courses. The natives turned out to be particularly adept at hockey, somewhat to the Englishmen's discomfort, as well as their joy. Tourists began to arrive, almost entirely for shooting animals. "Princes, peers and American magnates poured out in one continual stream," wrote Lord Cranworth. Most famous of the guides and hunters was the legendary R. J. Cunningham. He was guide to the most famous visitor to the territory in those years—Theodore Roosevelt, who left for East Africa less than two weeks after his successor had been inaugurated as President of the United States. "I am not in the least a game butcher," Roosevelt declared before leaving; "my interest is that of a faunal naturalist." He spent eight months in British East Africa collecting specimens and killing four lions, two giraffes, two wildebeests, two rhinoceroses, one gazelle, and other creatures. He was impressed with the administration. On his way home, he spoke at Oxford University on "British Rule in Africa," saying: "I grew heartily to respect the men whom I there met, settlers and military and civil officials. . . . Your men in Africa are doing a great work for your Empire, and they are also doing a great work for civilization."

In 1909 the ubiquitous Percy Girouard arrived as governor. Predictably, he decided that more railway building was required. The Colonial Office did not agree, but Girouard went ahead. "He had a very proper and worthy conceit of himself," said Cranworth, "and his view was that if he lost employment in one direction, he would very speedily build up an equally good position in some other sphere of action. I haven't the slightest doubt that he was correct." In 1912, under Girouard, the colony became self-supporting.

The main purpose of the railway which had opened up Kenya had been to open up Uganda. But comparatively few whites settled there, and nearly all were traders. Certainly the railway improved Uganda trade with the outside world—the only successful export prior to the railway had been ivory. Sir Harry Johnston, after six years' running Nyasaland, came on the scene. Under him, from 1899 to 1901, the country recovered from the shameful religious wars that had followed the ascendancy of the white man. Christianity percolated peacefully across the land. Another Rhodes friend, the monocled Sir Frederick Jackson, further stabilized the protectorate between 1911 and 1917. The Kabaka was not deposed, and much of the traditional system remained. There were few racial problems.

The two leading personalities in South Africa after the South African War were both Afrikaners, and both were men of unusual stature and goodwill: Louis Botha, forty, a successful farmer and general with an Irish wife, and Jan Christiaan Smuts, thirty-two, a smaller man with trim beard and keen, penetrating eyes. Botha came from Natal and Smuts from Cape Colony; both had therefore been born British. Perhaps this helped give them their extraordinary ability to deal with their recent enemies of the war. Botha was inclined to the view that by cooperating with the British in South Africa, the Afrikaners, by weight of numbers, would eventually control it. Smuts, who had lived in England and knew the British better than any other Afrikaner leader, genuinely came to like them. He was one of the few who really understood the British and their divided attitude toward their Empire.

As his army broke up, Botha told his men: "The sacrifices we had to make were terrific, but we are going to see a greater South Africa." The condition of the country was indeed appalling. Peace brought economic depression, and when the decimated Afrikaner families returned to their lands from the concentration camps, they found their farms in ruins. The grim saying of the time was: "My wife and children died in the camps, my home is burned down and my cattle gone, but otherwise there is nothing to complain of." One of the greatest difficulties the new British colonies of the Transvaal and the Orange River had to face was the enmity that the war had brought among the Afrikaners themselves: between the bitter-enders and the hands-uppers. It was in an attempt to solve these wounds that Botha and Smuts founded their Het Volk ("The People") Party. The party, some of whose officers were of British stock, flourished.

In 1905 the Liberals were returned to power in Britain. It was the signal the Afrikaners had been waiting for. Liberals like Gladstone and Sir William Harcourt had often been sympahetic to Afrikaner claims, and the party had opposed the South African War. Smuts went to London. At first the new Prime Minister, Campbell-Bannerman, seemed uninterested when Smuts explained that self-government was essential. Then he said: "Smuts, you have convinced me." He was convinced to such an extent that at the decisive Cabinet meeting the next day, at which a majority of the members were at first against him, Campbell-Bannerman swayed opinion with a speech so moving that one minister was reduced to tears. The two Afrikaner colonies were to be granted internal self-government with virtually all the privileges already enjoyed by Natal and the Cape. Smuts was impressed. He said: "They gave us back, in everything but name, our country. After four years! Only people like the English could do it. They make mistakes, but they are a big people."

One problem, on granting self-government, was how to obtain for Africans even the limited privileges they enjoyed in the Cape and Natal. The government did not really stand up to the problem, and little was done to ensure the future of the Africans. The undersecretary of state for the colonies was Winston Churchill. Announcing self-government for the Orange River colony in the House of Commons, he said of the Africans: "I think we could not do more; we could not, I am sure, have done less."

Het Volk ruled both states, with British stock voting for it and even with English-speaking candidates. In Botha's Transvaal Cabinet of six members, two were British. Botha and Smuts were determined to end the racialism that had bedeviled South Africa for so long. Their enemies said they were merely becoming "more British than the British," that their regime was backed by the British army. A young army officer, Richard Meinertzhagen, saw the two leaders in the capital. "Several of us lunched at the Union Club in Pretoria. At the next table to us sat Botha and Smuts, also having lunch. During the course of conversation I remarked what a good club it was and wondered if we could become members. Smuts apparently overheard this, and after lunch very kindly told me that if we were members of the garrison it was simply a matter of sending our names in to the secretary. I did not recognize him at the moment, but thanked him, told him my name and asked him his. He replied: 'I am Smuts, let me introduce you to General Botha.'"

Meanwhile, there had been trouble in Natal. An attempt had been made to raise a poll tax of £1 per male head in the colony—including Africans, but not Indians. The Africans, especially the Zulu, had received little from the administration and did not think that the tax was at all a good idea. There was a rebellion; Cetewayo's son was accused of taking a leading part but he had had little to do with it. The old fear of the Zulu was rampant again. The rebellion was easily put down. A commission was appointed, and its report indicated the chasm between black and white had been broadening instead of narrowing, that policies to accustom the Africans to the new conditions had been ineffective.

An addition to British territory in South Africa was the protectorate of Swaziland, northern near neighbor of Zululand. There had been a gold rush to the area, which had not fulfilled expectations. For a time Kruger had annexed the territory. The king had granted concessions liberally in exchange for grey hounds and supplies of champagne (he died of drink in 1889). His widow granted a British protectorate in 1906 (she lived till 1925).

Most of the Indians in South Africa lived in Natal. A determined and compassionate lawyer from Bombay, M. K. Gandhi, had been fighting on their behalf with some success. By 1914 he had rectified some of the worst injustices, and he returned to India. More than once he had been imprisoned for his pains. The problem of the Chinese, who had been imported to work the Transvaal gold mines, was yet another aspect of race among the smoldering fears and suspicions of South Africa. Sir William Butler, who had been right about South Africa before, returned on a visit for a London newspaper. He reported: "Johannesburg must in the near future become practically a Chinese town—a town in which Chinese will be the most important language." He was wrong, for most of the Chinese were transported home. Butler found the labor system at Johannesburg and Kimberley unsatisfactory: "The best thing that can be said of it is that it is a compromise between free labour and slavery. That it comes nearer the latter system most people who know both systems will admit." At two mines 240 Africans had died or were killed out of an average labor force of 1,600 at any one time.

Butler's notes of a survey of old battlefields give a good
picture of a country steeped in history:

Train starts for Dundee down slope all the way. Dundee
usual little Natal town, two hotels, three churches. Breakfast.
Old coloured man, Adam, ready with "spider" trap and four
horses. Start for N'Gutu at nine. Adam shows battlefield. Down
from nek into great plain of Buffalo river and round eastern
end of Biggarsberg to Vant's Drift twenty miles. Dine at small
inn and Kaffir-store combined; civil people. Cross Buffalo and
enter Zululand. Begin thinking many thoughts, as Adam takes
his team up the long slopes from Buffalo river. There, a few
miles south, that dark ridge marks Rorke's Drift; there to left
of dark ridge rises a curious abrupt cone, Isandhlwana by name.
Every now and again Adam stops his horses and turns their
heads round so that the cool breeze can blow into their panting
nostrils. It is at these times that he points out the landmarks
and names them. It is all a vast panorama of old wars; wars
between Zulus and Dutch, between English and Zulus, between
Dutch and English. . . .

With self-government, Botha and Smuts did not consider
their work finished. They now campaigned for a union of the
two self-governing Afrikaner colonies and the two self-governing British colonies. Others—particularly some of Milner's old
protégés (known as Milner's Kindergarten), and most especially Lord Selborne, the "proconsul" in South Africa, 1905–10
—had been working for the same end. Smuts' ambition was a
dominion, like Canada or Australia. "What use is there in these
tin-pot shows in South Africa?" he said. "Start a Union to rule
the country from Table Bay to the Congo, and even beyond
that." It had been the aim of many—Frere, Rhodes. Now the
idea was strengthened by intense railway and tariff rivalry
among the four states to tap the wealth from the Rand, which
threatened economic anarchy. But would the suspicion of Afrikaner for British, the long history of Afrikaner isolation, the
desire to live apart from the world, the religious independence
really allow such a union to take place with the old enemy?
Only, perhaps, if the whole union could be converted to the
Afrikaner way. Then the Boers would have won, after all.

The Union of South Africa was established on May 31, 1910.
Many were the avowals of goodwill, declarations of trust and

friendship, professions of loyalty to the king. The first governor general, aptly enough, was Gladstone's son Herbert, while the Colonial Secretary was Sir William Harcourt's son Lewis. The Prime Minister of the Transvaal, Louis Botha, became the first Prime Minister of South Africa. His chief colleague was Smuts who took three portfolios: Defense, Mines, Interior. By the South Africa Act, the whites of all four territories received equal status, but the Africans were guaranteed virtually no rights at all. Africans had been able to buy land in the British colonies, but not in the Afrikaner states. When the Union came into force, the Afrikaner restrictions applied to all South Africa. As a result of the Union, therefore, the Africans of the Transvaal and the Orange Free State were no better off, and the Africans of the Cape and Natal were worse off. There was no provision in the Union for an eventual vote for the Africans. Although ostensibly a victory for the Empire and the Anglicanization of South Africa, the Union was really a victory for the Afrikaners.

Many of the Afrikaners themselves did not realize this, nor did the leader of these malcontents, Jan Hertzog, a member of Botha's Cabinet. He believed the old Afrikaner values were being contaminated by this mixing and proximity with the British, believed they would in time be destroyed. Hertzog called his policy one of two streams. He was a highly cultivated man, a classicist, an able lawyer, and a persuasive speaker. His basic position was that of all Afrikaner leaders since the arrival of the British over a century before: The main danger was from the Africans who surrounded them and among whom they lived, while the British attitude to the Africans was wrong-headed, soft, and thus dangerous. Hertzog was forced out of the government, resulting in bitterness between his Nationalist Party and Botha's South Africa Party. When troops were called in to control a general strike in Johannesburg, the government had some difficulty in controlling the old commandos, so strong was nationalist feeling.

Botha and Smuts had worked hard for peace among the two white races, but Smuts in particular, a "Cape Boer," had gradually become identified with the hated British. If the Union had been intended as a panacea, it had not worked. The old wounds were too deep, the old fears too strong.

✦ XIII ✦

A Place in the Sun

JULY, 1914, was a pleasant month in Dar es Salaam, capital of German East Africa. Dhows idled in the harbor as the sun went down with breathtaking beauty. Trade was increasing, and profits were coming in at last. The greatest event in the thirty-year history of the colony was about to occur: the official opening of the Central Railway, 770 miles of track from Dar es Salaam to Ujiji on Lake Tanganyika—the railway for which Stanley had so fervently wished while marching along the same route in 1871. There were many visitors from the fatherland in town for the celebrations, sipping drinks with friends in the small hotels and on the verandas of houses in the outskirts.

It was German East Africa, of course, which was the missing link in the old dream of a British Africa from the Cape to the Mediterranean. . . .

In the Officers' Club, where the whirring fans did something to lessen the sticky, oppressive heat, sat the newly arrived German commander in chief in East Africa, Colonel Paul von Lettow-Vorbeck. Von Lettow, at forty-four, was a tall, arrogant-looking man, with a small but firm jaw, tight lips, a long, sloping forehead, and close-cropped hair. He had a great deal of varied military experience, including colonial wars in South-West Africa and China. He was the most experienced colonial commander in the German army. To control and defend his population of 8,000,000 Africans and 5,000 Europeans, he had an army of 216 Europeans and 2,540 askaris (trained soldiers); there were also 45 European and 2,154 African police. The two centers of civilization were along the Central Railway and along the only other railway, 270 miles long, which connected the chief port of Tanga with the foothills of the magnificent, haunting mountain of Kilimanjaro. The rest of the colony was undeveloped and not entirely known. To the west the colony was bounded by the great lakes and the Belgian Congo; to the south by Rhodesia and Portuguese East Africa; to the north by British East Africa (Kenya), where the King's African Rifles (KAR), now seventeen companies strong, were engaged in "a punitive expedition" against remote tribes in Uganda.

News arrived from Europe. It was war between Austria-Germany and the Anglo-French Entente. The governor of German East Africa, Dr. Heinrich Schnee, was horrified, not interested in war. His only concern was in developing the colony without irrelevant distractions from Europe. He made his position clear to the authorities in British East Africa, and a truce was arranged. This did not at all please Von Lettow, who was very much a professional soldier. Relations between the two were strained, and Von Lettow, on his own responsibility, made preparations for war. Communication with Germany was lost when the telegraph stations at Cairo and Khartoum no longer relayed messages. Weeks went by and no one in "German East" had any idea of what was happening in this distant war in Europe. There was some shooting on the border with British East Africa. Would the British try to invade the colony? Von Lettow wondered. And, if so, could he successfully defend such a vast area with so few men?

The outbreak of a world war had inflamed the already dangerous situation in South Africa. When Botha had declared his support for Britain, many of the Afrikaner Nationalists had been outraged. The rebellion that had threatened for years at last occurred. Botha and Smuts called out 40,000 men to quell it, taking care to ensure that most were loyal Afrikaners—in order to preclude another Anglo-Boer conflict. Botha spoke of "the necessity that is upon us of proving that popular government is not an absurdity. We must settle this question now whether in a free government the minority have the right to break up the government whenever they choose." Smuts defended the British case in the war against Germany with vigor. The rebels, who included the old hero De Wet, assembled a force near German South-West Africa, which they used as a source of supply, a base and a refuge. They attempted to set up a provisional government. But after a few skirmishes the rebellion disintegrated in piecemeal surrenders. Because of possible inflammatory consequences, clemency was generous in the extreme; De Wet, for example, though sentenced to six years' imprisonment, was released after a few months. The Union, which was lauded in London as a great example of the strength of the British system, was so weak that none of the ringleaders could receive anything more than the merest token punishment for armed revolt against the crown. "Saddest experience of my life," said Smuts. An election was fought with bitterness unusual even for South Africa. Smuts was despised as one who had sold out to the old enemy, while Botha, only fifteen years previously a supreme hero to every Afrikaner, was called "Judas, traitor, bloodhound, murderer."

With the conclusion of the rebellion, Botha embarked on the conquest of German South-West Africa, for which he had taken the entire responsibility from the British government. The Germans had evolved a careful defense with a system of blockhouses linked by telephone and 6,000 mostly locally raised troops (including a camel corps) under Colonel von Heydebreck. Botha raised an excessively large force, 67,237 strong, all Europeans. About 20,000 actually entered enemy territory, but few of them heard a shot fired. The main obstacle was the desert terrain and the resulting lack of water. The campaign opened with a humiliating reverse for Botha, but using well-tried Afrikaner tactics, he eventually cut off the German retreat, while another column of 3,000 marched nearly 500 miles across the desert from Kimberley through "loose, heavy, heart-breaking sand," transporting its own water—a considerable achievement. Von Heydebreck capitulated. Because of the ever-present fear of a native rising, and its possible effects on South Africa, most of the whites were released and returned to their civilian posts.

There were two other German colonies in Africa: Togoland and the Cameroons. In Togoland there were about 350 Germans. The acting governor suggested to the British that the colony should remain neutral, "having regard to insecurity of native tribes. . . . Warlike enterprises likely to have no bearing on decision arrived at in Europe." The British Cabinet considered his request and rejected it. Within a month the colony had been occupied and was split between France and Britain.

The conquest of the Cameroons was more arduous. The first British column to enter the colony was thrust back. Disease was as great an enemy as the German askaris. After a wretched campaign, fought by a sick army of French, British, Belgian, Indian, and West Indian troops, the Allies gained the colony, but the main German force escaped into Spanish territory, where it was interned. Most of the colony went to France, but on this occasion also the appetite of the British Empire for territory and responsibilities in Africa proved unsated.

German East Africa and Colonel von Lettow-Vorbeck remained. It was decided in Whitehall that an expedition from India would attempt the conquest of this, the richest of German colonies. The Indian army had long been considered one of the prides of the Empire, but it had seldom proved itself against European-led troops. In command of the expedition was Major General A. E. Aitken. It was his opinion that "the Indian Army will make short work of a lot of niggers." There would be two brigades, under Brigadier General R. Wapshare, a fat man with a mustache, and Brigadier General M. I. Tighe, a thin man forever sucking at a pipe. The intelligence officer was Captain Richard Meinertzhagen, of Danish extraction (later a friend of T. E. Lawrence, who described him as "a silent, laughing masterful man"). The force seemed formidable enough, certainly, for its task, for there had long been a belief in England that the Germans conducted their colonies with brutality and that their Africans would thus give them no loyalty at all. At a committee in London, it was said: "The smallest inducement would tend to make the whole of the German native troops desert to us." The plan was to land at Tanga and to proceed up the railway while another invasion was launched from British East Africa. Kitchener, back in London from Egypt as Secretary of State for War, promptly agreed to the plan and arrangements. The great German cruiser *Königsberg* was lurking in East African waters, raiding British shipping lanes, and it was even more essential to gain the German-held ports than the important colony itself.

The expeditionary force assembled at Bombay. Meinertzhagen ran his eye over the troops: "Constitute the worst in India and I tremble to think what may happen." The force steamed into the Indian Ocean, on board fourteen ships, on October 16, 1914, to conquer a land twice the size of Germany itself. The voyage was a nightmare. Some of the troops had never seen the sea before. There was a gentle but persistent swell, which provoked miseries of seasickness. The ships were crowded, the heat belowdecks was intense, and exercise of any kind was difficult. Aitken was as confident as ever: "The German troops are ill-trained, ours are magnificent and, bush or no bush, I mean to thrash the Germans before Christmas."

The convoy arrived at Mombasa, in British East Africa, where a conference was held. There Aitken learned that the main German force was near Kilimanjaro and Tanga was almost undefended. The question of the administration of German East after its conquest was discussed. General Aitken issued his orders. "From reliable information received," he began, "it appears improbable that the enemy will actively oppose our landing."

Von Lettow, meanwhile, had been preparing for attack at both Tanga and at Kilimanjaro. "It became more and more apparent that a hostile offensive was imminent," he said. Tanga, he believed, was the "obvious objective." Rushing up and down the railway, he prepared the defense. His army near Kilimanjaro was ready to dash down the line at a moment's notice.

The British convoy plowed its way south from Mombasa, within sight of the coast. The accompanying naval craft was HMS *Fox*. The commander of the *Fox*, Captain F. W. Caulfield, insisted that he could not support the landing unless a warning was first given to the civil authorities at Tanga, feeling he must honor the agreement made early in the war with Dr. Schnee, when there had been some suggestion of neutrality for German East. At this even Aitken was a little dismayed. HMS *Fox* accordingly steamed into Tanga Harbor, through twisting channels, flying the white flag. It was early dawn, misty, promising great heat later in the day.

The *Fox* anchored near the quay. The head of the local German administration came aboard. He listened to what the bearded Caulfield had to say: He was being given one hour to surrender the town. Leaving the ship, he ran to his office, sent a telegram to Von Lettow, who was at Moshi, donned his uniform

as an officer in the reserve, and reported for duty with the garrison. The *Fox* idled in the harbor, the dark green water slapping
on her old gray sides—waiting. The scorching sun was rising in
the clear morning sky. The German flag remained on top of the
government buildings, fluttering lazily in the breeze. Apart
from the water and the distant calls of tropical birds ashore,
there was no sound. Caulfield radioed Aitken: "No surrender.
Rejoining convoy." HMS *Fox* left the harbor.

Caulfield was reluctant to bombard the town or to return to
the channel leading to the harbor. He was worried about mines.
"Not at all inclined to help," Meinertzhagen said of him,
"always referring to the safety of his blasted ship, ignoring the
fact that it is his business to protect us even if he loses his ship."
Captain Caulfield transferred himself to a minesweeper and
personally conducted minesweeping.

Aitken decided to forget about the harbor and chose a neighboring beach for the landing. He gave his final order: "The
town of Tanga is to be seized tonight."

Many miles up the line, Colonel von Lettow-Vorbeck was
clattering down the railway at full speed. A thousand of his best
troops were ahead of him. Trains panted through rocky gorges
toward the distant sea, wagons packed with askaris, rifle barrels
glistening.

By 10 P.M. the first Indian troops were splashing ashore.
Tighe's brigade was to make the initial assault. Signal lamps
flashed from ship to beach, and by dawn the majority of the
brigade was on shore. All were weary, after weeks of seasickness
and a night without sleep. Most of the troops had not walked on
land for a month. Everyone was surprised at the thickness of the
bush offshore—palm trees, bramble, and grass higher than a
man. Pushing through the dense undergrowth, the brigade
moved tentatively forward.

At that very moment the leading askaris were jumping from
the wagons and lining the approach to the town. They let off a
withering fire into the bush and launched a fierce counter-
attack. The unhappy Indians, who had received no relevant
training at all, turned and fled, shot at by snipers in the trees.
Soon the force, in some panic, was back on the beach. Tighe,
smoking his pipe contemplatively, waited for the askaris to
arrive and annihilate his force. Fortunately, the Germans did
not follow up their attack. Wapshare's brigade and great quan-

tities of stores were now brought onto the crowded and confused beach, while the *Fox* lobbed an occasional shell into the
town. All busied themselves with the muddles and problems of
disembarkation, and no one thought of sending out patrols. It
was a pity, for the Germans, impressed by the size of the British
force, had withdrawn—Tanga had been evacuated. Confusion
on the beach was increased by hundreds of undisciplined
bearers, who had been shipped from Zanzibar. When a rifle was
fired accidentally, panic among troops and bearers was considerable. "Jolly fellows to go fighting Germans with," commented
Meinertzhagen. The force got what sleep it could under the
starry African sky.

The next morning Aitken took personal control. But it was
not until after midday that he was able to give the order to
advance, so great was the disorder on the beach. Movement was
slow, the heat oppressive, and many dropped from the ranks.
After a long, unnerving struggle through the bush, the force at
last arrived in front of the German position, where Von Lettow,
who had recently arrived, had brought his troops back again to
the edge of the town. An attempt by Aitken to launch a frontal
attack dissolved into chaos. Some Indians made for the rear,
while others pushed forward, and casualties were high as Indian
shot Indian. Officers shot their troops. British officers shot Indian officers. Meinertzhagen noted of the Indians: "All gibber-
ing like terrified monkeys, and were clearly not for it at any
price."

There was one British battalion in the force, the Second
Loyal North Lancashires, the same regiment that had endured
the siege of Kimberley under Kekewich fourteen years previously. The Lancashiremen actually broke through, reached the
center of Tanga, and brought down the German flag, but
receiving no support and presented with mounting house-to-
house resistance, they withdrew.

All other troops were now fleeing for the beach as fast as they
could run. A final push to the terrified troops was given by a
vast swarm of angry bees. The local custom was to hang hives
from the branches of trees, and the hives had become riddled
with shots. The bees were enraged, and they were on the war-
path. They chased the unfortunate Indian and British troops to
the edge of the sea. "I myself got stung twice," said Meinertzhagen, curtly. One member of the Royal Signals continued

taking a message while being attacked by bees; he later had more than 300 stings removed, and was awarded the Distinguished Conduct Medal. The legend persisted for months that the wily Von Lettow had laid wires in the bush which, when trodden on, released the bees.

On the beach, officers tried to stem the stampede by firing again on their troops, and this did not improve the situation at all. Aitken lost control. Only the fall of darkness brought some respite. The German force, meanwhile, had made no attempt to advance to the beach. When a distant trumpet call wafted across from the German lines, a staff officer called: "My God, that's the charge!" In fact, it was the retreat, for Von Lettow had decided to withdraw to a better defensive position. Aitken seemed "tired out and disgusted with the whole business." He ordered an evacaution the next morning. Another nervous night was spent in the open.

Soon after midday the reembarkation began. The 2,000 chattering bearers were the first to leave. Because of the tide, the men had to wade out up to their necks, and all stores and most equipment, including all the machine guns, were left behind. Some shots from a German patrol caused a renewal of panic, and according to the official account, written after the war, troops "fled in chaos into the sea, swimming out to the boats, half-swamping them and producing general confusion." Order was restored—"not without violence."

Meinertzhagen was still ashore attending to some unfinished business. After a refresher of warm water and rum—"drunk out of a bucket, and mighty good it was"—he approached the German lines with a letter from Aitken; this was an apology for a shell from the *Fox* that had hit the town hospital. He was cordially welcomed and entertained to "an excellent breakfast which I sorely needed. . . . It seemed so odd that I should be having a meal today with people whom I was trying to kill yesterday. It made me wonder whether this really was war or whether we had all made a ghastly mistake." On his way back a German askari fired at him, not understanding the white flag, and the bullet went through Meinertzhagen's helmet. "I went for him with my flag of truce and rammed him in the pit of the stomach, which doubled him up. I then wrenched the rifle out of his hand and stuck him with his own bayonet. I was furious."

The reembarkation was completed during the afternoon.

Some 7,200 men were taken off, but 130 seriously wounded had to be left behind. The force had suffered well over one-tenth casualties (359 killed). One of the ships was hit by the German artillery (two guns of 1873 pattern) and set ablaze. Caulfield was begged to bombard the town, but wouldn't do it. "Don't wish to stir them up again," he said.

The next morning Meinertzhagen was back in Tanga. He had been given the curious task, perhaps unique in war, of officially "handing over" the stores which had been left behind. An inventory was carefully made and signed by himself and a German officer. Meinertzhagen was then entertained to a meal: "good beer, ice, plenty of eggs and cream and asparagus."

The convoy was now ready to depart. Leading it into the Indian Ocean was HMS *Fox*.

Von Lettow jumped on his bicycle and watched the departure from the shore. About 1,000 of his men had beaten off 8,000. His reputation soared. Whereas previously he had been unpopular, now he could do no wrong. The morale of his troops had reached formidable heights, and it would remain high for four years.

The overland column to the Kilimanjaro area, marching through its own cloud of dust, watched by excited giraffes, zebras, and ostriches, had also been sent scurrying back to British East Africa. The attempt at invasion had ended in catastrophe.

The convoy arrived at Mombasa. The customs officers refused to let the remaining stores be landed without a duty of 5 percent. Recrimination and accusation about the disaster were fierce. Kitchener was beside himself. Aitken was ordered home, his command taken over by the rotund Wapshare, known to his men as Wappy. It was decided that a defensive role would have to be adopted until reinforcements could arrive in British East Africa.

Wapshare had great respect for Von Lettow's capabilities, which the result of border skirmishes seemed to increase. "He is terrified of him," wrote one officer, "and the mention of his name at mess sends him off into a shivering fit." Kitchener appointed his brother and Lord Cranworth to make up a commission to discover what could be done. Kitchener's brother said that no increase in locally raised forces was possible, and Cranworth reported that "the main line to pursue must lie in the most rapid expansion possible of the existing King's African Rifles." Things continued fairly peacefully. The governor spent most of his time fishing at Mombasa (his capital was at Nairobi). His staff took leave as usual. A remarkable unit, known as the Legion of Frontiersmen, arrived from London; it included famous hunters like D. P. Driscoll, George Outram, Selous, W. N. Macmillan (an American millionaire), at least one other millionaire, circus entertainers, a servant from Buckingham Palace, and Cherry Kearton, a photographer who had made a name photographing big game. "Wappy" left and was replaced by Tighe.

Von Lettow was successfully running a siege economy. Cut off from the outside world, the Germans had improvised brilliantly and greatly improved the economy of the colony. Automobile and bicycle tires were produced, candles and soap manufactured, tobacco grown, rum and whiskey (92 percent proof) distilled, and boots made from the skins of cattle. Quinine, most important of all, was produced by a chemical institute from wood bark (those who were dosed with this *Lettow-schnapps* swore its effects were worse than malaria's). On the Kaiser's birthday, Dr. Schnee told a crowd at Dar es Salaam: "The enemy cannot crush us economically. We get all we require from the country. The value of our colony shines forth in this war." By the end of 1915 Von Lettow had raised his force to 3,000 Europeans and 11,300 askaris.

The much-feared *Königsberg* had still not been sunk. Indeed, it had not been sighted or heard of for months. There were many theories on its whereabouts. Then a British cruiser stopped and boarded a German hospital ship; papers on board revealed that coal had been going up the Rufiji River, south of Dar es Salaam. There seemed no reason why coal should be needed in that wild region, except one, and 10 miles up the complicated, steamy channels of the Rufiji the *Königsberg* was found at last. There were no detailed charts of the labyrinthine delta, and British warships could not get at the German raider. As an alternative, a ship was sunk to block the exit to the sea, trapping the *Königsberg*. A telegram was sent to Smuts in South Africa: "Have you an elephant hunter Pretorius in South Africa? We would like him for a special mission." Pretorius, who knew the region well, arrived and was put ashore to determine the exact location of the ship. Seaplanes arrived and found the ship half-hidden by enveloping jungle. For six months the *Königsberg* survived, like a resilient but trapped wolf. Then two flat-bottomed craft arrived from England and blasted the proud German ship. (Her hulk still lies at the water's edge—her rusted side under the sun, fish swimming in and out of ports, and crocodiles slithering from her into the water.) Some of the crew, after twelve months, reached Germany by way of dhows to Arabia and thence via Turkey to Germany. The remainder provided valuable reinforcements and artillery to Von Lettow.

There was more naval activity on the great lakes which bounded so much of German East Africa. During the early weeks of war some regular boat services on Lake Victoria had continued, "it being considered essential to maintain the usual communications." But Lake Tanganyika was the most important of the lakes; 450 miles long, it accounted for almost the entire frontier of German and Belgian territory in Central Africa. The Admiralty took the responsibility of capturing it for the Allies. At the suggestion of another big-game hunter, twenty-eight naval officers were sent out to South Africa with two small armored launches, each almost 4½ tons and 40 feet long. From Cape Town they went by rail to the railhead of Rhodes' magnificent dream, at Elisabethville in the Congo (since Rhodes' death, a dozen years before, the railway had completed the crossing of Rhodesia from south to north). They were hauled and lugged through 150 miles of jungle, some of it untracked and unknown; then they were taken down the Congo. Five months after leaving England, they arrived at Lake Tanganyika. After a few shots had been fired at the converted German ferries, the lake was "within the sphere of British naval power."

Soon after this it was decided in London to revitalize the campaign in East Africa. None other than Smuts himself would take command, and a considerable army from South Africa would be transported to British East Africa for an invasion of German East. Tighe was at the Mombasa quayside to welcome Smuts on February 19, 1916. The trim, well-knit figure, his red beard jutting from beneath his red-banded British general's cap, stepped quickly and purposefully down the gangplank. Within hours he transformed the languid air of the campaign. On arrival at Nairobi, he ignored the receptions and functions in his honor and within twenty-four hours was off on a personal reconnaissance, not far from the enemy lines, studying the land through his battered favorite field glasses. Within five days he had decided on an immediate offensive to clear the German concentration around Kilimanjaro. He had brought with him 18,700 South Africans, all volunteer recruits. It might have been a strange situation for the British officers, some of whom found themselves in a position of serving under officers they had been fighting only fourteen years previously. Brigadier General Jacob Louis van Deventer's husky voice, for instance, was the result of a British bullet in his throat, but in his uniform, he looked the very caricature of a bluff English professional soldier. The British had encouraged this aping of themselves as a facet of their Empire, but whether it had really gone very deep with the South Africans remained to be seen. One officer told Meinertzhagen: "Though we would sooner be under British rule than German, we do not love the British. Our dream is eventual independence . . . we all hope that when this war is over we shall receive it. If you don't give it, we shall take it."

Smuts realized that Von Lettow, hopelessly outnumbered, would not want a stand-up battle. This, too, was his wish. Impressed by news of the heavy casualties on the western front in Europe, he had, as he said, no wish to become "Butcher Smuts." He planned to outmaneuver Von Lettow in typical Afrikaner fashion, avoiding static battles and gradually conquering the colony. Many of the British officers believed him wrong, thinking that a hard fight now, if Von Lettow could be cornered, would settle the issue and avoid casualties from sickness in a long-drawn-out campaign. But Smuts favored his South Africans against the askaris, in any conditions.

Smuts' ponderous force of 45,000 men, with its huge supply column, crossed the border into German East. Opposition was momentarily fierce, then faded away. The pattern for the campaign had been set. Smuts followed Von Lettow deep into German East, once the settled Kilimanjaro area had been taken, like a steel bar drawn along by a small but powerful magnet. Skirmishes were fought where and when Von Lettow decided. Smuts realized it: "Merely to follow the enemy in his very mobile retreat might prove an endless game." He attacked the colony from many quarters, gaining territory easily. But Von Lettow and his little army remained unconquered. He was

playing the Boer at his own game. And Smuts' men began falling sick.

It was a hard campaign, although the fighting was only
intermittent. Driscoll, commanding the Legion of Frontiersmen, wrote home:

> Wild animals, mind you, as well as wild devils to fight; the
> sun burning your very flesh; the flies intolerable. Imagine a
> camp at night under these conditions. Round and about the
> lions are roaring with hunger. Hyenas howl in the hope of snap-
> ping up a sentry or leaping in and carrying off a wounded man.
> . . . All this sounds bad enough, but, believe me, it gives you
> but a poor account.

The campaign appeared increasingly successful, although
large numbers of troops were languishing in hospital. Smuts
realized that a speedy end was essential, for the South African
troops were needed in Europe. Von Lettow realized it, too. He
had few supply problems, owing to a remarkable traveling
arsenal and the ability of his troops to live off the land. Medical
problems were also comparatively small. His personality and
inspired leadership bred intense loyalty in his troops.

At last Smuts was forced to give a strange order: "Refrain
from attacking the enemy—not only on military but also on
medical grounds." But Dar es Salaam was captured before the
advance came to a halt. There was considerable argument about
whether the army or the navy had achieved the conquest of the
capital. An official court had to adjudicate; an award was made
on behalf of the navy. The occupying forces made Dar es
Salaam their headquarters for the campaign, and staff officers
arrived by the hundreds. They found it an attractive place,
beside the glistening green waters of the Indian Ocean, with a
white strip of coral and sand, shady treelined streets, handsome
public buildings, fine homes with verandas screened by mosquito nets, up-to-date wharves, and red-tiled roofs. There was
some looting. A staff officer wrote of even generals being in the
stampede "for pictures and every class of loot."

Von Lettow now had left to him only the southeast corner of
the colony, squeezed up against the border of Portuguese East
Africa, which, of course, belonged to one of the Allies.

After continual pressure from the medical services, Smuts

agreed that the campaign could not be finished till the South African, Indian, and British troops had been replaced by African. A large expansion of the KAR was begun. As Meinertzhagen said: "Our battlefield casualties have been negligible. What Smuts saves on the battlefield he loses in hospital." Apparently still unaware of the kind of man he was up against, Smuts at this stage got a message through to Von Lettow suggesting the Germans surrender. It was Governor Schnee who replied, and he "declined." Later Smuts contacted Von Lettow again. He wrote a personal letter, informing the colonel that the Kaiser had awarded him a high decoration and expressed the hope that his "cordial congratulations" would not be unacceptable. Von Lettow replied with cold formality.

Skirmishing continued while the South Africans embarked. One man never to return was Selous, who had come back to the campaign after being invalided home: "Shall try and hold out to the end, if possible, or at any rate as long as my health and strength last." Fellow officers had been surprised to come across him in the bush, after an action, hunting butterflies with a net and specimen box. Aged sixty-five, he was shot dead, sewn up in a blanket, and buried beside a tamarind tree.

Smuts sailed for Europe only a few days after his departure from the campaign was anounced, a tired, thin figure, wasted with malaria. Before leaving, he said that all that remained to be done was to "sweep up the remnants of the enemy force." In London, he said: "The campaign may be said to be over." This was somewhat embarrassing for his successors. Eventually the command passed to Van Deventer, who could speak little English and write none.

When the British advance was renewed, Von Lettow crossed the Ruvuma River into the Portuguese colony with 300 Europeans, 1,700 askaris, and 3,000 followers and bearers. His askaris, in torn, faded uniforms, singing their monotonous songs, rifles reversed on their shoulders, seemed inexhaustible. Behind them went the long supply train and then the wives with children slung from their shoulders. The Germans prized their personal stores as treasure—brandy was as rare as gold. Every group of three companies had its own supply train and field hospital, and the number of doctors per man was far higher than in the chasing British columns. "How long can it go on?" a German wrote. "Have we not been through enough for

German East Africa? . . . Nobody has the slightest idea of what's happening in Europe. We fight in a silence, and we die with a silence all round." As one officer bitterly said: "This war has given us a place in the sun, anyway."

Van Deventer suggested to Von Lettow that it would be sensible to stop the campaign. There was no reply. For ten months Von Lettow's force fought through the wilderness of Portuguese East Africa, often mauled by superior British forces attacking from the coast, but never defeated. Then it returned across the Ruvuma and tramped across German East, completely outwitting the pursuers. In October, 1918, the world at large, which had long since forgotten about the campaign in East Africa, was surprised to hear of a German force threatening British territory.

From captured newspapers in towns they passed through, the Germans at last gained news of the war in Europe. There were few British in the area. Von Lettow crossed into Rhodesia unopposed, for there was no Cecil Rhodes to galvanize a defense. The British towns of Kasama and Fife were taken, and officers slept in houses for the first time in years. On November 11, while much of the remainder of the world was rejoicing in the streets at the end of the most terrible war mankind had ever known, Von Lettow toured his positions on his bicycle. Few people that day knew anything of Clause Seventeen of the Armistice signed that morning in a train in France; it provided for the surrender of the German army in Africa at such time as it could be contacted. It was not until two days later that a British motorcyclist arrived at Von Lettow's headquarters with the information. Von Lettow was 150 miles into Rhodesia and 450 miles north of Salisbury. At first he was disinclined to believe the news, and he sent a cable to the Kaiser personally, asking for verification. Receiving no reply, he formally surrendered at a parade at noon on November 25, 1918. Van Deventer allowed all the Europeans to retain their arms, "in consideration of the gallant fight you have made." British officers jostled to take photographs of Von Lettow, wrote of him in the highest terms, entertained him when, a "prisoner of war," he reached Dar es Salaam. One British officer, anticipating a future war and a future German general in Africa, wrote: "We had more esteem and affection for him than our own leaders." In Africa, it seemed, Europeans fought one another differently from the way they did on their own continent; it was as if they were on show.

Von Lettow had brought against him at least 130,000 troops and many generals, of whom almost 1 in 3 had died from disease, and he had caused an expenditure by the British alone of £72,000,000. But Britain had won the war. Van Deventer, the old Boer enemy, was made a Knight Commander of the British Empire, Smuts a privy councilor. The survivors staggered home and were congratulated for having "missed the war." The Belgians and Portuguese got small slices of Germany's share of the cake made during the scramble. But Britain got a vast new chunk, under mandate, and called it Tanganyika. The all-British way from the Cape to Cairo was complete at last—a broad belt of nearly 5,000 miles through the continent of Africa, from the Southern Ocean to the Mediterranean.

✦ XIV ✦

High Noon of Empire

In 1918 Britain had more territory in her African empire than any other country and ruled by far the greater proportion of the continent's inhabitants. Six years after the war an Englishman and his wife, Major and Mrs. C. C. Treatt (with hot-water bottles for the cold desert nights) drove from Cape Town to Cairo, in one year and four months—without once leaving British territory. The nomenclature for British rule was wide: dominion, company territory (later self-governing colony), crown colonies, mandates, dependencies, protectorates, condominium. Did the name really make much difference? The governor of Tanganyika, a mandate, who had just come from spending seventeen years in the protectorate of Nigeria, said the differences, if any, "did not trouble or preoccupy my mind in any way." Officially, inhabitants of the colonies were British subjects, of the protectorates "protected persons" (and aliens in any part of the Empire outside their own country). Indirect rule applied to all the protectorates, and to many of the colonies as well, and matters were not simplified by the fact that some territories were part colony and part protectorate.

Although there was some depression following the war colonies were soon showing modest surpluses. This allowed some room for the expansion of the Colonial Service and for improvements generally. The African territories were taken more seriously than ever before. This mood was also partly brought on by the establishment of the League of Nations, which had passed the old German colonies to the victors under mandate but required them to be ruled in the interests of the native population at least as much as in the interests of the administering nation. It was Smuts who was behind the League, with its high hopes for a civilized world, as much as anyone, although President Woodrow Wilson got most of the credit or blame. "Lloyd George says Wilson now talks of the scheme as if he is the author of it," Smuts said in 1919, "and may yet give it to the world as his own special creation! Who minds, so long as the work is done?" Smuts, contrary to all innate Afrikaner traditions, had become an extremely outward-looking statesman who fought tirelessly for the British Commonwealth, as he preferred to describe the Empire, and for the League.

Lugard retired to Surrey after the war but kept near the center of African affairs. Parties of chiefs visiting the capital of the Empire felt obliged to call on him, and sometimes he took them to see the animals at the London Zoo. In 1922 he published his important *The Dual Mandate in British Tropical Africa*. In it Lugard propounded the theory that Britain had a double responsibility in Africa—to the Africans and to the outside world (in the form of trade). For governing, he still advocated indirect rule, which would eventually produce a system fit for self-government. The argument was long and intense, lasting through the interwar years. Lugard had his followers, including the influential Margery Perham of Oxford, and he was read by a whole generation of colonial administrators. No one could now accuse the British of not giving thought to their African territories; they worried over them, debated them, and set up numerous commissions to study them. Writers, like Elspeth Huxley, specialized in British Africa.

In Nigeria, indirect rule was fragmented—suitable in the west and, in theory at least, in the north, but not in the east, where tribes and peoples were hopelessly mixed. Despite all efforts, the colony showed little sign of molding itself into an entity. The system was applied in Zanzibar, the Sudan and in Uganda (under Sir William Gowers, governor, 1925–32, who had worked closely with both Rhodes and Lugard). Tanganyika seemed to provide little scope for it, but it was applied there, too. British East Africa, renamed Kenya after the territory's greatest mountain, was different; the governor, 1925–31, was Sir Edward Grigg, and settlers were still arriving from home, as in

South Africa and Rhodesia—it was not just peopled by administrators and traders.

The hoped-for and, by some, expected end was self-government, but it seemed far away. There was no sense of urgency. The British had been in India for centuries, and it was more advanced when they had arrived than Africa was even now. The time available seemed almost endless—certainly many generations ahead. Even Leopold Stennett Amery, that enlightened "Africa man," Secretary of State for the Colonies, 1924–29, said: "In the course of the next century there will be a more or less continuous white population from the Cape to the borders of Abyssinia forming, in all probability, part of a single political entity. Throughout that area the white man will inevitably be the directing and governing element for any future, at any rate, that we can envisage."

Trade increased over the period, in some cases dramatically, although the slump affected Africa for a time almost as much as Europe and North America. There was a tremendous increase in the export of cocoa, for which Europe and America had developed an insatiable appetite in the form of bars of chocolate, and a considerable thirst for it, too. Prominent among traders was the United Africa Company, a subsidiary of Unilever Ltd., the product of the son of a Lancashire grocer, William Lever, who had made a fortune manufacturing soap. He had acquired the old Royal Niger Company for his raw material. Lever, who believed in cooperation in his English factories, was a late proponent of the white man's burden. "The African native," he said, "will be happier, produce the best, and live under the larger conditions of prosperity when his labour is directed and organized by his white brother." Unilever seems to have made an effort to monopolize the merchandizing of produce and entered the French West African colonies as well as the British. It associated itself with the aspirations of the emerging nations and plowed money back into West Africa. Two great banks, Barclays (D.C.O.) and Standard, also contributed to the economic expansion of British Africa.

During these interwar years the Colonial Service was greatly strengthened and under its permanent undersecretary, Sir Samuel Wilson, 1925–33, it developed an *esprit de corps*. Most new entrants were university graduates. With their long short trousers, open-necked shirts, and pipes stuck into the tops of their high white socks, they virtually ruled areas larger than England and hoped one day to take up residence in Governor's Houses. There was a feeling of contributing, in one's own small way, to the betterment of a whole continent. They ruled with mild firmness, taxing from time to time, improving agricultural techniques where it seemed worthwhile, adjudicating, explaining simple cattle husbandry . . . and retaining as much of the English way of life as possible, particularly a drink in the evening—the sundowner. African servants, even when they were grizzled old men, were known as boys, and it was as boys that they were treated. The frustrations at all levels were colossal, but at the end of the day the work had been useful, more full than suburban commuting at home. The life itself was better and could be expected to last longer than in the old days. The death rate fell from 20.6 per 1,000 in 1903 to 5.1 in 1935. Isolated as they were, hardly a man was killed, except, occasionally, when he shot himself with his own game gun. Their way was a peaceful one, based on instruction and persuasion rather than on force. To that extent the Empire in Africa had become a voluntary one, but the wars of occupation, which had so clearly shown that African war machinery was no match for British, were not all that long ago. The district commissioner was not a propagandist for any particular form of government. His motto appears to have been Pope's lines:

> For forms of government let fools contest;
> Whate'er is best administer'd is best.

The governor, if he was good, was in a curious, ambiguous position, supporting the interests of the home government, often representing the interests of the natives as he saw them, and trying to fulfill whatever the terms of Britain's presence were, were it mandate, trusteeship, or whatever, and his responsibilities very often conflicted. Above the governor, far away and remote, was the king, George V, who, like his father and grandmother, never saw his African possessions. Governors returning home would call on him at Buckingham Palace, and he always inquired "of the people and their well-being." One told him "how deeply impressed the townsfolk of Lagos had been by his message over the air on the preceding Christmas Day."

William Ormsby-Gore, an authority on fine arts, became

colonial Undersecretary responsible for the African territories in 1922 and with one short break remained in the post for seven years; he also served as Colonial Secretary, 1936–38. Ormsby-Gore had come under Milner's influence early in his career and believed wholeheartedly in the Empire, as well as in the ideals of service and responsibility. Under him, education, in particular, was improved when at last the government joined with the missionary societies in the great task of education. Primary education had to come first, and in 1939 there were fewer than 100 secondary schools in British Africa for Africans. It was from these secondary schools, however, that a new elite was beginning to emerge, to join or to challenge the privileged chieftain class through which British rule was being ordered. Some went abroad to take their education still further, and they were not satisfied with the opportunities offered them. They did not care to be governed by the old tribal methods that Britain supported through indirect rule. Above all, they felt patronized, and they rejected the idea that progress, the English way, was better than progress in a purely African way. Jomo "Johnstone" Kenyatta arrived in London from Kenya. In 1930 he wrote an impressive letter to the *Times* explaining that the Kikuyu felt seriously wronged in respect to land, education, tax, representation, and the "wholesale" abolishment of tribal customs. He asked for changes in Kenya, "so that we may all march together as loyal subjects of His Britannic Majesty along the road to Empire prosperity."

Nnamdi Azikiwe returned to West Africa from studies in America and founded a popular press for Africans, first in the Gold Coast and then in his native Nigeria. Kwame Nkrumah worked as an elevator boy in America to pay for his studies; already very politically minded, he followed Kenyatta at the London School of Economics, where he was a considerably less impressive pupil. A National Congress of British West Africa was formed, and it demanded African participation in government. But no one took a great deal of notice.

Smuts, after two and a half years in Europe, returned to South Africa. He had helped found the RAF, had been on several special missions for David Lloyd George (including ending a miners' strike at Tonypandy, Wales), and had, of course, inspired the idea of the League of Nations. Lloyd

George had been impressed by the thin man with piercing eyes from South Africa: "One of the most remarkable personalities of his time. . . . Of his practical contributions to our counsels during these trying years it is difficult to speak too highly."

Many Afrikaners had fought in France and Flanders, but the personality of the country was still hopelessly split. Hertzog was as bitter as ever. South Africa, he said, was "the spittoon of the Empire." Hertzog had kept alive the flame of Afrikaner hatred of the British, based on fear of the Africans, till his own party could rule and eventually hand it on to others.

South Africa was the first country in Africa to have to struggle with the changeover from a rural to an industrial economy, and that at a time when it had to struggle simultaneously with other great problems, especially that of race. The complex on the Witwatersrand had already become comparable with the industrial regions of Europe and the United States—in the working life of one generation. After Cairo, Johannesburg was the largest city in Africa. By 1939 there were nearly 500,000 Europeans on the Witwatersrand, where fifty years previously there had been fewer than 100. Gold flowed to the banks of the world. In 1935 South African exports to the United States were $52,864,813, while imports from the same country were $3,610,972. But the benefits of all this were not widely spread, and even the white workers did not gain sudden improvements in the standard of living. In 1922 there was an explosive strike of Rand mineworkers when Africans were being considered as skilled labor at lower wages than the whites. There was talk of a republic being proclaimed in the Rand. Troops were called in.

Johannesburg itself was not a city to please the sensitive. It had all the worst aspects of the great industrial metropolises and none of the best. One traveler described it in the 1930's thus:

> A city of a quarter of a million white people, many of them extremely rich and most of them prosperous, that could not support a single theatre. Super cinemas, yes. A city hall in which the most spectacular all-in wrestling matches took place. Chromium-plated milk-bars on every corner. But a theatre—with real live actors? An orchestra? Not likely. . . . They stand, swilling indifferent liquor, transpiring manly friendliness, talking of nothing else in the world except sport in which they themselves so seldom take part. Or discussing the best way of "keeping the niggers in their place."

In the twenties and thirties, Empire communications were speeded up by the introduction of air services. With the advent of the Handley Page Heracles in 1931 and the Hannibal soon afterward, long-distance routes became feasible. The London–Cape service, via Cairo and Rhodesia, was inaugurated in 1932. It was by no means unknown for the aircraft to land in outlandish spots, when faced by a bad head wind. In 1936 Imperial Airways began a new service, with massive Empire flying boats which contained wide bunks, a bar, promenade deck and smoking room, and a cruising speed of 145 mph. Hot meals were served, not on trays, but at tables. For overnight stops, passengers were advised to take mosquito boots, silk pajamas, and sun helmets. The importance of Egypt, as a refueling place for both South Africa and India, remained.

Botha, worn out with work, died in 1919, and Smuts became Prime Minister. He had little idea of what to do about the native problem. "I sympathize profoundly with the native races of South Africa," he said, "but I don't believe in politics for them. . . . When I consider the political future of the natives in South Africa, I must say I look into the shadows and darkness; and then I feel inclined to shift the intolerable burden of solving the problem to the ampler shoulders and stronger brains of the future."

Smuts lost the election of 1924, partly as a result of his handling of the disturbances in Johannesburg in 1922. He was succeeded by Hertzog, who remained Prime Minister for fifteen years. Unlike Smuts, Hertzog had very definite ideas of what to do about the Africans: He believed in separation. But Hertzog was no fool. He admitted the policy of his party was based on fear: "The European is severe and hard on the Native because he is afraid of him. It is the old instinct of self-preservation. And the immediate outcome of this is that so little has been done in the direction of helping the Native to advance." The only answer, he believed, was to overcome the fear by creating two South Africas, one white and one black—for the benefit of both. This became the policy of his National Party. The opposition was equally adamant. Smuts' friend Jan Hofmeyr, elder statesman of the Cape Dutch, said: "We have many educated and semi-educated Natives in South Africa. Many of them have attained to, and many more of them are advancing towards, European standards. They have been trained on European lines.

They have been taught to think and act as Europeans. We may not like it, but those are the plain facts. Now what is the political future for those people? . . . We drive them back in hostility and disgruntlement." Hofmeyr, who also was not a fool, predicted "disaffection and revolt." Although the fear of the African had been admitted as the basic cause of South African unease, the hatred of the British remained among many Afrikaners, and politics remained split, despite all the efforts of Smuts, between English-speaking and Afrikaans-speaking. During the world slump Smuts joined with Hertzog to form the United Party, but the hard-core Nationalists, led by Daniel F. Malan, remained outside, to wait for another day.

The proud Zulu pondered their fate, in their crowded native reserves—at a density of 33.7 per square mile, compared with 20.7 in the Union. There were no serious disturbances among the Zulu between the wars, but there was a deterioration of their native communities and way of life. Dressed as shabby Europeans, in torn trousers and greasy hats, many left their reserves to find work in domestic service in Natal, Johannesburg, and the Cape.

Also in southern Africa were three protectorates which Britain had kept apart from the Union: Bechuanaland, Swaziland, and Basutoland. All were ruled through existing chiefs, now termed royal families. In 1933 the Khama, or ruler, of Bechuanaland caused some concern by convicting a white man for rape and sentencing him to be flogged. A party of Royal Marines saw to the Khama's abdication, but he later apologized and was restored to power.

The British South Africa Company's charter in Rhodesia had run out in 1914. In 1922 there was a referendum among the electorate on whether it should join South Africa; 5,989 voted for entry into the Union, 8,774 voted against. It is estimated that some 60 voters were Africans. The company agreed to accept £3,750,000 for Rhodesia, north and south, retaining its mineral rights. It was paid in cash, which it was glad to get, for its operation had been far from successful. On September 12, 1923, the thirty-second anniversary of the arrival of the pioneer column at Fort Salisbury, Southern Rhodesia was annexed to the crown and became a self-governing colony. As a colony it was unique, for real power resided not in the governor but in the legislature, elected almost entirely by the white settlers. In its reaction to the racial problem, it was dissimilar to South Africa in theory (there being, in fact, little theory), but similar in practice: identification laws, industrial color bar, taxation without representation, social color bar based at first on custom, becoming more and more based on law. The economy of the country depended largely on the European population. It was developing steadily, but slowly by the standards Rhodes had envisaged. In 1936 the population of Salisbury was 32,846, of whom 11,392 were Europeans. By 1939 the white population of the whole colony was only about 60,000.

Northern Rhodesia, which had become a separate and more traditional colony, was different in character. There were few settlers—13,155 Europeans altogether, 97 percent of whom worked in the copper mines near the railway. Most stayed a few years, made some money, and departed. They did not look on themselves as Rhodesians in the same way as those in Salisbury and Bulawayo. The other 3 percent were the administrators, missionaries, and traders who lived with the million and a quarter Africans in the bush. The few permanent Northern Rhodesians, who also practiced a strong color bar (stricter, in some respects, even than in Johannesburg at that time), were naturally jealous of the independence enjoyed by their southern neighbors. One who worked in the railway as an engine driver and who was becoming politically active was "Roy" Roland Welensky; he was planning to found a Northern Rhodesia Labour Party, but his greatest fame to date was as heavyweight boxing champion of the colony. In Southern Rhodesia, from a more conventional background—local private school, university, tobacco farming—was emerging a similarly inflexible character: Ian Smith.

Squashed between Rhodesia and Lake Nyasa was Nyasaland. It was stubbornly poor, and no one really knew what to do with it. Should it join up with Northern Rhodesia, with which it had ties through the old British South Africa Company? Or did it really belong with Tanganyika, Kenya, and Uganda? The governor was all-powerful, but from 1933 indirect rule was followed. Twenty district commissioners administered more than 2,000,000 Africans. By 1938 education was still 65 percent in the care of missionary societies; there were 4,171 primary schools in 1942, with an enrollment of 173,692 children (attendance being extremely irregular). In 1940 there were only 1,812 Europeans in the whole territory, many of them employed by the societies. It was, of course, Livingstone's old country, and the Church of Scotland was still a significant power in the land (its mission was the most notable building in the main town, Blantyre). The chief burden on the country was its railway, completed in 1935, which proved uneconomic.

The Tanganyika railways, in contrast, were paying their way by 1925. The governor, Sir Donald Cameron, was an old Lugard man from Nigeria and a confirmed believer in indirect rule. At first no Germans were allowed in to the old territory (many had returned to Europe, their lands having been confiscated), but during the 1930's they came back to the sisal, coffee, and tea plantations in strength. By 1940, in many areas of Tanganyika, Germans were more in evidence than British. All this was confusing to the Africans, some of whom had mastered German and were now expected to learn yet another foreign language. A mission arrived from Germany to honor the debts to Von Lettow's askaris, who had not been paid during a large part of the war. There was a great deal of suspicion about its motives, and it was only allowed to carry out its task after much argument and under the supervision of British officers. "Trade was bad at the time," admitted Sir Donald, "and I had no objection, naturally, to the German government circulating a considerable amount of money amongst the people." Indians were much in evidence, their numbers increasing nearly three fold between the wars; they controlled between 70 and 80 percent of the retail trade and owned much of the urban land. In 1938 less than 8 percent of the native children attended school (fewer than half of whom were at government schools). There were 820 colonial civil servants on the Tanganyika List administrating over 5,000,000 people (about 14,000 Europeans). The legislative council was typical of British institutions in Africa: 13 official members from the administration and 10 nonofficial members also appointed (including 3 Indians and a clergyman). In 1936 only 493 persons were reported to having incomes of more than £600 a year (more than half of them government officials). In 1937 Africans paid £672,050 in poll taxes. Despite the favorable tax rates, the influx of British settlers was small and not particularly encouraged by the authorities (after all, the territory was meant to be in trust, on behalf of the League of Nations, for the Africans), and Cameron and the government had to put up with a lot of criticism over this policy. Those who did come were usually retired and living on small pensions. A visiting journalist described three retired colonels at the Southern Highlands Club: "Holding a bitter post-mortem over their daily nine holes of golf. Sunk in the chintz-covered chairs, each with a glass of whisky in his hand, the flames from a freshly lighted log fire playing on their swarthy faces, they were fighting the game over, stroke for stroke; it might have been Bognor Regis."

The island of Zanzibar was an even more classic case of indirect rule. About 11,500 Arabs lorded it over nearly a quarter of a million Africans. The Arabs, who had formerly been slavers, were not loved, but at least an Anglican cathedral now stood on the old slave market. The British resident ruled through the sultan (Sir Seyyid Khalifa bin Harub). In 1926 a legislative council was established—with nominated members. The Establishment which the British propped up was old; surely it would last.

There was much talk of joining Tanganyika to Kenya and Uganda in some form of federation, and from London it seemed a good idea. In Uganda, the "model colony," it seemed outrageous. In Kenya the settlers were appalled. The fight to produce a "white man's country" was really on. As Churchill had predicted, the triangular conflict in Kenya between African, Indian, and Briton looked as if it would tear the country apart. The Indians wanted the colony for Indian settlement, and believed they were being discriminated against, while the British settlers wanted to preserve it for themselves and believed they were being let down by their own government at home. The Africans, understandably, believed they ought to have some say in the matter. In 1919 the governor announced: "This country is primarily for European development." It sounded simple. In the same year one boatload brought 1,500 new settlers and their families from England. Banks were generous, as they always had been in Kenya. The economy tottered along between financial crises, although the territory had first become self-supporting in 1914. Most settlers relied on substantial overdrafts. When Lord Delamere died in 1931, he was financially embarrassed, a by no means unusual condition. "Curse all this work," he said near the end. It was almost impossible to believe that the puckish, sarcastic, indomitable leader of the settlers, who had been known to shoot out the Nairobi streetlights with his revolver, had gone at last; no European could remember a time in Kenya without him. "Caution was unknown to him," said Lord Cranworth, "and the only limit set to him was the limit of his purse or power of borrowing."*

The problems remained. Said Lord Milner, in London: "It is clear that if the limited areas on which alone European settlers can live were thrown open to the competition of Asiatics, who are physically fit to settle in other areas from which Europeans are by nature excluded, there would be, taking the protectorate as a whole, a virtual discrimination in favour of Asiatic as against European settlement." The Kenya Indians' leader said: "I would go so far as to advocate the annexation of this African territory to the Indian Empire, with provincial government under the Indian Viceroy, and let it be opened to us, and in a very few years it will be a second India." At the end of the First World War there were 5,362 Europeans and 14,693 Indians in the protectorate; by 1937 the respective figures were 19,211 and 46,026. At one point a vigilance committee of settlers had contemplated kidnapping the governor, setting off an armed rising and deporting all Indians. They were intensely patriotic— "For King and Kenya" was their motto and they dutifully sang "God Save the King" at all their secret meetings. Any threat to their "White Highlands," in which lay their substantial estates and rambling country houses, led to fierce reaction. The Masai and the Kikuyu watched it all with little surprise, for the tribes of Africa well understood the reactions to fear.

Nairobi, with its distant prospect of Kilimanjaro to the south and Mount Kenya towering to the north, prided itself on being the "Paris of Africa." Potentates, from both East and West, visited it regularly on their way to shoot big game, which had become a major attraction. A safari in Kenya was almost obligatory for affluent European and American sportsmen, although the lions were now less easy to come by. The dashing Prince of Wales was among those who came to shoot. Smart cafés in Delamere Avenue were packed at lunchtime. Shops rivaled Kensington stores in the quality of their wares. A daily train

---

* The present Lord Delamere still lives in Kenya.

from Mombasa disgorged relatives, tourists, sportsmen, and visitors from Europe. One who arrived, his name a sigh from the past, was Baden-Powell. Africa, he said, was "home"; said his wife, "utterly and supremely happy here"; he died three years later, with Mount Kenya rising "through the clouds of sunset." Golf, polo, tennis, cricket were played at the clubs. It was not all happy-go-lucky, for while the white Kenyans played hard, they worked hard, too. As early as 1918 Nairobi boasted private nursing homes, a YMCA, a Chamber of Commerce, two theaters, a Masonic temple, and motor garages. Between the wars its population rose from 19,000 to more than 50,000. The governor ruled over all, in imperial grandeur and calm. An American journalist, Negley Farson, was invited to lunch at Government House:

> The room was spacious. Its cream walls were hung with the portraits of former governors. The servants wore scarlet, gold-embroidered jackets, with blue puggarees. The food, strangely enough, was excellent. There were some splendid alligator pears. The conversation was such as it was expected to be; neither witty nor dull, nor over-serious on any topic. And throughout it all the governor sat with that courteous attention which a gentleman in his position is expected to display through hundreds and hundreds of such meals which must have bored him to death.

It was the calm before the storm. By the Second World War suffrage included Europeans, Indians, and Arabs, less than one-fortieth of the population, and elected members as distinct from nominated, were in a minority in the Assembly, thus leaving real power in London rather than with any one group in Kenya. Education proceeded as fast as money, mainly from charity via the missionary societies, would allow, which was not very fast. Delamere had been saying for years that it was better to teach the Africans skills than book learning, but whereas many children knew the date of the Fire of London and the names of Henry VIII's wives, older ones even struggling with Elizabethan drama, very few were taught about soil fertility, nutrition of humans and animals, local history, or the basic principles of economics. Those who were educated found jobs to use their talents difficult to get. Cranworth described, in 1939, "a tragedy that one of the most notable results of our education and Christian teaching is the increase of crime and vice."

Uganda, on the basis of a cotton industry which had expanded dramatically since the arrival of the British, was experiencing some prosperity. Great efforts, as elsewhere in British Africa, had been made to eliminate the tsetse fly. The road system was the best in East Africa. Of greater importance was an extensive system of village schools. There were hardly any settlers; the 2,100 whites were mostly Colonial Office officials, missionaries and their families. The Kabaka ruled in Buganda with considerable autonomy (and slowly drank himself to death). There was not much trouble with the 17,300 Indians. The British capital at Entebbe, set discreetly apart from that of the Kabaka at Kampala, was the enclave where 500 Europeans lived in neat white houses among well-cut lawns and shady trees, beside the waters of Lake Victoria. "The atmosphere of Entebbe is one of altruistic administration," wrote Farson. "It speaks of unhurried research. You feel, suddenly, that this is the way things ought to be in Africa. This is a native country, left as native by the British as it is possible. If there is any oppression, it is the oppression of one native over another." It had been Lugard who had negotiated the original treaty with Buganda, and thus it was apt that Uganda should be the pride of all those who proclaimed the virtues of indirect rule. But how long, in increasingly changing conditions, would Africans tolerate being oppressed by Africans without at least a change of oppressors? Perhaps the research was a little too unhurried.

British Somaliland, at the strategically important Horn of Africa, was the disgrace of the Colonial Office. The place showed no likelihood at all of ever paying its way. The trade balance was in seemingly permanent deficit, and revenue was well below the modest expenditure (1937) of £195,568 for a population of more than a third of a million. Annual grants were made from the Colonial Development Fund. For twenty years development had been hindered by the warlike activities of a religious leader, known to the British as the Mad Mullah. "I like war, but you do not," he complained to the governor. The Mullah was sane enough. At one point he pushed the British back to the coast and was only finally defeated in 1920 when the RAF was brought in to bomb his army to bits. The Mad Mullah escaped, only to die of influenza a few weeks later.

The British did not much like Somaliland and were only there to protect the route to India. In 1937 there were 549 Europeans in a territory twice the size of England. It was the least sought-after post in the Colonial Service, and considered something of a dead end, in contrast with adventure novels set in the place which featured the romantic local camel corps.

In Egypt there was restlessness and ferment. No territory of the Empire gave Britain more trouble between the wars. The two peoples disliked each other. The Egyptians saw the British as cynical oppressors, the heirs to the Ottoman Empire, while the British saw the Egyptians as lazy, immoral, and untrust-worthy. The Egyptian had become a stock figure of fun in England, dressed in a nightshirt and selling pornographic pictures; the fez is to this day considered a ridiculous headgear, and comedians find it a reliable prop. The old servility of Egypt, acquired during long years under the Turkish yoke, brought out the arrogance in the English upper class, and in their relations with the Egyptians, the British revealed a curious lack of sympathy not noticeable elsewhere in the Empire. When it became evident that Egypt was not to get independence after the war, there was serious rioting in 1919. The remaining interwar years were a story of Britain gradually and reluctantly giving way to demands for independence, while attempting to prop up the increasingly unpopular dynasty. The king, as the sultan was now known, was Italian in speech and outlook, although of Albanian origin. The ruling class was Turkish or French-oriented Egyptians. The Egyptian masses were Arab, and they were poor, although, thanks to Cromer, better off than before. The first proconsul after the war was Lord Allenby, who did not have the traditional distaste for the Egyptians. Allenby was a remarkable man who had been given the job because it was thought he would be firm and tough. In fact, he forced a reversal of British policy within three weeks of his arrival and obtained the return from exile of the nationalist leader Saad Zaghlul Pasha.

The main problem was the presence of British troops and the security of the Suez Canal. Churchill, always obsessed by the canal, was the chief advocate of a hard line in Egypt. At length Allenby found it impossible to get Egyptian support. A professional soldier who was unaccustomed to diplomatic procedures, he stormed into London in fairly sensational manner. Allenby was popularly known as the Bull. Arriving at Victoria Station early in the morning, he got a friend to drive him to the Foreign Office, where he produced twenty-nine pages of type-written foolscap from his briefcase, addressed to the Foreign Secretary, which he left with a porter. Allenby's memorandum on Egypt, which amounted to an ultimatum, was very much more strongly worded than was usual in official exchanges. At a meeting later the same day the Foreign Secretary, Lord Curzon, attempted to reprimand Allenby for addressing him in un-acceptable terms, but Allenby refused to budge. Allenby's for-midable presence when he was roused had in the past reduced hardy colonels to being sick on the carpet. The Foreign Secre-tary ended his interview in tears. At 10 Downing Street, Allenby told Lloyd George: "Well, it is no good disputing any longer. I have told you what I think is necessary . . . I have waited five weeks for a decision and I can't wait any longer. I shall tell Lady Allenby to come home." Lloyd George had given Allenby "special powers" to solve the problem; moreover, he was the most important man in the Empire after the viceroy of India and his resignation would have been a serious political crisis. The Prime Minister said: "You have waited five weeks, Lord Allenby; wait five more minutes." He then gave way to Allenby's demands for Egypt.

There had been considerable concessions: The "protector-ate" was ended, as was martial law. But within three weeks the British government had informed the great powers that Britain would maintain a "special relationship" with Egypt. It could permit no question or discussion of the relationship, and any interference in Egypt by another power would be considered an unfriendly act by Great Britain. The British kept more dis-creetly behind the scenes. Egypt had domestic home rule with Zaghlul as Prime Minister. But Allenby spoiled all his good work by losing control of himself and the situation when the governor general of the Sudan, Sir Lee Stack, was murdered in 1924 while passing through Cairo on leave. Allenby immedi-ately assumed it had been the work of nationalists and held Zaghlul's government responsible. He decided to demand a fine of half a million pounds and the virtual loss of Egyptian influence in the Sudan (something for which Britain had long been maneuvering). He sent off a cable to the Foreign Office for authority. When the time came for him to leave to present his demands, a reply from London still had not arrived. As he left the residency, an aide ran out to tell him a message had arrived from the Foreign Office, but it had not yet been decoded. The Bull was not a man to be unnerved by such a situation. He left, escorted by an entire jangling cavalry regiment, the Sixteenth/Fifth Lancers. Zaghlul was having his afternoon sleep when Allenby burst in upon him and read his demands. When he returned, he saw the Foreign Office cable; it advocated a milder approach.* Allenby was finished; He was maneuvered into resignation six months later. "I cannot ask to be retired with a view to relief from a strain which I do not feel," he insisted. He was the best friend Egypt had had since Cromer, but it is doubtful if he could have achieved much more.

Sporadic rioting and widespread discontent continued. A young student named Gamal Nasser wrote in an essay: "The disputes among the parties are being fomented by Imperialism, the Palace, and the party leaders themselves. Thus they hope to keep the country divided and busy with the race for lucrative posts." There was a growing disgust with politics, and the dynasty was discredited, although the British continued doggedly to support it. Opposition gathered in the uncompromising and nationalist Moslem Brotherhood, which sought a return to a truly Moslem state without extremes of wealth and poverty. The next notable proconsul was Lord Lloyd, who gained a great reputation in Britain and almost as much in Egypt. He, too, found himself fighting the government at home as much as the extremists in the streets of Cairo and Alexandria. In 1936 Egypt assumed full independence. Britain agreed to confine her troops to the Canal Zone (but was laggardly in withdrawing them there), and Egypt was allowed to revive her influence in the Sudan, always precious to her because of the Sudanese hold over the Nile.

Sudan was administered by a cliquish body of colonial civil servants who quietly devoted their working lives to improving the territory with few funds. "Boys, fresh from Oxford and Cambridge, and away from home for the first time, were put in complete charge of a district that might be twice the size of England," wrote a Sudanese. Under British supervision, there was a great expansion of the cotton industry, especially the

---

* The fine was accepted, however. It was used on medical services in the Sudan.

Gezira scheme, a vast irrigation project in a formerly arid area. Khartoum had been rebuilt, largely according to Kitchener's plan, with impressive buildings along the river esplanade, Gordon Avenue and Victoria Avenue. The street system was laid out in the design of the Union Jack. An electric tramway served the city and also Omdurman.

Newspapers found plenty of material in Egypt, and Allenby and others complained that riots had been grossly exaggerated, claiming that only the city dwellers were politically roused. But one story from Egypt riveted the attention of the world. For years Lord Carnarvon had been supporting the excavation of ancient Egyptian places; many wonderful discoveries had been made, indicative of a fascinating civilization 3,000 years before the time of Christ. Howard Carter discovered the tomb of Tutankhamen on November 4, 1922. A rumor gained ground that if the tomb were disturbed, those responsible would die. Carter opened the entrance on February 16, 1923. Sure enough, Carnarvon was bitten by a mosquito and died three weeks later. His brother, who had also been associated with Egypt, died soon after. Howard Carter, however, carried on the digging, and a remarkable treasure-house was discovered, the finest ever uncovered in Egypt. Despite the superstition, he died in 1939, aged sixty-six.

In West Africa the problems seemed comparatively mild. They were there, but there was nothing, it seemed, which time would not solve. The coastal strips were still carefully styled colonies, the hinterlands protectorates, but it did not make much difference so far as the inhabitants were concerned. The West African territories seldom reached the news, and a generation of colonial servants sweated out the best part of a lifetime's career in them between the wars. Rivalries between colonial servants were keen, but not entirely frivolous. The commissioners in Nigeria praised their "boys" as the best in Africa; the commissioners in the Gold Coast did the same.

In Nigeria it was still largely a matter of disentanglement and of producing an entity (in one province as many as sixty different languages were spoken), and tribal distrust between Ibo, Yoruba, Fuli, and others showed no signs of disappearing with the advent of railways, blackboards, Guinness, and trousers. Some 1,000 Europeans lived in an area nearly seven times the size of England, among 20,000,000 Africans. Order was preserved by 3,599 troops and 3,365 police. By 1929, 1,900 miles of railway had been constructed, and 3,000 miles of tolerably good road were being maintained. The administration was still complicated; some areas had a measure of representation, others not. The territory was self-supporting, exporting palm oil, palm kernels, cocoa, tin, groundnuts, and cotton; much of the cotton returned in the form of garments, and another major import was cigarettes. In an effort to improve production and protect health and morals, gin was prohibited in 1919. Trade had always been a major reason for "opening up" Nigeria, and now the day had come. In 1927 Britain supplied 62 percent of the imports and took 45.6 percent of the exports; most of the companies, particularly in the tin fields, were registered in London. Up till the Second World War education was still mainly in the hands of the missionaries, but there was a government secondary school at Lagos and a few technical and teacher-training colleges. Owing to the adherence to indirect rule, public beheading did not cease until the late 1920's. "The condemned man, his hands tied to his sides, was led through the market place," wrote a district commissioner; "the sword whistled round the unfortunate's head but still he was led on—and the fatal blow was given. Eye witnesses have told me of the headless body continuing to walk for many paces." Flogging continued into the 1930's, particularly for the nonpayment of tax (it had not been abolished in the British regiments in Africa till the late twenties).

The organization of the Gold Coast was as diffuse as that of Nigeria, only the coastal strip being officially described as a colony. There were about 3,000 Europeans. Cocoa was proving far more valuable than gold—the export value of cocoa was £9,181,000 in 1926, more than ten times the value of gold exports. From producing approximately one-fourteenth of the world's cocoa in 1906 the Gold Coast was producing nearly one-half only twenty years later. It was produced by self-employed African planters. Britain supplied two-thirds of the imports but took only one-third of the exports (the Americans were also proving to have a vast taste for chocolate). By 1926 the attendance at elementary schools was about 30,000; by the Second World War there were two teacher-training colleges. The Prince of Wales visited the site of a new college devoted to that favorite British concept, "character building." Trade had brought about a considerable middle class of Africans; the color bar was nowhere as conspicuous as in South Africa, the Rhodesias, and Kenya. In Ashanti, no further attempts were made to usurp the Golden Stool, which was rediscovered in 1920. In 1925 Prempeh returned to Kumasi from exile; the chief who had once presided over sacrifices returned as a mild-mannered Christian in a lounge suit. In accordance with indirect rule, he traveled about his former country by saloon car to preside at meetings, served on a sanitary committee, and made telephone calls, whereas once he had sent messages by drum. In 1935 he was succeeded by his nephew, Lieutenant Colonel Sir Osei Prempeh II. The Gold Coast and Ashanti were not heaven, but they were a lot better than they had been, by any standards.

The two remaining colonies in West Africa, Sierra Leone and Gambia, were also being brought into the currents of world trade. Sierra Leone exported cotton and agricultural produce, and more than half the imports came from Britain. The legislative council was mainly nominated by the governor, but there were three elected members. Indirect rule was religiously applied through the chiefs and native courts. It was an odd anomaly that the colony founded for freed slaves did not successfully abolish slavery in its hinterland until 1928 (some 200,000 persons becoming free on January 1 of that year).

Gambia consisted of a strip of land along each bank of the Gambia River and a dusty, ramshackle little town called Bathurst, where fewer than half the 265 Europeans were British. It had been self-supporting since 1871. Almost the entire male population was engaged in the production and export of the groundnut, the cultivation of which had been much improved.

Such was the situation in British Africa by 1939. An efficient, honorable administration ruled through existing institutions, even when they were based on old oppressions. Many of the British loved their Empire, all were proud of their reponsibilities abroad, but they preferred them not to cost too much. It was not, as compared with other periods of history, at all a bad time to be an African in one of those territories. Few people were aware of the volcano rumbling beneath.

In 1939, this scene of comfortable imperialism from Table Mountain to the Nile Delta was shattered by another world war. Strictly speaking the war was not Africa's affair, for it had nothing to do with Africa except that some of the powers involved had African territory. Hitler had said that although the loss of the German colonies in Africa was the only quarrel he had with Britain, he would not go to war over them. It was a question of ambitions and fears in Europe, resulting from the previous war. But there was always the Suez Canal. And in May, 1940, Winston Churchill became Prime Minister. His public career had stretched so long that he could claim to be both "India man" and "Africa man," as few others could, having been politically and personally involved with both parts of the Empire since his youth. The Suez Canal still haunted him, although from early in the war, ships and convoys to India had no longer used it, anyway, but had gone around the Cape. And since the First World War he had gained a great interest in the strategic importance of southern Europe. His other interest in the area was to bring Turkey into the war. He spent much of the war fighting for these three pet ideas about the Mediterranean and the Middle East, for he could find few to share his preoccupations, especially when America became an ally. North Africa and the Mediterranean, therefore, came much into his view and considerations.

Hitler, on the other hand, was always bored by North Africa. Insofar as he had ambitions toward India, it appears that he would have approached the subcontinent through the Caucasus. His main interest in the Middle East was Iraqi oil.

Italy entered the war on June 10. The British army had returned to Egypt; some of it had never left. The Egyptian monarch, Farouk, was hostile to the British, but the British occupation was supported by the once anti-British nationalist party, the Wafd, which returned to power in 1942. The Eleventh Hussars drove their armored cars into the Italian colony of Libya, from Egypt, within twenty-four hours of the outbreak of war with Italy. The Italians were surprised because they had not known anything about being at war. Soon Italian troops were pouring into North Africa, about a quarter of a million of them against some 50,000 British. But the first major conflicts were in the Horn of Africa, where the Italians already held Ethiopia and had invaded British Somaliland, which they occupied for nearly eight months. They were beaten back and defeated in 1941, after difficult and rigorous campaigning in which many colored African troops took part. Churchill was uninterested in this campaign ("petty"), which he thought was a distraction from the serious affairs farther north. This was a curious attitude, for the Horn of Africa had always been thought of as strategically important in relation to India.

The British in Africa were well led by General Archibald "Archy" Wavell, a one-eyed authority on desert warfare and a great admirer of Allenby. Wavell early on set the style for the desert war; he was not a stickler for discipline, and caring little for the appearance of his troops, he sported a short-sleeved pullover over a long-sleeved one and a rather battered cap. Officers began to conform to a pattern: They cultivated eccentric mustaches, suede shoes, and voluminous sheepskin jackets (the nights were cold). It became a kind of uniform and remained as a supposedly rakish fashion a quarter of a century after the war. All this brought some glamor to a nerveracking war in which civilians at home were often in greater danger than the armed services. The North African campaign produced perhaps the two best British poets of the war, Keith Douglas and Sydney Keyes, both killed. The campaign had a character of its own. Each side respected the enemy to a degree they never did in Europe itself, and conduct regarding prisoners, wounded, and Red Cross vehicles was of a high standard. When the Germans arrived, they and the British army shared a popular song, "Lili Marlene."

Owing to Wavell's success, Hitler was reluctantly obliged to support his ally, and the famous Afrika Korps was formed under the German commander General Erwin Rommel, the "Desert Fox," a very able tactician. The front went backward and forward, always dominated by the long supply lines, "the long road back," as Churchill called it. A lonely little port, Tobruk, of which few had previously heard, assumed an exaggerated importance as British and Australian troops were twice left there by the retreating army to face sieges. One of Rommel's staff said: "Tobruk had become an obsession with him [Rommel]. For over a year its capture had been the dominant desire in his mind, even though he engaged in other operations. He said he could not take Egypt if he left Tobruk behind." This was what Churchill, who was also obsessed with Tobruk, had hoped he would think. In the event, Tobruk had little effect on the campaign. Wavell, prompted by Churchill and Anthony Eden, the Foreign Secretary, grossly overextended his resources and failed. He could not get on with Churchill, whom he believed had finished Allenby in Egypt. He was replaced by General Claude Auchinleck, who held Rommel only 60 miles from Alexandria. At the beginning of July, 1942, there was considerable likelihood that Rommel would reach the Nile and Egypt would be lost. But, as one reporter wrote, "The atmosphere among ordinary civilians in Cairo continued so carefree that one had difficulty in believing such things." He continued: "One of the most curious and least expected legacies of British rule which this crisis brought out was a tendency among the peoples of Egypt to their own variant of British phlegm, and even to that famous British complacency. Without a doubt the behaviour of the very mixed town populations during the period when Rommel was bearing down on them with apparently irresistible momentum was admirable. It was quite obvious that the enemy radio was doing its best to create panic in the rear. But the people did not panic." Fortunately for the British, Rommel went over to the defensive on July 4.

Churchill was completely committed to the North African campaign. He was now in a difficult position politically, under considerable criticism in the House of Commons and some in the press. There was pressure to remove him, not so much as Prime Minister but as Minister of Defense, a position which, as a general *manqué,* he valued much more. Churchill took the closest day-to-day interest in the campaign—far too close for some commanders, who thought they should be allowed to get on with their jobs without detailed interference from politicians. Occasionally he even received copies of messages from young tank commanders. Auchinleck was replaced by Generals Harold Alexander and Bernard Montgomery. Montgomery had unusual powers of leadership and was an efficient commander; moreover, he inspired the force with determination and fitted into the style nicely, soon sporting two badges in his cap and a pullover only just surviving at the elbows.

He attacked the length of Rommel's line near the little railway halt of Alamein, where an old poster still fluttered in the desert wind with the message "Spend Your Holidays in Sunny Palestine." Montgomery had considerable superiority and began with an enormous barrage from nearly 1,000 guns. The Afrika Korps faced the equally famous Eighth Army, with their insignia of a desert rat. "If we are beaten in this battle, it's the end of Winston," said a senior minister in London. It was a hard-fought engagement, but Montgomery broke the Germans after twelve days. Churchill was overjoyed. The victory did mark a turning point in the war in that the British never again suffered a serious reverse.

The eyes of much of the world watched the desert war with fascination, but the main struggle was taking place in Europe on the eastern front.

Two days after Alamein, American and British forces invaded the French territories of Morocco and Algeria, to attack Rommel from the rear. German troops fought stubbornly, but after six months Rommel was cornered in Tunisia. On May 13, 1943, it was all over. "Africa was clear of our foes," Churchill wrote. "One continent had been redeemed." But the continent had only contained three poor, sparsely populated enemy colonies, nearly all sand. Europe remained. At least its "soft underbelly" was now fully exposed. Churchill claimed: "No one could doubt the magnitude of the victory of Tunis. It held its own with Stalingrad." The king, George VI, sent a personal message to the Prime Minister: "The African campaign has immeasurably increased the debt that this country, and indeed all the United Nations, owes to you." Churchill had to hurry off to Washington to persuade his doubting allies to follow up the campaign in Africa. "What should we do with our victory? Were its fruits to be gathered only in the Tunisian tip, or should we drive Italy out of the war and bring Turkey in on our side?" The Americans found it difficult to move Churchill from his strategy, and he got his way, but decreasingly so as the war went on and as the American part in it outweighed the British.

Churchill had already made it clear that Britain had no more territorial ambitions in Africa or, indeed, anywhere owing to the war. Italy had not achieved military conquest in Libya until as late as 1928, but she had already settled some 50,000 Italians along the coastal belt. The colony now came under a British administration, under which it remained for nine years. There were internal difficulties—the British backed a Cyrenaican monarchy which was not wildly popular in the rest of the country—but no one doubted that the new conquerors were not there to stay. The British had promised the Senussi, the major inhabitants of Cyrenaica, that they would not be returned to Italian rule, in return for their help in the war. After independence,

British administrators stayed on in many parts to guide the flegling country, and Britain supplied an annual grant to balance the budget. Montgomery had set the tone of British rule in North Africa when he said, in a message to the inhabitants at the end of 1942: "The military government will endeavour to rule with firmness, justice and consideration for the interests of the people of the country." Eritrea, at the Horn of Africa, had been rapidly colonized, the Italian population increasing from 4,188 in 1931 to nearly 50,000 by the war. The British administration took on many problems, including a threat of famine and severe unemployment. In their stay of eleven and a half years, they did much to better the area: They improved sanitation and public health and increased the number of schools. In nearby Italian Somaliland, also occupied by Britain in 1941, there was a similar administration, based at first on Nairobi. There Britain had a nine-year rule. In Ethiopia, which had been freed from the Italians, the British stayed only nine months; some 40,000 Italian civilians had been at the mercy of the Ethiopians. Emperor Haile Selassie returned to his country, but the British insisted on retaining a "military mission," advisers to the emperor, and on the presence of British judges in the courts. In return, she provided a £6,750,000 grant.

The Second World War had a great effect on imperialism and thus on Africa. Africans had fought on behalf of the Allies, they had been educated by travel and by the army, they could read newspapers, they had enjoyed a higher standard of living than before, and they returned home to conditions which did not satisfy them—even though the war had brought much capital into the colonies, with new roads, bases, airfields and harbors. They had seen white men killed in battle, they had gained confidence from becoming proficient at the white man's weapons, and they had heard of the humiliation of the British, French, and Dutch in the Far East. As the Rhodesian leader Ndabaninghi Sithole wrote: "After spending four years hunting white enemy soldiers, the African never again regarded them as gods." In addition, British troops training or in transit in the colonies had shown the African an unfamiliar kind of white man, one who went out with local girls and recognized no color bar.

If the war had brought unprecedented activity and some

prosperity to much of Africa, it had brought Britain down to the economic essentials. It was difficult to realize that the land of the white-helmeted governors, of the great fleet, of the raj, with colonial territories in every portion of the globe, one of the Big Three who were presuming at conferences to shape the future world, was bankrupt. It seemed incredible that a British ambassador to Washington, Lord Lothian, once a member of "Milner's Kindergarten," an old imperialist who had advised Lloyd George on the Empire, had actually said to the American press: "Well, boys, Britain's broke. It's your money we want." But it was true.

On the wider stage, the scene had utterly changed. There was a confrontation between the two great power groups, East and West, led by Russia and the United States, called the cold war. It left little room for the colonialism of prewar years, which seemed already, and was, a distant age. The European powers were faced with new problems, and they could not afford the grandiose schemes of old. Above all, the great British Empire, which had seemed so powerful, so permanent, so mighty only fifty years before, was quaking everywhere with protest. The brotherhood which had seemed so strong was revealing bonds which were so slight that they looked incapable of holding back the forces gathering ahead. The world waited to see what Britain would do about it.

PART FOUR

WIND OF CHANGE

❖ XV ❖

Striking the Flag

AT the end of the Second World War Britain ruled over a truly vast area of the African continent, including most of the ex-Italian colonies. On the roads to Berlin and Tokyo, the military tentacles from the island in northern Europe had stretched out across the deserts, mountain ranges and forests of Africa. Jeeps, RAF planes, trucks full of singing soldiers—they had been everywhere. But when the floor was swept clean for peace, the carpet appeared to be different.

The approximate European links with Africa immediately after the Second World War, including the temporary administration of the former Italian Empire, were as follows:

Great Britain	..	4,750,000	square miles (including South Africa, but not Egypt)
France	..	4,450,000	square miles
Belgium	..	930,000	" "
Portugal	..	788,000	" "
Spain	..	135,000	" "

The war had brought money into Africa, and in the postwar period this trend was increased. Africa's natural resources were developed as never before. Hydroelectric schemes, as at Kariba and on the Volta, transformed the industrial capacity. Roads were reconstructed and tarred across the continent to carry a new volume of traffic. Agricultural and veterinary improvements, especially the rotation of crops, were much greater than in the prewar years. There was a great increase in the building and staffing of schools and colleges.

That Britain took her full part in all this, despite her impecunious state, was to her credit, but many of the improvements were financed by the colonial territories themselves. The Gold Coast became the largest exporter of cocoa in the world and, after Malaya, the second richest colony in the Empire.

In Britain there was a Labour government, pledged (as, indeed, had been the wartime government) to self-government for the colonies. There was never any doubt of that, even among African nationalists. The Empire was to be a Commonwealth of Nations—a sort of Empire Old Boys' Club (an association of some standing, but previously for white members only). The Colonial Secretary was a mild, almost nondescript man, full of good intentions, who had made a long study of colonial problems: Arthur Creech Jones. The Labour government was adamant that self-government would have to be planned. First of all, economic development would have to be accelerated by massive injections of capital. In 1940 Britain had made available £5,000,000 per annum for development in the Commonwealth and Empire, but between 1946 and 1966 the nation spent about £450,000,000 for this purpose. The Overseas Food Corporation was set up to organize a great groundnut industry in East Africa. It was a catastrophe. Africa was not a place for such planning. For one thing, it was as yet far too unpredictable. The Colonial Development Corporation set up less ambitious schemes, also with its measure of failure.

At first progress in self-government also seemed to be going along at a speed about which few could complain. Legislatives were set up or improved. The Gold Coast was to be the showpiece. In March, 1946, there was a majority of African members in the legislature and a majority of elected members over nominated members. It was the first colony to experience such a situation, and to many at the time it seemed revolutionary. Final powers remained with the governor. Nigeria took a similar step forward in January, 1947.

Creech Jones toured African colonies, called a conference of governors, another of African MP's, and generally busied himself with Africa as no Colonial Secretary had done before him. But it was not enough for the nationalists, and they remained suspicious. In the Gold Coast, Nigeria, and Tanganyika there were political murders. Azikiwe's newspapers, for the small educated class in Nigeria, kept up a wild mood of dissatisfaction. Trade unionism was growing with distinctly nationalist overtones. There were strikes and riots, particularly in the Gold Coast (on one day twenty-one persons were killed). The discontent was not confined to Africa; there was a feeling among some at home that Britain was still not doing enough for Africa. It was certainly true that the Colonial Service, under new and demanding conditions, was absurdly overstretched, for there were still only about 2,000 officers to administer the 25,000,000 people of Nigeria. The colonial servants got on with their jobs as best they could. They were not overpaid. In 1956 the salary of the governor of British Somaliland, was £2,250 (entertainment allowance £650), while the head of police received £1,435. The director of medical services in Sierra Leone received £1,950; the director of education in that colony, £1,750. Portraits of colonial officers in Africa at this time appeared in two distinguished novels: *The Heart of the Matter,* by Graham Greene (1948), and *Consul at Sunset,* by Gerald Hanley (1951).

Everywhere the talk was of independence and of freedom. There was a feeling in Africa that independence was a word of almost magical qualities, the granting of which would solve all problems (the reverse was that the colonial powers were the source of all the problems). In 1944 the novelist Joyce Cary, who had wrought some fine literature out of British Africa having been a colonial servant, 1913–20), had written: "Freedom, power in the people, is a nuisance to rulers; it is insolent, enterprising, vulgar, inconstant, ungrateful. It produces in any state an everlasting confusion and turmoil. It has the manners of a yahou and the vitality of a mad dog. . . . It offers to every ambitious man, good or bad, the challenge of its opportunity. He can become great and glorious at one stroke by uniting that power in the name of the people."

Such a man had appeared in Africa: Kwame Nkrumah.

When "freedom" came, it came with speed. After the war here were nine ruling powers in Africa: Britain, France, Portugal, the Union of South Africa, Egypt, Belgium, Spain, Ethiopia and Liberia; by 1970, there were forty-four.

In a few years the whole concept of Africa had changed. It could no longer be regarded as the black man's home and the

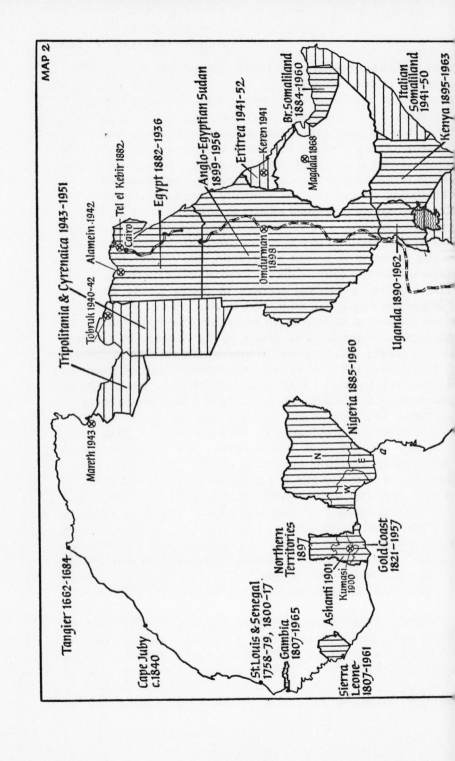

MAP 2

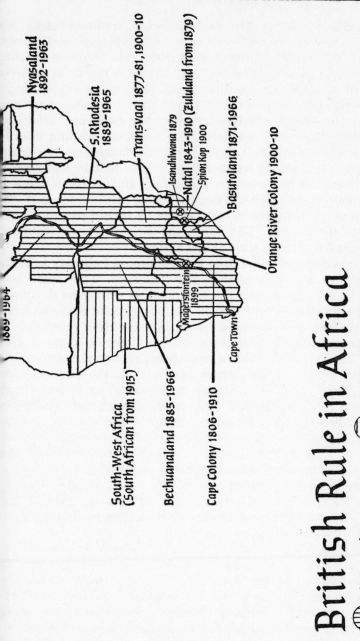

British Rule in Africa

⬭ Colonies and Protectorates   ⬭ Mandates and Trusteeships

The Cape-to-Cairo Railway ═══ COMPLETED ╌╌╌ PROJECTED

| 0 | 500 | 1000 | 1500 | 2000 miles | 2500 |

© CASSELL & CO LTD 1970

Nyasaland 1892-1963

S. Rhodesia 1889-1965

Transvaal 1877-81, 1900-10

Isandhlwana 1879

Natal 1843-1910 (Zululand from 1879)

Spion Kop 1900

Basutoland 1871-1966

Orange River Colony 1900-10

Magersfontein 1899

Cape Town

1889-1964

South-West Africa (South African from 1915)

Bechuanaland 1885-1966

Cape Colony 1806-1910

white man's preserve. African nationalism, confined before the war to a few intellectuals in London and America, had caught hold of the masses, and it showed every sign of being violent. From the Cape to Cairo there was a shiver of unease as settlers, colonial servants, businessmen from Europe considered their future and the safety of themselves and their families. Fear was back to the African continent. Perhaps the awful predictions of the Afrikaners had been right, after all. The speeding of self-government, under the Labour Party, had bought an inevitable swing to the right in South Africa, where Britain had always been suspect in her relations with Africa and Africans. Sensing the danger, Smuts, who had become Prime Minister again at the start of the war, suggested that George VI should pay an official visit to the Union. The king, the British Prime Minister (Clement Attlee) and the Cabinet agreed.

King and queen sailed from Portsmouth on February 1, 1947, in Britain's newest battleship, the *Vanguard*. They spent ten weeks in the Union, and the king worked with great devotion and energy to help heal the old wounds, despite anxieties over other matters. He presented Smuts, now the elder statesman of the Commonwealth, with the exclusive Order of Merit on the day of his arrival. He paid an unexpected visit on the eighty-two-year-old widow of the former President of the Orange Free State, Steyn. At Groote Schuur he returned to South Africa Kruger's Bible, which had been captured with the President's effects when Roberts had entered Pretoria nearly half a century before. He quoted Kruger in his broadcast to the South African people: "Take from the past all that is good and beautiful." He spoke to nationalists who had voted in 1942 for a complete rupture with the British crown. He stood beside Rhodes' grave. He tried to neglect no aspect, and no one cheered the royal party more enthusiastically than the flag-waving Africans who lined the roads.

The visit coincided with the coming-of-age of Princess Elizabeth. She spoke from Cape Town, in a clear, vibrant voice, to the 500,000,000 people of the new Commonwealth: "I declare before you all that my whole life, whether it be long or short, shall be devoted to your service and the service of our great Imperial Commonwealth." Few could have remained unmoved by the obvious sincerity and dedication to service of the king and his family, and by the end of the tour the king had won over most of those nationalists who had been hostile to his visit. The king wrote to Smuts: "Now that our visit is over I don't mind confessing to you alone that I was rather fearful about it, after reading various books and reports on South Africa. . . . If, and I firmly believe it has, our visit has altered the conception of monarchy to some South Africans, and has given them a new viewpoint from our personal contacts with them, then our tour has been well worth while."

But as it turned out, it was a personal matter only.* The Afrikaners respected the king as a man, but it was not enough. The following year Smuts was defeated, and the blatantly racial Nationalist Party came to power (but on an overall minority of votes). It began immediately to put effect to its policy of apartheid. It appealed also to the old anti-British hatreds of the Afrikaners. It also assuaged a new fear in South Africa, now dominated by industrial business, the fear of Communism. As some three-fifths of the population were Afrikaans-speaking, the combination seemed to be irresistible for many years, and so it proved. The Prime Minister, Dr. Malan, was succeeded by Johannes G. Strijdom, who was as straightforward as Hertzog had been. Strijdom was followed by Hendrik F. Verwoerd. The course of South Africa was not difficult to discern. The country became a republic in 1960. In 1961 it left the Commonwealth, thus severing the last remaining links with Britain. In South Africa this was frankly looked on as the final and victorious outcome of the old struggles with an old enemy, particularly of the South African War. The dream of Milner, Rhodes, and others to bring the Afrikaners into the British system had never really come true, for the Afrikaners had proved far too strong. They got on with their age-old affairs, which had been interrupted, less likely to be moved by isolation from the world, which had always been their wish, than any other people on earth. Strijdom said: "I am being as blunt as I can. I am making no excuses. Either the white man dominates or the black man takes over."

Strijdom's words shocked the world. But they were only the simple truth, as was being amply demonstrated elsewhere on the continent.

* Shortly before his death, the king was offered a private visit to South Africa, for his health, by Dr. Malan, as a guest of the South African government.

The first colonial territory in Africa to be released into a violent and confused world after the war was the Sudan. The speed there was due more to the ambitions of the Egyptians than to those of the Sudanese. Egypt was anxious to gain sole control over the area. The first Sudanese general election was held in 1953. Two years later the assembly voted for a republic, and this was set up on January 1, 1956. The Sudan left the Commonwealth but inherited a British city, British administration, and much else besides. The Mahdi, who to the British had been a bloodthirsty, fanatical tyrant, was revered as a national saint. The main difficulty in the Sudan, as in so many other subsequent nations in Africa, was that it was not really an entity at all, having been carved out of Africa by Europeans fairly arbitrarily many years before. Within two years of independence the democratic government had given way to a military *coup d'état*. The country was deeply split between two races, and little progress had been made toward integration. Under the British, the country had remained largely cut off from the rest of the world. "Visitation was not encouraged," wrote John Gunther, in 1955. The United States had not been allowed any representation until as late as 1951.

The example of the Sudan was a great boost to nationalism in Africa. Nkrumah was the man who seized the hour. He had returned to his country from London in December, 1947, after twelve years abroad. He had a certain aura about him: aloof cold, with a slightly cynical smile, and considerable powers of oratory. He was a hard political realist, the first modern African politician of stature.

Nkrumah was called home to be secretary-general of the United Gold Coast Convention, a mainly middle-class nationalist organization, at a salary of £20 a month. He made it into a considerable political machine but found it too timid for his approach. Nkrumah believed in violent protest, was convinced it would work. When an all-African assembly was elected in 1949, he said it was not enough, "an imperialist fraud." He began the policy of positive action. Nkrumah was ruthless tireless, and utterly convinced. His vast appeal was not to the middle class of Africans, but to a whole new area of society which had hardly been politically conscious before, and he appealed especially to youth. He formed a new party, and strikes and boycotts proliferated. Nkrumah helped found a aggressive nationalist newspaper. He was charged with inciting others to strike illegally, was convicted and sentenced to twelve months' imprisonment with hard labor. In prison, he wrote editorials, on a toilet-paper roll, between mending fishing nets.

At a general election in 1951, Nkrumah's party won a majority of seats. Nkrumah was released from prison and faced representatives of the press from all over the world. "I would like to make it absolutely clear that I am a friend of Britain," he said. "I come out of jail and into the assembly without the slightest feeling of bitterness to Britain. I stand for no discrimination against any race or individual, but I am unalterably opposed to imperialism in any form." Within twenty-four hours of being released he was offered the post of leader of government business by the governor. Later the British were able to bring themselves to call him Prime Minister. For six years Nkrumah ruled the Gold Coast, with his radical Marxist party, in conjunction with the Colonial Service and under the sovereignty of the queen. The world watched this strange partnership with bewilderment. An excellent relationship developed between the rebellious Prime Minister and the governor, Sir Charles Arden-Clarke. Arden-Clarke was a typical "Africa hand"; for sixteen years he had been in the Colonial Service in Nigeria, followed by six years in Bechuanaland and four years in Basutoland. When, at last, news arrived from London that the British government was ready to grant dominion status (which was what Nkrumah had always sought), the governor was as moved as the former rebel. "He handed me a dispatch from the Secretary of State," wrote Nkrumah. "When I reached the fifth paragraph the tears of joy that I had difficulty in hiding blurred the rest of the document." He said to the governor: "It is the end of what *we* have been struggling for, Sir Charles." It was a tribute to the postwar Colonial Service, and not undeserved. Britain had hardly expected to hand over power (through indirect rule), to men like Kwame Nkrumah and his party who represented not the chiefs but a totally new generation of Africans.

The queen did not go to Accra for the independence ceremony, but she was represented by her aunt, the Duchess of Kent. The Duchess read a message from the queen: "That Ghana has been able to achieve her freedom by constitutional and peaceful methods, in collaboration with my Government in

the United Kingdom, is a matter of profound satisfaction."
Nkrumah addressed the largest crowd ever seen in Accra, at the
old polo ground: "Free now forever," he said. It sounded good.
The London *Times* declared the future of the new country
depended on how many British officials would remain: "in the
long run the best officials will only stay if they feel that they are
furthering an ideal." That night the British Prime Minister,
Harold Macmillan, spoke on radio and television: "Today we
see the fruition of a long effort, to which British men and
women have made a great contribution. They are not always
very well known names, or even very well recognized in our
own country, but they have done years of patient and devoted
service and many of them, especially in the earlier days, gave
their lives to the work."

Nkrumah became a Commonwealth statesman, stayed with
the queen at Balmoral, and was made a member of the privy
council. But he did not, or could not, give up his fight against
imperialism. He presented himself as the "Redeemer" of all
Africans and rejuvenated the old ideal of Pan-Africanism. His
capital, Accra, became the center for revolutionary Africa and
enjoyed a brief period of heady excitement. There was talk of
its being the headquarters of a new, free Africa (the "United
States of Africa," the "Third Force") which would become a
vital new element in the structure of world power. The first
Pan-Africa Conference to be held on the continent took place in
Accra in 1959 in an atmosphere electric with excitement and
hopes. The conference motto was "Whites Scram Out of Africa."
Nationalist delegates from French and British colonies talked
feverishly to each other through interpreters, while propaganda
cars toured the streets with slogans such as "Forward Ever,"
"Africa Free Equals Heaven on Earth," and "Hands off Africa."

Nkrumah's was a strange dichotomy—the friend of the queen
and the flag-bearer of the revolutionaries—but on the whole he
carried it off. It seems, however, that he began to believe the
claims made by his most fervent admirers on his behalf and
came not to care for the system of democratic opposition that he
had inherited from the British, whereas others did care for it.
Most serious of all, when left on his own, he was not as good a
running a country as he had been with the British at his shoulder. In 1960, Ghana, as the new state was called, became a

republic but remained in the Commonwealth. Nkrumah became President, with wide powers. Ghana began to founder.

Soon after Nkrumah had been released from jail to take up office, the Conservatives, under Winston Churchill, had been returned to power. Creech Jones' remarkable period of office had already come to an end when he had lost his seat the previous year; he received no honors, made little further mark in public life but returned to Parliament and remained an MP till 1964. The most important Conservative Colonial Secretary of this period was Alan Lennox-Boyd. Like Creech-Jones, he had made a long study of African affairs. He, too, had determined views. He strongly believed that the European still had an important part to play in Africa and that a place had to be preserved for him. His policy was racial partnership. His detractors saw this as a way of retaining imperial influence and white men's privileges when, in fact, it was an honest attempt to save Africa from chaos. His three greatest problems were the Rhodesias, Nigeria, and Kenya.

It had been assumed that East Africa presented the government with more time than West Africa, for the economies were less advanced, the Africans less politically aware and educationally more backward. In Kenya, moreover, the ambitions of the settlers were seen as the main problem rather than those of the Africans. Jomo Kenyatta had returned in 1947, after a fifteen-year absence. His work on anthropology had come to be respected by academics. During the war he had worked on a farm in Sussex and had become an accepted member of the community, drinking brown ale by the stove in the White Horse, attending village hops, marrying a local governess, and picking up his son from nursery school when cycling home from work in the evening. Back in Kenya, he had become politically active and was soon addressing mass meetings of several thousand. His demands, by Nkrumah's standards, were fairly moderate and had hardly changed since his letter in the *Times* in 1930. "I don't want to make a lot of black Englishmen," he said. Negley Farson described him at this time: "A big, paunchy man, bearded, with slightly bloodshot eyes, a theatrically monstrous ebony elephant-headed walking stick, a gold-rimmed carnelian signet ring about the size of a napkin-ring, an outsize gold wristwatch fastened to his hefty arm with a gold strap, dressed in European tweed jacket and flannel slacks—with as pleasant, ingratiating and wary a manner as you have ever met." He drank heavily.

Kenyatta appealed particularly to his own tribe, the Kikuyu. These people had suffered from the growth of the European farms and were in a dangerous condition. Although they had increased in population, their land had decreased. There was unemployment, and many loitered about with little to do, eyeing with envy and fear the expanding European farms thriving on land which they believed was their own. Many turned to petty crime. In 1953 the approximate average annual income in Kenya was: Europeans $2,000, Asians $880, Africans $80. The approximate annual sum spent on primary education was: European child $150, Asian $3, African 60 cents.

That perceptive observer Negley Farson wrote in 1952: "The settlers seem bent upon holding down the safety-valve until the hatred mounts in Kenya to a point where that love and understanding, even between individuals, will be gone forever. This love was never felt between the races. The thing that is most lacking in all Africa today is *heart*."

During 1951 a violent campaign broke out, under a secret military wing of the Kikuyu called the Mau Mau. At first the members confined themselves mainly to arson and the mutilation of cattle, but the murder of a few isolated farmers gave notice of things to come. The Mau Mau held the white settlers responsible not only for the land problems but also for deliberately retarding the political advancement of the Kikuyu. They began a campaign of terror against both whites and loyal Kikuyu, with the object of overthrowing the European-dominated society of Kenya. It was the old African ploy of attempting to strike terror into their opponents and not at all dissimilar to the Matabele rising of 1896. They used guerrilla techniques, returning after raids to well-nigh impenetrable forests on the slopes of Mount Kenya. Some had served in the British forces during the war, and others were criminals. The desire for secrecy was fanatical and was further inculcated by oath-taking ceremonies in which the drinking of blood was prominent. The white settlers armed themselves and, infuriated at what they said was British inaction, threatened to take their own measures.

Just as the terrorism was mounting, Princess Elizabeth and her husband, the Duke of Edinburgh, visited the colony, despite protests from the local commissioners. "Absolutely terrified," said one of the possible consequences. The royal couple stayed at the famous Treetops Hotel. Then it was announced that George VI had died, and the new queen hurriedly returned to London—the second reigning monarch to have been in her African Empire. (In 1954 she returned to Africa for an official visit to Uganda, the only colony thought sufficiently "safe" for such a visit.)

A new governor, Sir Evelyn Baring, was sent out to Kenya in order to take a firm stand against terrorism. Baring was Cromer's son, and had just spent nearly ten years' service in Rhodesia and South Africa. He declared a state of emergency, banned African political parties, and arrested 183 suspect African leaders, including Kenyatta. Kenyatta underwent a five-month trial and was sentenced to seven years' hard labor for having been associated with Mau Mau. The trial was unsatisfactory, for much evidence was conflicting and none of it conclusive. Kenyatta spent the seven years in a hot, stuffy, flyblown little prison in a remote, little-known area in the far north of the colony. There he read philosophy and cooked for the other prisoners. He was now not only the most famous Kikuyu, but also assured of future leadership.

The Mau Mau situation immediately got worse. Chiefs, most of whom were friendly to Britain (in that their authority had been supported by the British), were murdered. Kikuyu who worked for the administration were slaughtered in the streets. Police stations were attacked and their occupants hacked to death. White farmers and their families were overrun and hideously massacred. The worst atrocity was at the Kikuyu village of Lari, where mothers were forced to drink the blood of their decapitated babies and where eighty-four Africans were killed.

The army fought the war by herding the loyal Kikuyu into fortified villages, surrounded by a ditch and fence. This proved successful, and loyal Kikuyu fought courageously. At a time when the world was seriously contemplating the possibility of its destruction through nuclear weapons, an important colonial war was being fought with spears, knives, and axes.

Against the Mau Mau, Britain brought eleven battalions,

including the Devonshire Regiment, the Lancashire Fusiliers, the Black Watch (in which was Wavell's only son, who was killed), the Royal Inniskilling Fusiliers, the Royal Northumberland Fusiliers, and the Buffs. A Kenya Regiment was raised from the settlers. KAR came from Tanganyika and Uganda, as well as Kenya. The RAF also took part. After the villages were defended, a concerted effort was made to push the Mau Mau into their lairs and destroy them there. Suspects were rounded up and put into detention camps which were far from civilized (in February, 1959, eleven men were beaten to death in Hola Camp, the cause of a considerable scandal). Terror lasted for four tense and horrible years (the "emergency" was not officially ended till 1960), during which more than 12,000 Mau Mau were killed or hanged. They killed nearly 2,000 Africans, 63 troops and police, and only 32 European civilians.

The troops went home. Kenyatta waited in his whitewashed primitive prison to return to a Kenya that was never to be the same again. The white settlers had learned at last the single fact of their lives which they had evidently not appreciated before: In their isolated farms, they were at the mercy of the surrounding Africans unless defended by considerable British forces. They began to readjust their thoughts. The Africans, on the other hand, were now deeply split among themselves, and the bloodiness of the conflict made the divisions difficult to heal. But now there was a bond of common experience for those old enemies, black and white in Kenya. In the "emergency" all had suffered.

In his quest for multiracial societies and racial partnership, Lennox-Boyd had encouraged the idea of a federation of the two Rhodesias and Nyasaland. This idea had come from Rhodesia, after the 1948 victory of the Nationalists in South Africa. The Rhodesians wished less than ever to share their future with a nation which was certain to reject the queen and Commonwealth. They believed their loyalty to the crown was second to none, as they frequently said. Roy Welensky, of Northern Rhodesia, was anxious to join forces with them, and so were most of the few whites of Nyasaland. A dominion, like Canada or Australia, was envisaged, with Europeans safeguarded politically from the preponderance of Africans. It was very much the sort of thing Rhodes had dreamed of sixty years before. Eco

1omic benefits were also expected to result from such a federation. When the Central African Federation came into being in
.953, it was meant as Britain's answer to the racialist solution of
South Africa. It was doomed from the start. African nationalism
1ad progressed too far elsewhere, and educated Africans were
:ertain they were being tricked into everlasting white rule.
\ware of these fears, Britain stopped at federation and did not
:arry through complete amalgamation as some wished.

The forecasts of economic growth from federation proved to
)e correct and rapid. Salisbury flourished. But improvements
or Africans were hardly noticeable. By 1961 the average annual
ncome for Europeans was £1,209, for Africans £87. Nyasaland
·eceived a grant of £4,000,000 a year from the federation, but
ittle else. Interests of the three territories and their populations
vere utterly divergent. The Rhodesians were adamant that
)olitical control could not be handed over to the Africans until
hey were "civilized;" to them this seemed only common sense
ind for the good of the Africans, as well as of themselves. But
he forces of African nationalism were too strong to be entirely
lenied. Welensky, who became the second Prime Minister of
he federation, proved to be as determined and skillful a politi-
:ian as he had once been a boxer. His predecessor, Sir Godfrey
Huggins, a doctor, had been Prime Minister of Southern Rho-
lesia since 1933 (a British and Commonwealth record) .

Nyasaland was where the dam broke. The nationalist leader
vas Dr. Hastings Banda, who had left his country more than
orty years before as a youth, studied in America and Scotland,
1ad become a doctor and had recently spent the war in general
)ractice in Liverpool and on Tyneside during the blitz. He was
. forceful orator. Strikes, riots, and detention without trial fol-
owed his appearance. A commission under Sir Patrick Devlin
vas sent out from Britain to report on the situation. His report
vas a shock in Britain. "The opposition to federation was
here," it said; "it was deeply rooted and almost universally
ield." This contradicted the official explanation that the whole
ffair was the result of a few agitators. Banda ensured the end of
he federation.

A change had come over British policy. The Nyasaland dis-
urbances had been firmly put down. Lennox-Boyd was re-
)laced as Colonial Secretary by Iain Macleod, a politician who
1ad not particularly specialized in colonial affairs. He gave the

final push to the British exit from Africa. Lennox-Boyd was made a viscount and continued his contribution to Africa by joining Guinness, the famed purveyors of British stout. It was a time when the Belgians were in appalling trouble in the Congo and when General Charles de Gaulle was peacefully transferring independence to the former large French Empire in Africa. Macleod was apparently impressed by the loquacious Afro-Asian group in the United Nations. He and the Prime Minister Harold Macmillan decided that the multiracial concept would have to be dropped, although Macmillan had at first supported it. From now on it was "one man, one vote." Britain would support the flood of African aspirations—or perhaps be swept along before it.

In 1960 Macmillan made the first tour of a British Prime Minister in office to the Empire in Africa. He uttered a speech in Cape Town which was widely reported and seemed important: "The most striking of all the impressions I have formed since I left London a month ago is of the strength of this African national consciousness. The wind of change is blowing through this continent, and whether we like it or not this growth of national consciousness is a political fact and our national policies must take account of it."

The South Africans were not in the least surprised for it was what they had always expected of the British. The white Rhodesians and Kenyans believed it sounded the end of British support. They were right. Nyasaland and Northern Rhodesia were granted majority African rule, elected African prime ministers in the persons of Banda and Kenneth Kaunda, and broke up the federation. It officially ended on the last day of 1963. After nine months of internal self-government, Northern Rhodesia became, as Zambia, an independent state in the Commonwealth in October, 1964. Nyasaland, as Malawi, received internal self-government in February, 1963; it became independent but also remained in the Commonwealth in July 1966. In neither country had the British handed over to the powers they had anticipated; Malawi was founded as a one-party state. The vast and fabulously rich mining and financial empire founded by Rhodes (Kimberley diamonds, Rand gold, and Rhodesian copper) had passed to the Oppenheimers' Anglo-American Corporation, which uneasily retained its mines in Zambia.

Southern Rhodesia reverted to its former curious position as a self-governing colony. Independence was painfully sought, but after many discussions it was not granted, for the British were now completely committed to African majority rule, as in the other territories, despite Rhodesia's special situation in having a well-established European community of a quarter of a million—Europeans who considered themselves African. Sensing years of frustration, Rhodesia seized independence unilaterally on November 11, 1965. The only colony in British Africa to seize independence from the British was the only one in which large numbers of the British lived. For a while they continued to sing "God Save the Queen" and to fly the Union Jack. The governor lingered on in his residence, humiliated and almost alone. The loyalty of the Rhodesians had proved to be less strong than their fear.

It was during the 1960's, mostly under a Conservative government, that the Empire in Africa disintegrated in the Balkanization of the continent begun during the previous decade. The wind of change was too strong for the old dream of handing over power, via indirect rule, to chiefs who had been carefully nurtured for years. And there was no trace of the great multiracial partnerships that Lennox-Boyd had envisaged. All dreams except those of the African nationalists were swept away.

British rule ended in Somaliland on June 26, 1960. Soon after, British Somaliland became part of the republic of Somalia, outside the Commonwealth. It was much as the Mad Mullah would have wished it.

Lennox-Boyd's greatest achievement was the fairly peaceful transition to independence of federal Nigeria. This great country of 30,000,000 people, split into three states, was a fantastic hodgepodge of races and tribes with little in common except the short history of British rule and English as a common official language. The chances of its weathering its growing pains, especially in view of what was happening in the Congo, did not seem high. But in Lagos, the capital, young graduates of British and Irish universities revoked their customary lightweight suits and donned national dress with high hopes. The Union Jack was lowered in October, 1960, at an impressive ceremony. The country remained in the Commonwealth, the governor general being the old nationalist Azikiwe. Three years later Nigeria became a republic, with Azikiwe as President. Effect on trade had already been evident, for emergent nations in West Africa saw no reason why they should not merchandise their own raw materials. Unilever's United Africa Company (the successor to Goldie's Royal Niger Company), which had enjoyed almost monopolistic conditions in West Africa, had hurriedly to diversify.

Sierra Leone followed in April, 1961, and remained firmly in the Commonwealth under the "Queen of Sierra Leone" (also the Queen of the United Kingdom). The constitution was of the British system, with an assembly modeled on the House of Commons and a Speaker with suitable regalia. The first military coup took place in less than six years. In 1956 there were 357 primary schools in Sierra Leone and 17 secondary schools; two years after independence, 662 primary schools and 44 secondary schools.

As well as a Central Africa Federation, Lennox-Boyd had hoped for an East Africa Federation, an old prewar idea, of Kenya, Tanganyika, and Uganda, in which the Europeans position would be protected. An East Africa High Commission with a legislative assembly, had been established under Creech Jones in 1947; its chairman was the governor of Kenya. I hardly stood a chance. Multiracialism was given a try in Tanganyika. There were 8,000,000 Africans, 140,000 Asians and 20,000 Europeans, and each race was allotted seven seats. In 1954 the Colonial Office declared: "The suggestion that Tanganyika could achieve self-government in less than twenty years is based on erroneous assumptions." In the same year Julius Nyerere gave up schoolteaching and began a nationalist movement. Educated at Edinburgh University, he developed into a formidable politician, who insisted that the rights of European would be respected. Most of the Tanganyika whites came to trust him, and progress was rapid, after the abandonment of multiracialism. After only one year of training in internal self government, Tanganyika became an independent state in the Commonwealth on December 9, 1961. A republic was announced exactly a year later, with Nyerere as President, and Tanganyika became a one-party state. In December, 1963, Zanzibar was given independence, and sovereignty was handed back to the sultan. It was the only case in Africa till that time of Britain handing over rule in the fashion that had long been intended through indirect rule. The sultan's regime lasted just over one month. The African majority overthrew the Moslem leadership, the sultan fled the country, and a revolutionary "people's republic" was established. Zanzibar joined with Tanganyika to form the loose federation of Tanzania, in 1964.

With the independence of Tanganyika, all hope of an East Africa Federation, dominated by the Kenya settler, was over. So, indeed, were the chances of multiracial systems elsewhere in Africa. Uganda, so long thought of as the model protectorate, proved to be unexpectedly troublesome on its path to independence. The kingdom of Buganda, which formed about a quarter of Uganda, had an ambitious and proud king, or Kabaka—Sir Edward Frederick William Mutesa, KBE, a lieutenant colonel of the Grenadier Guards, who sported suede boots and a clipped English manner (much addicted to "Oh, jolly good show!") and had been educated at Cambridge—a century after Speke had first arrived at his forefather's court. At the time of the suggested East Africa Federation he fought the proposal to such effect that the British deported him (on an allowance of £8,000 tax-free). After two years, in face of strong public pressure, they allowed him back. Uganda received independence on October 9, 1962, and the Kabaka was made President but with little real power. Four years later he was deported once more. Almost penniless, the thirty-seventh and last of the proud Kabakas eked out an existence in London's East End—a strange victim of Britain's rule in Africa. He died in London's slumland in 1969, and was given an imposing military funeral.

In Kenya, Kenyatta, having served his sentence, was still restricted to the remote north. In 1961 he was allowed to return to Nairobi. After only six months' experience of internal self-government, Kenya received independence in December 1963. The governor general was Malcolm Macdonald, son of the first Labour Prime Minister, an amiable anticolonialist whose career had been officially connected with Empire and Commonwealth, almost without a break, for thirty-two years. Inevitably Kenya became a republic, with Kenyatta as President, a year later. The day that Lord Delamere had so dreaded had actually arrived. His Lordship's statue was removed, but otherwise nothing very alarming happened. Kenyatta, flicking at flies with his whisk, a look of understandable satisfaction on his features, appeared to be completely unembittered. Many of the old White Highlanders lingered on in their mansions, referring affectionately to the once hated and feared Kenyatta as "the old man."

The extraordinary fact was that relations were nowhere better between black and white in British Africa than in the one colony which had experienced bloody rebellion, and nowhere were they worse than in Central Africa, the one area where a multiracial society had actually been put into effect.

In the mid-1950's a Colonial Office paper had asserted that Sierra Leone, with a population of just over 2,000,000, was the smallest colony for which independence could be contemplated and that anywhere smaller could not be expected to survive as a state. But the turn of tiny Gambia, population 315,486, came as Britain departed from the continent. At the time of independence there were four secondary schools and one teacher-training college. The broadcasting service had begun only in 1962.

From the once vast African Empire, only the mostly empty protectorate of Bechuanaland and the two little enclaves in South Africa, Basutoland and Swaziland, remained. In 1935, Britain, in face of claims by South Africa, had stated that no decision would be made about these territories against the wishes of the native Africans. In these protectorates there was some small comfort for the ghost of Lugard and the old advocates of indirect rule. Bechuanaland, which had progressed little under British rule, achieved independence in September, 1966, under the name of Botswana. The President was Sir Seretse Khama, KBE, the first general election having been held the previous year. A scant sixteen years previously, Seretse Khama had offended opinion in Africa by marrying a white girl; for his transgression he had been deposed from his chieftainship by the embarrassed British and exiled. It seemed a long time ago.

Basutoland, a poor, mountainous, and undeveloped country, surrounded on all sides by the apartheid of South Africa, received its independence a month later, when sovereignty was returned to the Basuto royal family in the person of King Moshoeshoe II. Basutoland was considerably different from what it had been when it had fought the British for its survival in the previous century, but it was not the power it had been before the arrival of the white men in force. Mining and farming, indeed all ownership of land by whites, had been prohibited, and there were few European settlers. It was difficult to see how Lesotho, as the new state was styled, could retain its newfound integrity.

Swaziland, almost surrounded by the same antagonistic system, became independent on September 6, 1968. Parliament consisted of two houses; in the Senate, six members were elected and six appointed by the hereditary king; in the Assembly, twenty-four members were elected and six nominated by the king. There were few Swazis sufficiently trained to take over top posts, and virtually no middle class (at the first elections, six of the king's nominations for Parliament were local white residents). Flogging, "not exceeding fifteen strokes," was still an official punishment. There had been no postage till 1954. There was a powerful group of white settlers. All three of these new states had never paid their way, and they continued to receive substantial grants from British taxpayers after independence (more than half the annual revenue of Lesotho was in the form of a grant from Britain).

September 6, 1968, was a date to remember in African history. The withdrawal was complete, and fewer than 20,000 had lost their lives since the process had begun. It could have been worse.

Britons may not have been history's best colonialists, they were not the worst, but they were certainly the most eccentric. Perhaps, in the end, such eccentricity will confound the critics of posterity, reading through the years of bumbling goodwill, and will save the reputation of the British.

The whole history of Britain in Africa had been characterized by a curious division from the very beginning. There had always been those against even the idea of the British entering Africa and later those against all her actions there except departure. The nation had never been dedicated to the African dream—only individuals like Sir Joseph Banks and his circle, Livingstone, Lugard, and Rhodes. But it had been the governments more than the British people themselves which, faced with seemingly insoluble problems and rapidly decreasing time in which to grapple with them, lacked conviction in African imperialism. The peak of imperialism had been in the 1890's, but by then Britain had hardly got into Africa. The run down from the peak had been rapid. What it amounted to was that Britain had gone into Africa too late, and the preliminaries, particularly exploration, had been immense and time-consuming. There just had not been enough time for the white man's burden, insofar as that humanitarian concept had been part of Britain's presence in Africa, to be satisfactorily discharged.

During those decades of Empire a few thousand Britons from the home island had administered the millions of native inhabitants, sometimes with dedication, sometimes with languor, sometimes for the worse, often for the better. It had been easy to distinguish between rulers and ruled in many ways, but most easily by the color of their skins. If his skin were white, the most humble clerk had known himself to be one of the rulers, and he had acted accordingly. No matter how some of the native inhabitants had emulated the rulers, they had not been able to change the color of their skins. This simple fact of pigmentation bedeviled the last years of the British Empire in Africa. The colonizers could never become assimilated had they wanted to, and the Africans could never become identified with the white men. It was this consciousness, this indignation for which there was no hope short of a new skin, that was Europe's most important contribution to Africa and elsewhere in the world. This side effect of imperialism continued in the second half of the twentieth century, long after imperialism was dead. The dream of a few men in the Pall Mall coffee shops became a nightmare of racial distrust and antipathy among millions.

Britain's term in Africa had not been long, but neither had it been uneventful. The wild animals, having been carefully hunted for over half a century, were considerably diminished. Although Africans were not without their fears—far from it— they were less dominated by insecurity than they had been before the colonialists had arrived, for "protection" had evidently enjoyed some lasting effects. All African states born from the British Empire had experience of some basics of democracy to which, if discarded, they could return, and they had a common language. There were hospitals, sunglasses, schools, bottled beer, radios, brassieres, lawyers, false teeth, peaked caps, national anthems, books, desks at the United Nations, can openers, national airlines, motorcycles.

September 6, 1968—a date to remember.

For grandeur, it was not a ceremony to put beside others in the continent's history. The London *Times* refrained from comment on the occasion, and reported the event in a few inches on an inside page. The Commonwealth Secretary, in a neat lounge suit and horn-rimmed spectacles, represented the British queen. The sixty-nine-year-old king, in headdress of black and red feathers, represented the Swazis. The king's 112 wives arrived by car, barefoot and in identical robes. The king informed the assembly in the football stadium that "Her Majesty graciously welcomes us" to the Commonwealth. The Commonwealth Secretary warned of the hazards of the future: "days of inevitable change and adaptation." A new flag was unfurled above, while a wild traditional dance was performed. The white men from the island off the coast of Europe were going home.

The Empire in Africa

Population figures are approximate and prior to independence.

BASUTOLAND: Nation of Basutos established about 1824 by Moshesh (*c.* 1790–1870). Moshesh agreed treaty granting British protection in 1843. Interminable disputes between Afrikaners, British, other Africans, and Basuto led to Basuto Wars. Annexed to Cape Colony 1871; led to internal conflict and Basuto War of 1879. After further fighting, transferred from Cape control to Colonial Office, 1884. British commissioners worked with Moshesh's successors. Poor and backward colony. Population (1946) 561,000. Administered by nine district commissioners (salaries averaging about £1,250 in late 1950's). Plagued with alcoholism and wave of revolting "medicine" murders—*i.e.,* to obtain human relics for witchcraft. Became independent kingdom of Lesotho on October 4, 1966, under paramount chief, the successor of Moshesh.

BECHUANALAND: Bechuana tribes first visited by Europeans from Cape Colony about 1780. Scottish missionary Robert Moffat had success teaching, 1820–70. Occupied by British force under Sir Charles Warren, 1878, to forestall Transvaal interest in the area; withdrew 1881, whereupon occupied by Afrikaners. Friction led to another British expedition, 1885, also under Warren, and territory came under British control as a protectorate. Important rail route from Cape to Rhodesia built through eastern Bechuanaland. Ruled from Mafeking, in the Cape. Population (1966) 976,000. By independence there were 256 schools (an increase of more than 40 percent in the final twelve years). First general election held in 1965. Became independent republic on September 30, 1966, as

Botswana, under Seretse Khama, hereditary chief of the largest tribe, the Bamangwato.

BRITISH SOMALILAND: Peopled by nomadic tribes. Egyptian control 1865–84. British protectorate established on July 20, 1887, to protect route to India and source of supply for Aden. Boundaries remained ill defined. "Mad Mullah" resisted British occupation, with some success, 1901–20. Little done to develop the area. Italian occupation, 1940–41. Joined with former Italian Somaliland to form republic of Somalia, 1960. Population (1955) 600,000.

CAPE COLONY: Originally Dutch settlement, founded 1652. Temporarily occupied by Britain, 1795–1803. Britain took possession by conquest in 1806. White population at that time 73,633 (Cape Town 6,000). Gradually pushed north and east, expanding its territory. Dutch population dissatisfied and withdrew from colony, 1836–38. Followed by Kaffir Wars and defense of the frontier. Two-chamber Parliament set up in 1854, elected by those with minimum qualifications of property or income (*i.e.,* ostensibly not on race or color). By then 140,000 Europeans; exports mainly wool, £800,000. Discovery of diamonds at Kimberley, in 1870, transformed economy; exports, 1890, £7,000,000, more than half in diamonds. On May 31, 1910, became Cape Province, of Union of South Africa; contributed over half (583,177) of European population of the Union (total population at that date, 2,563,024).

THE COMPANIES: The following companies played an important part in British Africa:
Company of Adventurers into Africa, 1618 (Gambia).
Royal African Company, 1672–1725 (Gold Coast and Gambia).
African Company of Merchants, 1759–1821 (Gold Coast).
Sierra Leone Company, 1791–1807 (Sierra Leone).
African Lakes Corporation, 1878 (Nyasaland).
United African Company, 1879–81; National African Company, 1881–6; Royal Niger Company, 1886–1900; Niger Company, 1900–29; United Africa Company (Unilever), 1929–   (West Africa).

Imperial British East Africa Company, 1888–95 (Kenya and Uganda).

British South Africa Company, 1889–1923, 1923–33; Charter Consolidated Ltd. (Anglo-American Corp.), 1964– (South Africa, Southern Rhodesia, Northern Rhodesia, Bechuanaland, Nyasaland).

EGYPT: Long history of independence and Roman and Turkish subjugation. British expedition, 1801–3, against French occupation. Unsuccessful British expedition, 1807. French influence continued, but Britain built first railways from 1852. Suez Canal opened in 1869 as result of French initiative; transformed importance of Egypt, on route to India and the East. Anglo-French financial control from 1875, owing to chronic insolvency. Revolt against Egyptian hierarchy led to British invasion, 1882, the French having declined joint operation. Britain promised to retire as soon as order restored. Civilian control under Sir Evelyn Baring (Lord Cromer), 1883–1907. Improvement in law and order and, slowly, in prosperity; formation of large, British-trained Egyptian army. First World War brought about British protectorate, 1914–22. "Special relationship" maintained by Britain after 1922. Nationalist movement led to succession of crises. Complete independence granted August 22, 1936; Britain reserved defense of Suez Canal. British miltary reoccupation in Second World War. Disastrous Anglo-French expedition to Suez after nationalization of canal, November, 1956. War with Israel, 1967–.

GAMBIA: Territory on each side of the Gambia River. Queen Elizabeth I granted charter for company to trade there in 1588, but there was no success in doing so. Series of British forts at mouth of river. Recognized as British area in 1783, but not taken over till 1807, when it came under Sierra Leone. Separate colony created 1843. Slave trade long established, not wiped out till twentieth century. Economy entirely dependent on export of groundnuts. Primary schools doubled between 1945 and independence (when there were ninety). Population (1963), 315,486. Independent state February 18, 1965. Republic, 1970.

GOLD COAST: Portuguese brought back stories of gold from this coast in fifteenth century. Portuguese influence lasted about 150 years, followed by Dutch. English traders built fort at Cape Coast about 1660. This and other forts resulted in intense rivalry and some fighting with Dutch. Royal African Company and African Company of Merchants, the latter subsidized by the government, traded for slaves and gold. Garrisoned by West India Regiment for many years. Government took over trading posts and forts in 1821. British supported Fanti people against Ashanti of interior, 1824–26. Coast returned to subsidized private enterprise 1828–43. George Maclean consolidated British position 1830–47. Under Sierra Leone 1843–74. British jurisdiction defined with coastal chiefs 1844. Remaining Danish and Dutch forts purchased in 1850 and 1871 respectively. War with Ashanti, 1873–74. Combined with Lagos as colony independent of Sierra Leone, 1874–86. Gold Coast colony and protectorate from 1886. Explorers penetrated and claimed hinterland beyond Ashanti 1882–98. This region became Northern Territories, 1897. Ashanti War of 1901 led to final annexation of that territory. Cocoa planting began 1879; considerable growth of industry by 1900. Togoland annexed from former German territory 1920. By 1920 produced half the world's cocoa crop. Gold mines supplemented by other mineral mining. By 1954, 31 government hospitals (1,783 beds), 4,135 primary schools, and 20 secondary schools. 501 miles of railway built. Population (1954) 4,548,000; about 16 percent Christian. Independence March 6, 1957; republic, under Kwame Nkrumah, July 1, 1960; one-party state 1964; army coup 1966.

ITALIAN COLONIES: Cyrenaica and Tripolitania, under British administration 1943–51 (other part of Libya, the Fezzan, was under French administration). Eritrea, British administration, 1941–52, became part of Ethiopia; Italian Somaliland, British administration 1941–50, was returned to Italy by United Nations resolution; on July 1, 1960, Italian Trusteeship came to an end, and republic of Somalia was formed by amalgamation of former Italian Somaliland and British Somaliland. Britain ruled in all these former Italian colonies under auspices of the United Nations, which also settled their eventual determination.

KENYA: Inhabited by Masai, Kikuyu, Somali, and other peoples, with Arabs on the coast. Coast claimed by Zanzibar in nineteenth century. British at first uninterested in the sultan's domains, but began making treaties with chiefs of interior from 1884. British sphere of interest defined 1886 and agreed 1890, after Germany also began to take an interest in East Africa. Imperial British East Africa Company formed 1888; connected with British India Steam Navigation Company, to open up interior. William Mackinnon the moving spirit. Difficulties with German counterclaims and parliamentary opposition at home. Company transferred control to government 1895; territory to be known as British East Africa; coastal strip a protectorate, the remainder a colony. Railway from Mombasa to Victoria Nyanza built 1896–1903, at government expense; opened up country. Settlers arrived from 1902, owing to clement climate and good land. Conflict of interest between Africans, European settlers and Indian immigrants accelerated during interwar period. Renamed Kenya 1920. Whites given elected representation, but British government retained control. Highlands area reserved for European development. Mau Mau revolt 1952–56. Population (1961) 7,287,000 (66,000 Europeans). Railway built by independence (with Uganda), 3,490 miles; bitumen-surfaced roads, 920 miles; post offices, 230; telephones, 44,137. After six months of internal self-government, independent with majority rule constitution December 12, 1963; republic, under Jomo Kenyatta, December 12, 1964. Still 40,000 Europeans in 1970.

NATAL: Inhabited by Bantu; conquered by Zulu 1818–20. British, from the Cape, settled at Port Natal 1824, traded with Zulu. Durban founded near Port Natal by about 50 settlers, 1835. Afrikaners began arriving from the Cape in 1837; this led to war with Zulu and British military occupation at Port Natal. Afrikaners proclaimed republic of Natal (or Natalia). British took over the republic 1843, and most of the Afrikaners left. Made separate colony from Cape 1856; legislature with majority of elected members. Africans pacified by Sir Theophilus Shepstone. Indian immigration for labor in sugar plantations. By 1886 a state-owned railway and 20,000 Europeans. Zulu War, 1879, broke Zulu power; all Zululand annexed by 1897. Internal self-government granted 1893. African revolt 1906. Decided to join Union of South Africa, by referendum, June, 1910.

NIGERIA: Native kingdoms of Benin, Yoruba, Ibo, Oyo, Bornu, Fulani, Egba, and others. Scattered European trading posts appeared in seventeenth century; Portuguese already there. By 1800 most posts British. Preliminary explorations of Mungo Park, Lander brothers, Clapperton, and Barth lasted for more than half a century. Macgregor Laird attempted to increase trade. Lagos Island taken over as colony in 1862. Parliamentary committee of 1865 advised withdrawal of British interest. Lagos colony with Gold Coast 1874–86. French set up posts in early 1880's. Goldie formed United African Company 1879, amalgamated British posts and bought up French. British protectorate announced, 1885, of coastal strip. United African Company became Royal Niger Company 1886. Resistance of Moslem rulers of interior. Royal Niger Company handed over political and administrative responsibility to government January 1, 1900. Became colony of Lagos and two protectorates of Northern and Southern Nigeria; much of Northern taken by conquest. Lagos and Southern Nigeria amalgamated 1906. Lugard ruled Northern. Amalgamation of Southern and Northern Nigeria January 1, 1914; Lugard became governor general. Several peoples and many tribes with little in common thus brought together. Cameroons, part of ex-German colony, annexed 1919. Limited franchise for certain areas began 1923. Federation established 1954, with House of Representatives of 184 elected and 9 nominated as ex officio members. Between 1945 and 1955 British government gave £1,710,864 toward university. Population (1954) 31,800,000. By independence, 124 hospitals and nursing homes, 2,022 miles of tarred road, 1,903 miles of railway. Exported groundnuts, cocoa, palm kernels and oil, cotton, tin. Oilfields from mid-1960's. Eastern and Western Nigeria, internal self-government 1957; Northern Nigeria 1959. Federation of Nigeria became independent October 1, 1960; republic, October, 1963; military coup, January, 1966; civil war, 1967 to 1969.

NORTHERN RHODESIA: Two-thirds of British South Africa Company's Rhodesia, carved out of Central Africa by Cecil Rhodes in 1890's; all British South Africa Company's land north of the Zambezi, originally belonging to Barotse chiefs, who maintained some independence under the company and who had been glad to see the British. Rhodes never saw the country. Originally Northwestern and Northeastern Rhodesia; combined 1911 (when European population 1,434). Taken over as protectorate by British government February 20, 1924. Developed only along railway line; unsuitable for European settlers. Hilton Young commission of 1927 advised "association" with Southern Rhodesia and Nyasaland. Colonial Secretary said this could not "be regarded as practicable" (1944) but set up committee to promote cooperation in the same year. Franchise limited to Europeans with property qualifications (about one-third of whites) till after Second World War. Copper mines developed by Anglo-American capital in 1930's, greatly expanded after war. Population (1950) 1,816,000. European population more than doubled after the war, to 56,000 in 1954. One secondary school by 1954. Became part of Federation of Rhodesia and Nyasaland, September, 1953. Unrest, accelerated by industrial colorbar. Three Africans voted in first federal election. A breakup of federation 1963; became self-governing protectorate destined for majority rule. Independent republic of Zambia October 24, 1964.

NYASALAND: Bantu area west and south of Lake Nyasa, first visited by Livingstone 1859. African Lakes Corporation formed 1878, helped open up territory to Europeans, with Scottish missionaries already established for some years. British South Africa Company obtained charter to develop the country 1884, but became fully stretched in Rhodesia. Protectorate established 1892. Country subdued, with aid of gunboats and Indian troops, by Harry Johnston, who also administered Northern Rhodesia. Revolt under John Chilembwe 1915. Developed slowly. Under indirect rule, chiefs received some autonomy 1933. In 1944 "advisory councils" of

African chiefs established. Economy entirely reliant on export of tea, tobacco, loans and subsidies; many left to find employment in the Rhodesias. Population (1954) 2,495,800 (5,100 Europeans). Incorporated in Federation of Rhodesia and Nyasaland September 4, 1953; legislative council entirely nominated. Received internal self-government on breakup of federation, 1963; universal suffrage; independent republic under Dr. Hastings Banda, July 6, 1966.

ORANGE FREE STATE: Bantu country, between Orange and Vaal rivers, settled by Afrikaners from 1834. Republic established 1836. Britain claimed area 1848 and defeated Afrikaners at Boomplaats. Afrikaner republic reestablished 1854, at instigation of British. European population then about 15,000. Occupied by British troops in South African War 1900. Renamed Orange River Colony, under British rule, in the same year. Self-governing colony 1907. Bitter conflict between Afrikaans-speaking and English-speaking citizens, particularly on educational matters. Population (1921) Europeans 188,556, non-Europeans approximately 440,000. Entered Union of South Africa, as Orange Free State Province, May 31, 1910.

RHODESIA AND NYASALAND, FEDERATION OF: Federation of self-governing colony and two protectorates came into being September 4, 1953, with view to eventual dominion status. Long advocated, especially in Southern Rhodesia. Prime Minister was former Prime Minister of Southern Rhodesia. Assembly constituted: Southern Rhodesia seventeen; Northern Rhodesia eleven; Nyasaland seven. Nyasaland the most populous of the three. Franchise varied. Federal government responsible only for education of non-Africans. Population (1954) 6,876,000. Europeans: Southern Rhodesia 159,000; Northern Rhodesia 56,000; Nyasaland 5,200. Federation abandoned December, 1963.

SENEGAL: French West African territory. Coast claimed by Britain 1758–79. Restored to France, by treaty, 1783. British had done nothing in the area apart from take over and establish a few trading forts. Again held by Britain, 1800–17 (St. Louis from 1809).

SIERRA LEONE: First contacted by the Portuguese. Later afflicted by the slave trade. Settled by freed slaves from North America and Britain from 1787. Survived early disasters. First settlers joined by slaves freed from illegal slave ships. By 1807 population 1,871. In that year Sierra Leone Company handed over to the government, and territory became a colony. Governor, Zachary Macaulay. Further protectorate territory slowly acquired. Progress hampered by disease. Headquarters of British West African administration during much of nineteenth century. Higher education since 1876. Much enlarged after agreement with French, 1896. Twelve district commissioners administered the territory. Diamond industry, plagued by smuggling. Population (1948) 1,858,275. Has built 310 miles of railway, and 90 miles of bitumen-surfaced road. By independence about 50,000 children attending school. Independent state, under British crown, April 27, 1961; military coup, 1967.

SOUTH AFRICA, UNION OF: Established on May 31, 1910, after parliamentary votes in self-governing colonies of Cape, Orange River, Transvaal, and referendum in Natal. Efforts to avoid friction resulted in Afrikaans and English being official languages, and administration split between Pretoria (government), Cape Town (Parliament) and Bloemfontein (judiciary). Provision made for future admission of Rhodesia, Basutoland, Bechuanaland, and Swaziland. Union always under strain, increased by rebellion during First World War. Afrikaner and British split remained, based on attitude to Africans and remaining British ties. White female franchise introduced 1930. Louis Botha Prime Minister 1910–19, Jan Smuts 1919–34, James Hertzog 1924–33, Coalition (Hertzog and Smuts) 1933–39, Smuts 1939–48, Danil Malan 1948–54, Johonnes Strijdom 1954–58, Hendrik Verwoerd 1958–61. Population (1961) 15,982,664 (African 10,907,789; white 3,088,492, Coloured 1,509,258; Asian 477,125). No vote for Africans. Became independent republic, outside Commonwealth, May 31, 1961.

SOUTHERN RHODESIA: Originally Bantu gold-producing kingdom of Monomotapa, which had treaties with the Portuguese; later Kalanga, Matabeleland, and Mashonaland. Visited by hunters and missionaries during 1880's. Rhodes made agreement with chief of Matabele 1888. British South Africa Company received charter to develop area 1889. Pioneer column founded Salisbury, 1890. By 1892, 1,500 settlers. Named Rhodesia 1895. Matabele risings 1893 and 1896. Railway reached Bulawayo 1896, Victoria Falls 1905. Legislative council introduced 1899. Tobacco planting promoted, gold mines developed. Referendum resulted in majority against joining the Union of South Africa, 1922. Company gave up territory to crown for £3,750,000. Became self-governing colony September 12, 1923, thirty-two years after arrival of pioneer column. First general election April 19, 1924; franchise included Africans over twenty-one possessing £100 of property. By 1928 European population 50,000. Surviving mineral rights of company purchased by government for £2,000,000, 1933. Increased immigration after Second World War. Local self-government for Africans established. Controversy with British government as to majority rule. Grants for African education rose from £113 in 1901 to £1,901,313 in 1958; first secondary school 1946. Most powerful member of Federation of Rhodesia and Nyasaland, 1953–63. Population (1965) : Europeans 224,000, non-Europeans 4,101,000. Vote for fraction of Africans. Declaration of independence November 11, 1965; only British territory in Africa to seize its own independence. Republic, 1970.

SOUTH-WEST AFRICA: German protectorate 1884–1915. Mandated to Union of South Africa by Treaty of Versailles, 1919, and thus in Empire and Commonwealth. After the Second World War South Africa refused to consider ways of bringing mandate to an end. International Court of Justice confirmed mandate and obligations 1950. Population (1966) 610,000 (Europeans 96,000) .

SUDAN: Became Moslem country after Arab invasion of seventh century, except Negro south, which was exploited for slavery into twentieth century. Egyptian conquest 1820–21; Egyptian administration weak. Samuel Baker annexed southern part for Egypt 1870–73; followed by Charles Gordon 1874–76, who received governorship of all Sudan from Egypt 1877–79. Governor of southern part Emir Pasha, 1878–84. Mahdist rising 1883. Withdrawal of Egyptian occupation. Gordon besieged at Khartoum 1884–85. Mahdi succeeded by Khalifa 1885–98. Kitchener defeated Khalifa 1898. Anglo-Egyptian joint sovereignty proclaimed 1899. Francis Reginald Wingate governor 1899–1916. Railway built from Nile to Red Sea 1906. Cotton growing promoted. Unrest in Negroid south continued. Between world wars, Anglo-Egyptian controversy on future of Sudan. By 1955 2,071 miles of railway, a university college, four teacher-training colleges. Population (1955) approximately 9,000,000. Sudanese right to independence established 1953; first general election in the same year. Republic proclaimed January 1, 1956; army coup 1958; civil war in the south.

SWAZILAND: Bantu people who came under Zulu domination, but broke free 1843. Conflict with Afrikaners and a gold rush led to confusion. Transvaal took over administration 1894. British administration after South African War. Protectorate established 1906. Europeans took over large tracts of land for cattle-ranching companies. Asbestos mining promoted. By 1954, 221 schools for Africans, nearly all missionary (17 government schools). British ruled through paramount chief (or king); political advance slow. Population (1955) approximately 200,000 (3,500 Europeans). By 1964 140 miles of railway completed. Hydroelectric power. Constitution 1967, with half Senate and quarter of Assembly nominated by king. Independent kingdom came into being September 6, 1968.

TANGANYIKA: Territory, mainly Bantu, between great lakes and Indian Ocean, claimed by Sultan of Zanzibar in nineteenth century; Arabs and Swahili inhabited coast. German East Africa 1884–1917. Considerably developed by Germany in short rule, including the two major railways and European settlement in the Usambara Mountains. Britain given mandate of most of colony; renamed Tanganyika 1920. Depression followed war. German settlers repatriated; estates sold. Large Indian population produced conflict of interests. League of Nations required territory to be run for benefit of African inhabitants. Slavery abolished 1923. Germans allowed to return from 1925. Territory gradually recovered; education established; tsetse fly attacked. By 1938 about 7 percent of African children of school age attended school. British ruled through tribal organizations. Coffee and sisal principal exports. Population (1960) approximately 9,000,000 (Europeans 22,000). Independence December 9, 1961; republic December 9, 1962; loosely united with Zanzibar April 25, 1964, to become Tanzania, under President Julius K. Nyerere.

TRANSVAAL: Afrikaner republic (the South African Republic) established after Great Trek; recognized by Britain 1852 at the Sand River Convention. Great leaders Andries H. Potgieter and Andries Pretorius. Capital of Pretoria founded 1855. British rule 1877; brought to an end 1881 by First South African War. Rand goldfields discovered; Johannesburg founded 1886. *Vitlander* controversy, mainly electoral. Rhodes and others attempt coup 1895. Transvaal annexed as colony during Second South African War, September 1, 1900. Self-governing colony 1906. Population (1921): Europeans 543,485, non-Europeans approximately 1,500,000. Joined Union of South Africa, 1910, as Transvaal Province.

UGANDA: Territory north and west of Lake Victoria, dominated in nineteenth century by kingdom of Buganda, a comparatively advanced society. Traded with Arabs. Visited 1862 by Speke, the first European to reach it. Visited by Stanley 1875. Missionaries began to arrive 1877. Conflict by Anglicans, Roman Catholics, and Moslems led to religious persecution and wars. Rivalry between British, French, and Germans. British sphere of influence agreed 1890. Imperial British East Africa Company sent Lugard to claim and pacify territory 1890; religious wars. Company decided to withdraw, but government eventually declared protectorate of Buganda 1894. Extended over neighboring areas, including Bunyoro and Busoga, 1896. Civil and religious wars 1897–99. Pacification under Sir Harry Johnston 1899–1901. Railway from coast to Lake Victoria completed 1902; trade began to increase. Cotton cultivation from 1904. Nominated legislative council established 1921. Railway extended into Uganda 1928. Hydroelectric power created after Second World War. The four states of Buganda, Ankole, Toro, and Bunyoro retained considerable internal autonomy. University awarded degrees from 1953. By 1955 about 250,000 children at grant-aided schools. Population (1959) 6,538,175 (Europeans 10,000). First general election April 25, 1962. Independence October 9, 1962; republic October 9, 1963; Kabaka (king) of Buganda, first President, banished 1966.

ZANZIBAR: Two islands and some islets off east coast of Africa, the Arab rulers of which formerly controlled much of that coast. Long history of slave trading. Dominions dismembered by British, Germans, and Italians during scramble for Africa. British consul, Sir John Kirk, 1866–87, advised the sultan. By 1890 little remained but the islands and the coast directly opposite. British protectorate proclaimed in that year. Slavery abolished 1897. Nominated legislative council established 1926. British ruled through sultan. By 1962, seventy-four primary schools (sixty-two being government schools). Population (1948) 264,162 (Europeans 296). Independence December 10, 1963, after less than six months of internal self-government. Within four weeks sultan overthrown and People's Republic proclaimed. Union with Tanganyika April 25, 1964, to form republic of Tanzania.

ZULULAND: Bantu people of southeastern Africa who quickly grew by conquest in early nineteenth century, under Chaka and Dingaan. War with Afrikaners 1838. Kept apart from Transvaal and Natal under Mpande (1840–72); military system grew restless. Cetewayo (1872–79) resisted British pressure. Zululand invaded January, 1879; early British defeats, followed by overwhelming victory. Cetewayo restored 1882–83; civil war. Zululand annexed to crown, 1887. Rebellions under Cetewayo's son, 1888, 1906. Control transferred by British government to Natal, 1897.

Bibliography

Some of the many accounts, biographies, newspapers, and reference works consulted:

AGAR-HAMILTON, JOHN AUGUSTUS IAN, *The Road to the North.* Longmans, 1937.
———, *The Siege of Mafeking.* Methuen, 1900.
AMERY, LEOPOLD S., *The Forward View.* Bles, 1935.
———, ed., *Times History of the War in South Africa.* Sampson Low, 1902.
ARMSTRONG, HAROLD COURTENAY, *Grey Steel: J. C. Smuts.* Barker, 1937.
BADEN-POWELL, LORD ROBERT STEPHENSON SMYTH, *Lessons from the Varsity of life.* Pearson, 1934.
BARTH, HEINRICH, *Travels in North and Central Africa.* D. Appleton & Co., 1857.
BETTS, RAYMOND F., *The Scramble for Africa.* Heath, 1966.
BLAKE, ROBERT, *Disraeli.* Eyre & Spottiswoode, 1966.
BOVILL, EDWARD W., *Missions to the Niger,* Vol. I. Hakluyt Society, 1964.
BRADLEY, KENNETH GRANVILLE, *Diary of a District Officer.* Nelson, 1947.
BRELSFORD, WILLIAM V., *Handbook to the Federation of Rhodesia and Nyasaland.* Cassell, 1960.
BROWN, ROBERT, *The Story of Africa and Its Explorers,* Vols. I–IV. Cassell, 1892–95.
BURTON, SIR RICHARD FRANCIS, *The Lake Regions of Central Africa.* Longman, Green, Longman & Roberts, 1860.
BUTLER, SIR WILLIAM FRANCIS, *Autobiography.* Charles Scribner's Sons, 1911.
CALDWELL, THEODORE C., *The Anglo-Boer War.* Heath, 1965.
CAMERON, SIR DONALD, *My Tanganyika Service.* Allen & Unwin, 1939.
CARDINALL, ALLAN WOLSEY, *In Ashanti and Beyond.* Seeley Service, 1927.
CARY, JOYCE, *The Case for African Freedom and Other Writings.* University of Texas Press, 1962.
CECIL, LADY GWENDOLEN, *Life of Robert, Marquis of Salisbury,* Vol. IV. Hodder and Stoughton, 1932.
CHURCHILL, LORD RANDOLPH HENRY SPENCER, *Men, Mines and Animals in South Africa.* Sampson Low, 1892.
CHURCHILL, SIR WINSTON S., *My African Journey.* Hodder, 1908.
———, *The River War,* Vol. II. Longmans, 1899.
———, *The Second World War,* Vols. II, IV. Cassell, 1949, 1951.
CLAPPERTON, HUGH, *Journals of a Second Expedition into Africa.* Murray, 1829.

COHEN, MORTON, *Rider Haggard*. Macmillan, 1968.

COLVIN, IAN, *Life of Jameson*. Arnold, 1922.

Colonial Office Papers.

CONAN DOYLE, SIR ARTHUR, *The Great Boer War*. Smith Elder, 1901.

CRANWORTH, LORD BERTRAM FRANCIS GURDON, *A Colony in the Making*. Macmillan, 1912.

——, *Kenya Chronicles*. Macmillan, 1939.

CROMER, LORD EVELYN BARING, *Modern Egypt*, Vol. I, II. Macmillan, 1908.

CROSS, COLIN, *The Fall of the British Empire*. Hodder, 1968.

CROWDER, MICHAEL, *West Africa Under Colonial Rule*. Hutchinson, 1968.

CROWE, JOHN HENRY VERINDER, *General Smuts' Campaign in East Africa*. Murray, 1918.

CROZIER, FRANK PERCY, *Five Years Hard*. Cape, 1932.

DAVIDSON, BASIL, *The African Past*. Longmans, 1964.

Debates on the Great Slave Trade. London, 1806.

DELF, GEORGE, *Jomo Kenyatta*. Gollancz, 1961.

Dictionary of National Biography. Oxford University Press, 1921–27.

DRUMMOND, HENRY, *Tropical Africa*. Scribner & Welford, 1889.

ELTON, LORD GODFREY E., *General Gordon's Khartoum Journal*. Kimber, 1961.

Encyclopaedia Britannica, 1947 ed., 1968 ed.

FARSON, NEGLEY, *Behind God's Back*. Harcourt, 1941.

——, *Last Chance in Africa*. Gollancz, 1953.

Foreign Office Papers.

FURNEAUX, RUPERT, *The Zulu War*. Weidenfeld, 1963.

GARVIN, JAMES LOUIS, *The Life of Joseph Chamberlain*, Vol. III. Macmillan, 1934.

GIBBS, PETER, *A Flag for Matabele*. Muller, 1955.

GILBY, THOMAS, *Britain at Arms*. Eyre & Spottiswode, 1953.

GUNTHER, JOHN, *Inside Africa*. Harper & Row, 1955.

HAGGARD, ANDREW CHARLES PARKER, *Under Crescent and Star*. Blackwood, 1896.

HAGGARD, SIR HENRY RIDER, *The Days of My Life*. Longmans, 1926.

——, *The Last Boer War*. Kegan Paul, 1899.

HAILEY, LORD MALCOLM, *An African Survey*. Oxford, 1938, 1945, 1957.

HALLETT, ROBIN, *The Penetration of Africa*, Vol. I. Routledge, 1965.

——, *Records of the African Association*. Nelson, 1964.

HANCOCK, WILLIAM K., *Selections from the Smuts Papers*, Vol. IV. Cambridge, 1966.

HARDY, GEORGES, *Vue Générale de l'Histoire d'Afrique*. A. Colin, 1922.

HATCH, JOHN, *A History of Post-War Africa*. Deutsch, 1965.

HEADLAM, CECIL, ed., *The Milner Papers*. Cassell, 1931, 1933.

HILLCOURT, WILLIAM, *Baden-Powell*. Heinemann, 1964.

HILLIER, ALFRED PETER, *Raid and Reform*. Macmillan, 1898.

HOCKLY, HAROLD EDWARD, *The Story of the British Settlers of 1820 in South Africa*. Cape Town, 1948.

HODGSON, LADY MARY ALICE, *The Siege of Kumasi*. New York, Longmans, Green & Co., 1901.

HORDERN, CHARLES, *Official History, Military Operations East Africa*. H.M.S.O., 1941.

HUXLEY, ELSPETH, *White Man's Country*, Vol. II. Chatto & Windus, 1953.

JACOB, ALARIC, *A Traveller's War*. Dodd, Mead & Co., 1944.

JAMES, DAVID PELHAM, *Lord Roberts*. Hollis & Carter, 1954.

JEANS, THOMAS TENDRON, *Naval Brigades in the South African War*. Sampson Low, 1901.

KEITH, ARTHUR BERRIEDALE, *Selected Speeches and Documents on British Colonial Policy, 1763–1917*, Vol. II. Oxford, 1918.

KENNEDY, AUBREY LEO, *Salisbury*. Murray, 1953.

KRUGER, PAUL, *Memoirs*. Unwin, 1902.

KRUGER, RAYNE, *Goodbye Dolly Gray*. Cassell, 1959.

LAING, ALEXANDER GORDON, *Travels in Western Africa*. Murray, 1825.

LAIRD, MACGREGOR, OLDFIELD, R., *An Expedition into the Interior of Africa*, Vol. I, II. Murray 1837.

LANDER, RICHARD L., *Records of Capt. Clapperton's Last Expedition*. Colburn & Bentley, 1830.

LEGUM, COLIN, *Africa: A Handbook*. Blond, 1961.

LEHMANN, JOSEPH, *All Sir Garnet*. Cape, 1964.

LETTOW-VORECK, PAUL VON, *My Reminiscences of East Africa*. Hurst & Blackett, 1920.

LIVINGSTONE, DAVID, *Narrative of an Expedition to the Zambesi*. London, 1865.

LLOYD, ALAN, *The Drums of Kumasi*. Longmans, 1964.

LLOYD, LORD GEORGE AMBROSE, *Egypt Since Cromer*. Vol. II. Macmillan, 1934.

LOCKHART, JOHN GILBERT, and WOODHOUSE, CHRISTOPHER, *Rhodes*. Hodder, 1963.

LONGFORD, ELIZABETH, *Victorian R.I.*, Weidenfeld, 1964.

LUCAS, SIR CHARLES PRESTWOOD, *The Empire at War*, Vol. IV. Milford, 1926.

LUGARD, SIR FREDERICK D., *The Dual Mandate in British Tropical Africa*. Blackwood, 1922.

MAGNUS, SIR PHILIP, *Kitchener*. Murray, 1958.

MAJDALANY, FREDERICK, *State of Emergency*, Longmans, 1962.

MARAIS, JOHANNES S., *The Fall of Kruger's Republic*. Oxford, 1961.

MEINERTZHAGEN, RICHARD, *Army Diary*. Oliver & Boyd, 1960.

———, *Kenya Diary*. Oliver & Boyd, 1957.

MILLAIS, JOHN GUILLE, *Life of F. C. Selous*. Longmans, 1918.

MOOREHEAD, ALAN, *The Blue Nile*. H. Hamilton, 1962.

———, *The White Nile*. H. Hamilton, 1960.

MORAN, LORD CHARLES MCMORAN WILSON, *Winston Churchill: The Struggle for Survival*. Houghton Mifflin, 1966.

MORRIS, DONALD R., *The Washing of the Spears*. Simon & Schuster, 1965.

MORRIS, JAMES, *Pax Britannica*. Faber, 1968.

MOYSE-BARTLETT, HUBERT, *The King's African Rifles*. Gale & Polden, 1956.

NAVAL INTELLIGENCE, *Kenya Handbook*. H.M.S.O., 1920.

NEWTON, JOHN, *Journal of a Slave Trader*, Bernard Martin and Mark Spurrell, eds. Epworth, 1962.

Official History of the War in South Africa. Hurst & Blackett, 1906.

OLIVER, RONALD, and ATMORE, ANTHONY, *Africa Since 1800*. Cambridge, 1967.

OLIVER, ROLAND; ATMORE, ANTHONY; and FAGE, J., *A Short History of Africa*. Penguin, 1962.

O'MEARA, WALTER ALFRED JOHN, *Kekewich in Kimberley*. Medici Society, 1926.

PADMORE, GEORGE, *Africa: Britain's Third Empire*. Dobson, 1949.

PARK, MUNGO, *Journal of a Mission in the Interior of Africa*. London, 1815.

———, *Travels in the Interior Districts of Africa*. London, 1799.

PATTERSON, JOHN HENRY, *The Man-eaters of Tsavo*. Macmillan, 1914.

PERHAM, MARGERY FRIEDA, *Lugard*. Faber & Faber, 1959.

PLOMER, WILLIAM CHARLES FRANKLYN, *Cecil Rhodes*. Davies, 1933.

RANSFORD, OLIVER, *The Battle of Majuba Hill*. Murray, 1967.

———, *The Rulers of Rhodesia*. Murray, 1968.

REITZ, DENEYS, *Trekking On*. Faber, 1936.

RENNELL, LORD FRANCIS JAMES RODD, *British Military Administration of Occupied Territories in Africa.* H.M.S.O., 1948.

Report of the Royal Commission on the War in South Africa, 1903.

RHODES, CECIL J., *Letters, etc.,* 1900–02, Rhodes Papers. Rhodes House, Oxford.

RICHTER, WERNER, *Bismarck.* Macdonald, 1964.

ROSENTHAL, ERIC, *Stars and Stripes in Africa.* Routledge, 1938.

SAMKANGE, STANLAKE, *Origins of Rhodesia.* Heinemann, 1969.

SCHMIDT, HEINZ WERNER, *With Rommel in the Desert.* Harrap, 1951.

SHEPPARD, ERIC WILLIAM, *A Short History of the British Army to 1914.* Constable, 1940.

SMITH, EDWARD, *The Life of Sir Joseph Banks.* Lane, 1911.

SMUTS, JAN CHRISTIAN, *Jan Christian Smuts.* Cassell, 1952.

SPARROW, GERALD, *Gordon.* Jarrolds, 1962.

SPEKE, JOHN H., *Journal of the Discovery of the Source of the Nile.* London, 1863.

STANLEY, HENRY M., *How I Found Livingstone.* Sampson Low, 1872.

STANLEY, RICHARD, and NEAME, ALAN, eds., *The Exploration Diaries of H. M. Stanley.* Kimber, 1961.

STEAD, WILLIAM THOMAS, *Last Will and Testament of C. J. Rhodes.* London, 1902.

STEEVENS, GEORGE WARRINGTON, *With Kitchener to Khartoum.* Dodd, Mead, 1908.

TAYLOR, ALAN J. P., *Bismarck.* Hamilton, 1955.

———, *Germany's First Bid for Colonies.* Macmillan, 1938.

TAYLOR, DON, *The British in Africa.* Hale, 1962.

THEAL, GEORGE McC., *History of South Africa,* Vols. III, IV. London, 1891, 1893. *The London Times.*

TIMOTHY, BANKOLE, *Kwame Nkrumah.* Allen & Unwin, 1955.

TREVELYAN, GEORGE M., *British History in the 19th Century and After.* Longmans, 1937.

Letters of Queen Victoria, Third Series, Vol. III. Murray, 1932.

WALKER, ERIC ANDERSON, *The Cambridge History of the British Empire,* Vol. VIII. Cambridge, 1953.

———, *History of South Africa.* Longmans, 1959.

WAR OFFICE PAPERS, DIARIES, *Siege of Mafeking, 9100–01.* Public Record Office.

WAVELL, LORD ARCHIBALD PERCIVAL, *Allenby: Soldier and Statesman.* Harrap, 1940.

WHEELER-BENNETT, JOHN W., *King George VI.* Macmillan, 1958.

Whittaker's Almanac, 1956, 1964, 1966, 1968, 1969.

WHITE, STANHOPE, *Dan Bana.* Cassell, 1966.

WILLIAMS, BASIL, *Botha, Smuts and South Africa.* Hodder, 1946.

WILLIAMSON, JAMES ALEXANDER, *The British Empire and Commonwealth.* Macmillan, 1935.

———, *A Short History of British Expansion.* Macmillan, 1934.

WILSON, HERBERT WRIGLEY, *With the Flag to Pretoria,* Vol. I, II. Harmsworth, 1900, 1901.

WILSON, MONICA, *Oxford History of South Africa,* Vol. I. Oxford, 1969.

WINGATE, SIR FRANCIS REGINALD, *Ten Years' Captivity in the Mahdi's Camp.* Sampson Low, 1892.

WRENCH, SIR EVELYN, *Alfred Lord Milner.* Eyre & Spottiswoode, 1958.

YOUNG, FILSON, *The Relief of Mafeking.* Methuen, 1900.

ZETLAND, MARQUIS OF, *Lord Cromer.* Hodder, 1932.

Index